The Intimate Life
of Saint Thérèse

Portrayed by Those Who Knew Her

By

Rev. Albert H. Dolan, O. Carm.

Originally published in 1929 by Carmelite Press under the title of *Collected Little Flower Works*, which was a compendium of the following eight small books: *The Life of the Little Flower, The Living Sisters of the Little Flower, Our Sister Is in Heaven!, Where the Little Flower Seems Nearest, The Little Flower's Mother, An Hour with the Little Flower* (Little Flower Series—Number One), *An Hour with the Little Flower* (Little Flower Series—Number Three), *Scapular Facts*

Loreto Publications
Fitzwilliam, New Hampshire 03447

Nihil Obstat:
> Lawrence C. Diether, O. Carm.,
>> Censor Deputatis

Imprimatur
> George Cardinal Mundelein,
>> Archbishop of Chicago

Previously published in 1929 and 1944 by
Carmelite Press
First Loreto Printing 2003
Second Loreto Printing 2006

All Rights Reserved

Loreto Publications
P. O. Box 603
Fitzwilliam, NH 03447
603-239-6671
www.LoretoPubs.org

ISBN: 1-930278-34-9

Printed and bound in the United States of America

Publisher's Dedication

This work is dedicated to Saint Thérèse and her saintly family, with grateful affection, in appreciation of many favors and graces received.

The Loreto Family

Table of Contents

Book One: The Life of the Little Flower

Part One
The Little Flower's Home Life 3

Part Two
The Little Flower's Convent Life 23

Part Three
Beatification, Canonization, and Shower of Roses 45

Book Two: The Living Sisters of the Little Flower

Chapter One
Description of Lisieux, of the Little Flower's Convent and
of the Personal Appearance of the Little Flower's Sisters 51

Chapter Two
First Visit with Pauline 57

Chapter Three
First Visit with Pauline—Continued 63

Chapter Four
The Second Visit with Pauline 69

Chapter Five
The Visits with Marie and Céline 75

Chapter Six
The Visit with Léonie 85

Chapter Seven
The Visit with Jeanne Guérin, the Little Flower's Cousin
and Playmate 93

Chapter Eight
The Visit with Sister Francis de Sales, the Little Flower's Teacher 99

Chapter Nine
An Audience with the Holy Father Concerning the Little Flower . . . 107

Chapter Ten
Pierre, the Little Flower's Sacristan and Guardian of her Tomb 113

Chapter Eleven
Visits to Buissonnets, the Home of the Little Flower 125

Chapter Twelve
Visits at Alençon, the Birthplace of the Little Flower 135

Chapter Thirteen
The National Shrine of the Little Flower 145

Book Three: "Our Sister Is in Heaven!"

Chapter One
Holy Communion to the Sisters of St. Thérèse 153

Chapter Two
What the World Does Not Know About the Little Flower 161

Chapter Three
New Messages from Those Whose Sister Is in Heaven 171

Chapter Four
More Marvellous Relics Given to the National Shrine
of the Little Flower 177

Chapter Five
The Little Flower's Last Letter 183

Chapter Six
The World's Youngest Saint 189

Chapter Seven
"She's My Saint," Said the Holy Father 193

Indulgences 195

Book Four: Where the Little Flower Seems Nearest

Chapter One
To the Cloister Room 199

Chapter Two
The Infirmary 205

Chapter Three
The Chapter Hall 211

Chapter Four
The Cell 215

Book Five: The Little Flower's Mother

Chapter One
A Visit to the Little Flower's Mother's Home 223

Chapter Two
Her Parentage and Maidenhood 225

Chapter Three
Her Marriage and Early Married Life 227

Chapter Four
The Birth and Infancy of St. Thérèse 239

Chapter Five
The Mother During the Girlhood of St. Thérèse 249

Chapter Six
The Mother's Influence upon St. Thérèse .253

Chapter Seven
Twilight and Dawn 257

Book Six: An Hour with the Little Flower
(Little Flower Series—Number One)

Chapter One
The Little Flower's Secret of Happiness 267

Chapter Two
St. Thérèse, Our Guide in Sorrow 273

Chapter Three
The Mighty Promises of the Little Flower 281

Chapter Four
Comfort for Sinners from the Life of St. Thérèse 287

Chapter Five
The Little Flower's Love of Our Lady of Mt. Carmel 295

Chapter Six
Lovers of Thérèse Love Mary 301

Chapter Seven
The Veneration of the Little Flower 307

Chapter Eight
The Little Flower Still Lives 311

Book Seven: An Hour with the Little Flower
(Little Flower Series—Number Three)

Chapter One
The Special Vocation of the Little Flower to Love God 317

Chapter Two
The Little Flower's Oblation of Herself as a Victim of Love 327

Chapter Three
Practical Rules for the Practice of Love of God 345

Chapter Four
The Unselfishness of the Love of the Little Flower 353

Book Eight: Scapular Facts

Chapter One
Why Wear the Scapular? 359

Chapter Two
Brief History of the Scapular and of the Carmelite Order 365

Chapter Three
The Privileges of Membership in the Scapular Confraternity 371

Chapter Four
Some Practical Questions Briefly Answered 377

Supplement

Supplement
Description of the National Shrine of the Little Flower 383

The Life of the Little Flower

Thérèse at the age of eight, holding a jump rope.

Part One

The Little Flower's Home Life

Parents and Sisters of St. Thérèse*

Louis Martin, the father of the Little Flower, and Zélie Guérin, her mother, had in their early days both sought admission into religion, but God had other designs for them. He drew them together; they married and made it their earnest prayer that He would give them many children and to each child a religious vocation. Nine children blessed their happy union. Of these, four died in their infancy and five of them entered the convent. Entire sermons have been preached upon that truly Catholic household in which, as in a garden, the choice flower, Thérèse, grew up and blossomed. The father and mother of this family were examples of true Christian parents.

Every morning they were at Holy Mass and Holy Communion together. They strictly observed the fasts and feasts of the Church and kept Sunday sacred. From the cradle they dedicated all their children to Mary Immaculate, and each received Mary's name: Marie Louise, Marie Pauline, Marie Léonie, Marie Hélène, Marie Joseph Louis, Marie Joseph Jean Baptiste, Marie Céline, Marie Mélanie, and lastly

---

* Throughout this book, and in all the literature issued by the National Society of the Little Flower, united with the Confraternity of the Scapular, the Little Flower is termed Thérèse, rather than Teresa. The shorter, two-syllable word, is preferred, first, to distinguish the Little Flower from her Patron, St. Teresa of Avila, and secondly, because the shorter word better expresses the littleness of the Little Flower, who one day, when asked by what name she was to be addressed when in heaven, humbly replied, "You will call me—little Thérèse."

Marie Françoise Thérèse, who was to become the most beautiful flower in that garden of lilies.

Her Personal Appearance

In appearance, Sister Thérèse was tall and slender with a graceful, attractive form and very beautiful hands. She had bluish-gray eyes, and as a young girl, a wealth of blond curly hair. Her features were delicate and refined; her complexion unusually fair. When she spoke of God her face lighted up with a holy enthusiasm, and she became ravishingly beautiful. An expression of heavenly purity, meekness and blessed peace always rested upon her countenance. Her gait was dignified, but marked by simplicity and grace.

The Little Flower's Own Prelude to Her Life Story

Almost at the beginning of her Autobiography the Little Flower writes: "If a little flower could speak, it seems to me that it would tell quite simply what God had done for it, without hiding any of its gifts. It would not say, under the pretext of humility, that it was not pretty and had not a sweet scent, that the sun had withered its petals or the storm had bruised its stem—if it knew such were not the case."

"The Flower now telling her tale rejoices in having to publish the wholly undeserved favors of Our Lord. She knows that in herself she had nothing worthy of attracting Him. His mercy it was that filled her with good things—His mercy alone. He allowed her to see the light in a holy soil fragrant with the odor of purity. He caused eight fair white lilies to spring up there before she appeared. In His love He willed to preserve her from the poisoned breath of the world, for hardly had her petals unfolded when this good Master transplanted her to the mountain of Carmel, Our Lady's garden of delight.

"Throughout my life it has pleased God to surround me with affection; my earliest recollections are of tender caresses and smiles. And if He allowed so much love to be lavished upon me, He also endowed me with a warm and sensitive heart to return it. Of my affection for Papa and Mamma it would be difficult to convey an idea, and being very demonstrative I showed my love in a thousand little ways, though the means I employed make me smile now when I think of them."

Letters of the Little Flower's Mother Describing the Child, Thérèse

"In proof of what I said about my way of showing affection for my parents, here is what Mamma wrote:* 'Baby is the dearest little rogue; she will kiss me and at the same time wish me to die. "Oh, how I wish you would die, dear Mamma!" Astonished at being scolded for saying such a thing, she will answer: "It is because I want you to go to heaven, and you say that to get there we must die!" In her outbursts of affection for her Father she wishes him also to die. The dear little thing will hardly ever leave me: she delights in following me about, especially in the garden. If I am not there, she refuses to stay and is so inconsolable that she has to be brought back to me again. She will not even go upstairs by herself without calling at every step, "Mamma, Mamma!" and if I forget to answer, "Yes, darling!" she waits where she is and will not move.'

"I was nearly three years old when Mamma wrote: 'Little Thérèse asked me the other day if she would go to heaven. 'Yes, if you are good,' I told her. 'Oh, Mamma,' she answered, 'then if I am not good shall I go to hell? Well, I know what I will do—I will fly to you in heaven, and you will hold me tight in your arms, and how could God take me away then?' I saw by her look she was convinced that God could do nothing to her if she hid herself in my arms.

"Thérèse loves her little sister very much; indeed she is a child who delights us all. She is extraordinarily outspoken, and it is charming to see her run after me to confess her childish

---

* This is an extract from a letter of Mrs. Martin, the mother of Thérèse, to her other daughter, "Pauline," who is now Prioress of the Carmel of Lisieux.

Thérèse at the age of 15 with her father.

faults: 'Mamma, I gave Céline a push'; 'I slapped her once, but I will not do it again." The moment she has done anything mischievous, everyone must know. Yesterday, without meaning to do so, she tore off a small piece of wallpaper; you would have been sorry for her—she wanted to tell her Father immediately. When he came home four hours later and everyone else had forgotten about it, she ran at once to Marie, saying, 'Tell Papa that I tore the paper,' and she waited like a criminal for sentence. There is an idea in her little head, that if she accuses herself she will be the more readily forgiven."

"I see with pleasure in my Mother's letters that as I grew older I began to be a greater comfort to her. That is what Mother writes in 1876:

"'Even Thérèse is anxious to practice mortification. Marie has given her little sisters a string of beads on purpose to count their acts of self-denial, and they have really spiritual, but very amusing, conversations together. The other day Céline asked: "How can God be in such a tiny Host?" and Thérèse answered, "That is not strange because God is Almighty." "And what does Almighty mean?" continued Céline. "It means," said Thérèse, "that He can do whatever He likes." But it is still more amusing to see Thérèse continually putting her hand in her pocket and pulling a bead along the string for every little sacrifice.'"

Her Father's "Little Queen"

"Papa's name fills me with many happy memories As soon as he came home I would run to meet him and he would carry me about through house and garden. He would take me in his arms, lift me high up in the air, set me on his shoulder and load me with caresses. Mamma used to say, laughingly, that he always did whatever I wanted; and he would answer: 'Well, why not? She is the Queen!' Yet I cannot say that he spoiled me. I remember one day while I was merrily swinging he called out as he passed, 'Come and give me a kiss, little Queen!' Contrary to my usual custom, I would not stir, and answered pertly, 'You must come yourself for it, Papa!' But he wisely took no notice of me.

"'You naughty little girl,' exclaimed Marie, 'to answer Papa so rudely!' Her reproof took effect; I immediately got off the swing and the whole house resounded with my cries. As I hurried upstairs, this time not waiting to call 'Mamma!' at every step, my one thought was to find Papa and make my peace with him, which, needless to say, was quickly done."

The Little Flower's Faults in Childhood

"Here is a letter which will show you how much sweeter Céline was than I:

"Céline is naturally inclined to be good; as to that little puss, Thérèse, one cannot tell how she will turn out, she is still so young and thoughtless. She is a very intelligent child, but has not nearly so sweet a disposition as her sister, and her stubbornness is almost unconquerable. When she has said 'No', nothing will make her change; you might leave her all day in the cellar without getting her to say "Yes". She would rather sleep there than do so.'

"I had another fault, that of strong self-love, which Mamma did not mention in her letters. Here are a couple of instances: One day, wishing no doubt to see how far my pride would go, she said smiling, 'Thérèse, if you will kiss the ground I will give you a halfpenny.' In those days the sum was a fortune, and in order to gain it I had not far to stoop, for I was so tiny that there was not much distance between my lips and the ground; but my pride was up in arms, and holding myself erect, I replied, 'No, thank you Mamma, I would rather go without the halfpenny.'

"Another time when we were going into the country to see some friends, Mamma told Marie to put on my prettiest frock, but not to let me have bare arms. I did not utter a word, and appeared as indifferent as children of that age should be, but in my own mind I said, 'I should have looked much prettier with bare arms.'

"With such a disposition it is clear that had I been brought up by careless parents, I should have become very wicked, and perhaps have lost my soul. But Jesus watched over His little spouse and turned all her faults to advantage, since by being checked early in life they became a means of leading her towards perfection.

"A visitor once remarked on my beautiful hair; another inquired as she left the room, who was the pretty little girl? Such remarks, all the more flattering because I was not meant to hear them, left a certain feeling of pleasure which clearly proved that I was full of self-love. Once also when we were on the beach, a gentleman and his wife, after looking at me for a long time, asked Papa if I were his child, and remarked that I was a very pretty girl. Papa at once made them a sign not to flatter me, but I was pleased to have overheard, for I did not think I was pretty.

"One day, Léonie, under the impression that she was too big to play with dolls, brought us a basket filled with their frocks, and other trifles. On these she laid her doll. 'Here, dears,' she said, 'choose whatever you like.' Céline looked at it, and took a woolen ball. After a moment's thought I put out my hand, saying, 'I choose everything,' and I carried off both doll and basket without more ado.*

"This childish incident sums up, so to speak, the whole of my life. Later on, as in the days of my childhood, I cried out, 'My God, I choose everything—I will not be a saint by halves, I am not afraid of suffering for Thee. One thing only do I fear, and that is to follow my own will. Accept then the offering I make of it, for I choose all that Thou willest!'"

There, then, we have Thérèse, the baby of three and four years, vain of her beauty; proud of her pretty dresses; eager for praise and notice; inclined at times to fits of temper and stubbornness; so proud that when offered a coin to stoop humbly and kiss the ground, she refused to bend. Nevertheless, this very

---

* The reader will notice Thérèse's marvellous memory which permits her to record many incidents of her babyhood. It is worthy of remark, too, that her frank and sincere recital is as free from the slightest affectation as it is full of simplicity.

human little girl became one of the greatest of all the saints. No little of the Little Flower's influence over souls is due to the evil inclinations and other human imperfections which we notice in her youth. Her complete eradication of those faults has taught thousands, and should teach us, the possibility of complete victory over our faults if we imitate the Little Flower's Little Way of humility, prayerfulness, and trust in God.

The Little Flower's Love of Flowers, Sunsets and the Sea

From the Little Flower's Autobiography may be gleaned a sentence here and there which reveals her love of nature in all its moods. "Papa's name fills me with many happy memories. I think with delight of our Sunday walks when our beloved Mother always accompanied us. Indeed I can still feel the vivid and poetic impressions made on my childish heart by the vision of the cornfields studded with cornflowers, poppies, and marguerites. Even at that age I loved far-stretching views, sunlit spaces, and stately trees; in a word all the beauties of nature cast their spell upon me and raised my soul to heaven. Truly everything on earth smiled on me; I found flowers strewn at each step, and my naturally happy disposition helped to make life bright. But a new era was about to dawn. I was to be the spouse of Our Lord at so tender an age that it was necessary I should suffer from childhood.

"I was between six and seven when I saw the sea for the first time. I could not turn away my eyes; its majesty, the roaring of the waves, the whole vast spectacle impressed me deeply, and spoke to my soul of God's power and greatness.

"One evening, at the hour when the sun seems to sink into the broad expanse of waters, leaving behind it a trail of light, I sat with you on an unfrequented rock and let my gaze linger on this path of splendour. You described it as an image of grace illuminating the way of faithful hearts here upon earth. Then I pictured my own soul as a tiny barque, with graceful white sail, floating in the midst of the golden stream, and I determined never to steer it out of the sight of Jesus, so that it might make its way swiftly and tranquilly towards the heavenly shore."

Her Mother's Death

"All the details of Mamma's illness are still fresh in my mind. The touching ceremony of Extreme Unction made a deep impression upon me. I can see the spot where I knelt and I can still hear my poor father's sobs. With Mamma's death* began the second period of my life, the most sorrowful of all. It lasted for the space of ten years. Immediately after Mamma's death my naturally happy disposition deserted me. From being lively and demonstrative, I became timid and shy and so sensitive that a look was often sufficient to make me burst into tears. I could not bear to be noticed, or to meet strangers, and I was only at ease when with my dear ones at home. There I was always cherished with the most loving care. Papa's affectionate heart seemed endowed with a mother's love. If Our Lord had not lavished His sunshine upon His Little Flower, she never could have become acclimatized to this earth. Still too weak to bear either rain, or storm, she needed warmth, refreshing dew, and gentle breezes—gifts never denied her, even in the wintry season of trials."

Walks and Joys of Her Childhood

After her Mother's death, Thérèse and her Father moved from Alençon to Lisieux, in order to bring his girls nearer their mother's brother, M. Guérin, as well as to secure Madame Guérin's advice in the upbringing of the younger ones. Thérèse says of her reading lessons, "I remember that 'heaven' was the first word I could read alone.

"Each afternoon I went with Papa for a walk and made a visit to the Blessed Sacrament in one or other of the churches. It was in this way that I first saw the chapel of our Carmel: 'Look, little Queen!' said Papa. 'Behind that grating there are

---

* Madame Martin died on the night of August 28, 1877, when Thérèse was four years old.

holy nuns who are always praying to Almighty God.' Little did I think that nine years later I should be amongst them, that in this blessed Carmel I should receive so many graces.

"I was also very fond of flowers, and in a recess in the garden wall I used to make little altars and decorate them. When all was ready, I would run and call Papa. To give me pleasure, he would appear lost in admiration over the wonderful altar that, to me, seemed a masterpiece."

The tiny monstrance, chalice, missal, cruets, candle sticks and statues which were the toys of the Little Flower's childhood are still carefully treasured at her home in Lisieux and shown to visitors.

Her First Confession

Pauline, whom Thérèse chose as her second Mother, prepared the Little Flower for confession so well that Thérèse remarks, "You had told me that it was not to a man but to God that I was going to tell my sins, and this truth so impressed me that I remember to have asked you seriously whether I should tell Father that I loved him with my whole heart, since it was God I was going to speak to. I remember he exhorted me to be devout to Our Lady, and how I determined to redouble my love for her who already filled so large a place in my heart."

Various Incidents of Her Childhood

From her life at this time Thérèse selects many instances which are here briefly reproduced for the light they throw upon her character and disposition as a child.

Once, after having had her beads blessed, she stopped under a lamp, to the great amusement of Pauline, "to see how my beads look now that they have been blessed."

She loved processions of the Blessed Sacrament. "What a joy it was to strew flowers in God's path! But before letting them fall under His feet, I threw them high up in the air, and never was I more happy then when I saw my rose petals touch the sacred Monstrance."

Of the sermons at high Mass, which she attended every Sunday with her Father, she remarks, "I really did listen attentively though I must own that I often looked at Papa more than at the preacher; I read so many things in his noble face. Sometimes his eyes were filled with tears which he strove to keep back; and as he listened to the eternal truths, he seemed no longer of this world; it was as though his soul had soared to a higher sphere."

Of her walks with her Father under the stars she says, "I looked up at the stars with untold delight. Orion's belt, like a cluster of diamonds hung in the deep vault overhead, had a wonderful fascination for me because I saw in it a likeness to the letter T. 'Look, Papa!' I would cry 'My name is written in heaven!' Then no longer wishing to see this dull earth, I would ask him to lead me on, while with head thrown back, I gazed unweariedly at the starry skies."

Her Evenings at Home—Night Prayers

"There is much I could tell you of our winter evenings at home. After a game of draughts, Pauline or Marie used to read aloud from some spiritual book, during which time I always sat on Papa's knee. At length we went upstairs for night prayers. Once again my place was beside our beloved Father, and I had but to look at him to learn how the saints pray. Then you put me to bed, dear little Mother, and I invariably asked you, 'Have I been good today? Is God pleased with me? Will the angels watch over me?' 'Yes,' was the unfailing reply—were it not, I should have spent the night in tears. You and Marie then kissed me, and little Thérèse was left alone in the dark."

Saint Thérèse was always deeply grateful for the influence exercised over her life by the good example of her family and her careful home training. "Oh," she wrote in later years, "how many souls might attain to great sanctity if they were wisely guided from their childhood."

Father Dolan before the miraculous statue of the Virgin Mary, which smiled upon Thérèse and cured her of her childhood illness.

Surely there is a much needed message from God here to Catholic parents of our age, in which home life is so little calculated to produce saints. The peace and beauty of Thérèse's evenings at home; the family prayers; the spiritual reading and instructions; the virtuous behaviour and the holy example of the parents should inspire all parents, to whose attention these pages come to make their households more like that of the Martin family and thereby to bring down upon their homes the more abundant blessings of God.

Her Love of Her Father—Her "King"

"How I loved and admired him! When he expounded to me his ideas on the most serious matters as if I were a grown-up girl, I would say quite artlessly, 'It is certain, Papa, that if you spoke like that to the great men who govern the country, they would make you its King, and France would be happier than she has ever been. But you yourself would be unhappy, for such is the lot of kings, and besides, you would no longer be my king alone; so I am glad they do not know you'."

Her Lovableness

Is it any wonder that this little girl has won the love of hundreds of thousands? How calculated to inspire love for her are those lovely pictures she gives us of herself, pictures of a heart in which natural love of father and sisters was so deep and tender; pictures of a soul full of sweet poetry, thrilled by stars and trees, flowers and sunsets! Hers was a heart made to love and be loved; her soul was one of the most consummate masterpieces of Almighty God. No wonder that so many are caught by the spell of her charm; no wonder that so many choice souls, who have hearts that in a small way resemble hers, become enamored of her and spend themselves to make her known to others. Her childish heart, as revealed to us in her Autobiography, was fertile soil in which to plant the choicest graces. But her childlike soul, wonderful and lovable as it is, is not as great a marvel as the soul revealed to us later, a soul on fire with the full blaze of the love of God. Any one can understand and love the heart of Thérèse, the child, but more rare spiritual perception is necessary to appreciate fully the soul that later breaks forth into the Canticle of Love with which she concludes her Autobiography.

If, after reading so far, we find it in our hearts to love her let us follow her on in her development into a very Seraph of the Love of God; let us beg her to help us to understand and to imitate. We are not ready to delve into the deeper depths of her heart until we have pondered and understood all that is implied by these words of the Little Flower with which we will conclude this section: "From the age of three, I never refused our Good God anything; I have never given Him aught but love and it is with love He will repay." Yes, He has repaid; repaid with love, by fanning her love for Him into a great fire which has lighted the twentieth century and attracted the attention of the world; repaid by permitting Thérèse to win the love of thousands, first for herself and then for Him.

Parting from Pauline

To understand what a blow for Thérèse was Pauline's departure for Carmel, it is necessary to read Thérèse's account of the exquisitely tender friendship between the two sisters and to remember that Thérèse had turned the affection of her ardent soul upon Pauline, her "Little Mother," as the Little Flower called her.* Thérèse says, "The parting almost broke my heart when Our Lord took my Little Mother whom I so dearly loved. How can I describe the anguish my heart endured? In a flash, I beheld life as it really is, full of suffering and constant partings, and I shed most bitter tears. At that time the joy of sacrifice was still unknown to me."

---

* Thérèse was ten years old when Pauline entered Carmel.

Mary's Smile

The parting with Pauline was so severe a trial for ten-year-old Thérèse that in consequence she fell dangerously ill, and seemed at the point of death. "The Queen of Heaven, however," says the Little Flower, "was keeping a faithful and affectionate watch from above over her Little Flower and was making ready to still the tempest just as the frail and delicate stem was on the point of breaking."

Thérèse then proceeds to describe the agony of her sisters and her father when they realized the almost hopeless condition of their beloved Little Flower. They begged for a miracle to restore her to health and their cry of faith forced the gates of heaven.

"We were then," continues Thérèse, "in the lovely month of May* and earth was adorned with the flowers of spring. Only the Little Flower drooped and seemed to have faded forever. But close beside her was a radiant sun, the miraculous Statue of the Queen of Heaven, and towards that glorious Sun the Little Flower would often turn. At length my agony so increased that I could not recognize even Marie, who knelt in tears at the foot of the bed. Entirely exhausted, I then entreated my heavenly Mother with all my heart to have pity on me. Suddenly the statue became animated and radiantly beautiful with a divine beauty that no words can ever convey.* The look upon Our Lady's face was unspeakably kind and sweet and compassionate, but what penetrated to the very depths of my soul was her gracious smile. Instantly all my pain vanished, my eyes filled, and big tears fell silently, tears of purest joy. When Marie saw me gaze fixedly on the statue, she said to herself, 'Thérèse is cured.' It was true. The Little Flower had come back to life. A bright ray from her glorious

---

* Because Our Lady first smiled on Thérèse in May, and because May is the month of Mary, whose habit Thérèse wore and, because Thérèse was canonized in May, one of the five solemn novenas made by the members of the Society of the Little Flower, united with the Confraternity of the Scapular, is held at the National Shrine in May.

* The Little Flower was at this time ten years old, the date of Our Lady's first smile being May 10, 1883.

sun had brought warmth and light, and had delivered her forever from the cruel enemy. 'The dark winter was now passed, the rain was over and gone,' and Our Lady's Flower gathered such strength that five years later she unfolded her petals on the fertile mountain of Carmel."

Her Devotion to Mary

While we are on the subject of Mary's favor to the child Thérèse, it will be well to include here an account of the Little Flower's great love for the Immaculate Mother of God. Throughout her Autobiography, Thérèse refers very frequently to Mary and always with the most tender affection. In speaking of her first confession, for instance, she says, "I remember that my first Confessor exhorted me to be devout to Our Lady and I determined to redouble my love for her who already filled so large a place in my heart." "Oh!" she exclaims elsewhere, "how I love our Blessed Lady. Had I been a priest how I would have sung her praises."

On May 31, 1886, Thérèse became a sodalist of Our Lady and of this event she writes, "I resolved to consecrate myself in a special way to our Blessed Lady and therefore I sought admission into the Sodality of the Children of Mary."

Her devotion to Mary, especially under the title of Our Lady of Mount Carmel, was manifested by choosing a religious order especially dear to the Queen of Heaven. Of all the orders open to her, she chose the order of Mary, the Carmelite order, which was the first to be dedicated to Mary and which has given to the Church so many glorious saints, among whom was St. Teresa of Avila, the patroness of the Little Flower.

The members of the Carmelite Order wear the brown scapular of Mary as part of their habit and are called, popularly, Carmelite Nuns or Carmelite Priests, whereas their full official title is "The Brothers" or "The Sisters of Our Lady of Mt. Carmel."

As a novice mistress, Thérèse so often proved that she was aware of the most hidden thoughts of her novices that they expressed surprise, to which she answered, "This is my secret: I never give you advice without first invoking the Blessed Virgin Mary."

In a letter to her sister, Céline, Thérèse writes: "Sometimes I find myself saying to the Holy Virgin, 'Do you know, O cherished Mother, that I think myself more fortunate than you? I have you for Mother and you have not, like me, the Blessed Virgin to love. You are, it is true, the Mother of Jesus, but you have given Him to me, and He, from the cross, gave you to us as our Mother'."

As a further evidence of Thérèse's devotion to Mary, we must quote here the surpassingly beautiful words of the Little Flower which she wrote during her last illness: "Oh! Mary, were I Queen of Heaven and Thou Thérèse, I should wish to be Thérèse, that I might see thee, Queen of Heaven." This tribute of love to our Blessed Mother was the last sentence written here on earth by the Little Flower.

When we consider the Little Flower's love of Mary and Mary's love of Thérèse, we do not wonder that, since the Little Flower's death, she has obtained from Mary so many favors for nuns and priests of her own order of Our Lady of Mt. Carmel and that she has dispensed her favors so abundantly at Carmelite Shrines. Since the Little Flower's death the entire order of Carmel has experienced a remarkable revival of its old and glorious spirit, and its convents and monasteries throughout the world have been deluged with applicants for admission as priests and nuns. A great number of these applications have been attributed to the inspiration of the Little Flower.

The Little Flower's First Communion

For years Thérèse had looked forward to the day of her first Communion.* Once, when much too young for first Communion, she begged her eldest sister to take her to

---

* The Little Flower made her first Communion on May 8, 1884, when she was eleven years old. At this time children were generally obliged to wait until they were twelve or thirteen before they could be admitted to first Holy Communion.

midnight Mass on Christmas Eve, for she wanted to take advantage of the darkness in order to go to the Holy Table and steal the little Jesus. "I will slip in by your side," she said, "no one will see me. May I do that?"

Of her preparation for first Communion she writes: "Pauline taught me that I must in preparation stir up in my heart fresh transports of love and fill it anew with flowers. Every day, therefore, I made a number of little sacrifices and acts of love which were to be transformed into so many flowers; violets or roses, cornflowers, daisies or forget-me-nots—in a word, all nature's blossoms were to form within me a cradle for the Holy Child."

Of her first Communion day she writes: "At last there dawned the most beautiful day of all the days of my life. How perfectly I remember even the smallest details of those sacred hours! The joyful awakening, the reverent and tender embraces of my schoolteachers and older companions, the room filled with snow-white frocks, where each child was dressed in turn, and above all, our entrance into the chapel and the melody of the morning hymn:

"'O Altar of God, where the Angels are hovering.'

"How sweet was the first embrace of Jesus! It was indeed an embrace of love. I felt that I was loved and I said, 'I love Thee and I give myself to Thee forever.' Jesus asked nothing of me, and claimed no sacrifice; for a long time He and little Thérèse had known and understood one another. That day our meeting was more than simple recognition; it was perfect union. We were no longer two. Thérèse had disappeared like a drop of water lost in the immensity of the ocean; Jesus alone remained—He was the Master, the King. Had not Thérèse asked Him to take away the liberty which frightened her? She felt herself so weak and frail, that she wished to be forever united in the Divine Strength.

"And then my joy became so intense, so deep, that it could not be restrained; tears of happiness welled up and overflowed. My companions were astonished, and asked each other afterwards, 'Why did she cry? Had she anything on her conscience?' 'No,' some answered, 'it is because she has not her Mother here, or the Carmelite sister of whom she is so fond.' No one understood that all the joy of heaven had come down into one heart, and that that heart—exiled, weak, and mortal—could not contain it without tears.

"In the afternoon, I read the Act of Consecration to Our Lady in the name of all the First Communicants. Probably the choice fell upon me because my own earthly Mother had been taken from me while I was still so young. I put my whole heart into the reading of the prayer, and besought Our Blessed Lady always to watch over me. It seemed to me that she looked down lovingly, and once more smiled on her Little Flower.

"When evening came the little Queen walked hand in hand with Papa to Carmel, where I saw my beloved Pauline, now become the spouse of Christ and, like me, wearing a white veil and a crown of roses.* My happiness was without alloy, for I hoped soon to join her, and at her side to wait for heaven.

"At last, night fell, bringing to a close that beautiful day. For even the brightest days are followed by darkness; one alone can have no setting—the day of the eternal Communion in our only true home. The morrow seemed veiled in melancholy. The pretty clothes, the presents I had received, did not satisfy me. Henceforth Our Lord alone could fill my heart, and I only longed for the blissful moment when I should receive Him again."

---

* Pauline made her vows in the Carmel of Lisieux on the day of Thérèse's first Communion, May 8, 1884.

The sisters of Lisieux tending to the wash.

Part Two

The Little Flower's Convent Life

Efforts to Enter Carmel—Her Vocation

When Pauline was planning to enter Carmel, Thérèse, then eight years old, felt that she too had a vocation to Carmel. She says, speaking to Pauline: "You explained to me the nature of the religious life and one evening, while pondering all alone on the picture you had drawn for me, I felt that Carmel was the desert where God wished me also to hide. I felt it so strongly that there was no room for doubt. It was not the dream of an impressionable child, but the certainty of a divine call, and this sensation, which I am unable to describe, brought with it a wonderful peace. Next day I confided my desires to you, and seeing in them the working of God's Will, you promised to take me soon to interview the mother Prioress that I might tell her my secret."

When nine and ten years old Thérèse repeatedly begged to be received into the Carmelite Convent at Lisieux. She even persuaded her father to go with her to the Bishop and beg his permission to enter, but he would not consent. All the world knows the story of her daring appeal to the Holy Father when she was in Rome on a pilgrimage at the age of fourteen. She ran across the audience room and flung herself at the feet of Leo XIII saying, "Holy Father, in honor of your jubilee, permit me to enter Carmel at the age of fifteen." Everyone gasped at her audacity, as the Pontiff answered: "Well, child, you will enter if it is God's Will."

Carmel at Last

Even in the face of the Holy Father's refusal to interfere, she continued to hope and pray that she would be permitted to give herself to Our Lord without delay. The Divine Infant spoke to the heart of the Bishop who sent a special permission to the prioress of Carmel, which was received on the significant Feast of the Holy Innocents, and on April 9, 1888, when the Little Flower was fifteen, the doors of the Lisieux Convent swung open to receive her who was to make that convent known in every corner of the world.

Of her entrance the Little Flower says: "The following morning after a last look at the dear home of my childhood, I set out for the convent where together we all heard Mass. At the Communion when Our Divine Lord entered our hearts, I heard sobs on every side. I did not shed a tear, but as I led the way to the cloister door the beating of my heart became so violent that I wondered if I were going to die. Oh, the agony of that moment! One must have gone through it to understand it.

"I embraced all my loved ones, then I knelt for Papa's blessing and he too knelt as he blessed me through his tears. To see this old man giving his child to God while she was still in the springtime of life was a sight to gladden the angels. This is how my father announced my leaving home to one of his friends: 'Thérèse, my little Queen, entered Carmel yesterday. God alone could ask such a sacrifice, but He helps me so powerfully that my heart is overflowing with joy even in the midst of my tears.'

"At length the door closed upon me, and I found a loving welcome in the arms of those dear sisters who, each in her turn, had been to me a mother, and likewise from the family of my adoption, whose tender devotedness is not dreamed of by the outside world. My desire was now accomplished, and my soul was filled with so deep a peace that it baffles all attempts at description. This peace has been my portion during the eight and a half years of my life within these walls, never forsaking me amid the hardest trials."

The "Little Miracle" of Her Clothing Day

On January 10, 1889, she received the holy habit of Our Lady of Mount Carmel and received the name she so coveted, Sister Thérèse of the Child Jesus and of the Holy Face. On the day of her clothing Our Lord worked the "little miracle" of snow to grant a pleasure to His favorite child. The Little Flower was fond of snow; "even when quite small its whiteness entranced me. It was therefore natural that on the occasion of my clothing ceremony I should wish to see the earth arrayed like myself in spotless white. The weather, however was so mild on the preceding day that it might have been spring, and I no longer dared hope for a fall of snow. But after the ceremony, the moment I again set foot in the enclosure, my eyes fell on the pretty statue of the Holy Child smiling at me amid flowers and lights; then, turning towards the quadrangle I saw it was all covered with snow! What a delicate attention on the part of Jesus! To gratify the least wish of His little spouse He actually made her a gift of snow. Where is the creature with power enough to make even one flake fall, to please his beloved? Owing to the warm temperature everyone was filled with amazement, but, hearing of my desire, many have since described this event as the little miracle of my clothing day, while at the same time expressing surprise at the strange fancy I displayed. So much the better—such things help to show forth still more the wonderful condescension of the Spouse of Virgins, of Him who loves lilies white as the snow."

Her Profession

She made her holy vows in Carmel on September 8, 1890, and of this she writes: "The next morning, September 8, my soul was flooded with heavenly joy, and in that peace which surpasseth understanding, I pronounced my holy vows. Was not the nativity of Mary a beautiful feast on which to become the spouse of Christ? It was the little newborn Mary who presented her little Flower to the little Jesus."

A beautiful passage in the Autobiography follows the one just quoted: "Eight days after I had taken the veil, our cousin Jeanne was married to Dr. La Neele and at her next visit I heard of all the little attentions she lavished on her husband. I was greatly impressed and I determined it should never be said that a woman in the world did more for her husband than I for my Beloved. Filled with fresh ardor, I strove with increased earnestness to please my heavenly spouse, the King of Kings, who had deigned to honor me by a divine alliance.

"When I saw the letter announcing our cousin's marriage, I thought I would amuse myself by composing an invitation which I read to the novices in order to bring home to them what had struck me so forcibly—that earthly unions, however glorious, were as nothing compared to the titles of a spouse of Christ."

The invitation to which the Little Flower refers follows; it is modeled closely on the letters whereby French parents announce the marriage of their children:

"God Almighty, Creator of heaven and earth, Sovereign Ruler of the universe, and the most glorious Virgin Mary, Queen of the heavenly court, announce to you the spiritual espousals of Their August Son, Jesus, King of Kings, and Lord of Lords, with little Thérèse Martin, now Princess and Lady of His Kingdoms of the Holy Childhood and the passion, assigned to her in dowry by her Divine Spouse, from which kingdom she holds her titles of nobility—OF THE CHILD JESUS AND OF THE HOLY FACE. It was not possible to invite you to the wedding feast which took place on the Mountain of Carmel, September 8, 1890—the heavenly court was alone admitted—but you are requested to be present at the at home which will take place tomorrow, the day of eternity, when Jesus, the Son of God, will come in the clouds of heaven, in the splendor of His Majesty, to judge the living and the dead. The hour being uncertain, you are asked to hold yourselves in readiness and to watch."

This exquisitely worded invitation, written to amuse herself is certainly sublime in its imaginative power and its poetic beauty, and in the depth of the spiritual lessons which it contains. It will bear re-reading and careful meditation.

Thorns Amid Roses—Her Sorrows

Many, attracted by the sweetness of the Little Flower's words, by her cheerfulness and by her frequent protestations of her complete happiness, fail to realize that her life was one long record of sorrow. Few pages of her Autobiography fail to record some pain, some trial, some sorrow. About some of her sorrows before she entered the convent, notably, her mother's death, her parting from Pauline, the thwarting of her ambition to enter Carmel, we have already spoken. Of her convent life she writes: "I found the religious life just what I expected. Sacrifice was never a matter of surprise. Everything in the convent delighted me, yet from the very outset my path was strewn with thorns rather than with roses."

Only a few of the thorns of her convent life may be mentioned in this pamphlet. First, there was the thorn of spiritual dryness, aridity, which increased until, as she says, "I found no comfort in heaven or on earth." She was the prey to all kinds of interior trials. "The darkness within my soul was so thick that I no longer knew if God loved me." To this was added the prudent severity of her first superior who never met our little novice without scolding and finding fault. She was too slow; her dusting was not thorough; a cobweb was found in the cloister. Yet Thérèse could write, "Yet, dear mother, I thank God for having provided me with so sound and valuable a training: it was a priceless grace. What should I have become if, as the outside world believes, I had been made the pet of the community?"

Then, as a climax of grief, came the agony of her father's stroke of apoplexy which robbed her beloved king of his mind and necessitated his removal to an asylum. Oh, what a cross that cruel fate of the father must have been to his little Queen. She tells us that she suffered from it so intensely that she learned at that time how the agony of the crucifixion of Our

Lord pierced the heart of His holy mother. "I no longer protested that I could suffer more. As there are no words to express my grief I shall not attempt to describe it here. . . ."

Throughout the Autobiography we find that the Little Flower never mentions a sorrow without adding the startling statement that her cross caused her the greatest happiness. For instance, after telling us how she suffered during her father's confinement in an asylum she adds, "The three years of our dear father's martyrdom seem to me the sweetest and most fruitful of our lives. I would not exchange them for the most sublime ecstasies, and in gratitude for such a priceless treasure my heart cries out: 'Blessed be Thou for the days wherein Thou hast afflicted us.'"

This strange intermingling of the keenest suffering with the greatest happiness—this mystery of the Little Flower's falling in love with suffering—will become intelligible to us as we study her as an apostle of prayer and seraph of love, eager to save souls, and to help priests save souls, by prayer and sacrifice and sufferings borne in love and cheerfulness.

The Little Flower an Apostle of Prayer—A Victim for Sin

Our little saint had the soul of an apostle, of a martyr. "Like Thee, O my Adorable Spouse," she writes, "I would be scourged, I would be crucified! I would be flayed like St. Bartholomew, plunged into boiling oil like St. John, or, like St. Ignatius of Antioch, ground by the teeth of wild beasts into a bread worthy of God.

"With St. Agnes and St. Cecilia, I would offer my neck to the sword of the executioner and like Joan of Arc murmur the name of Jesus at the burning stake.

"Like the prophets and doctors, I would be a light unto souls, I would travel the world over to preach Thy name, O my beloved, and raise on heathen soil the glorious standard of the cross. One mission alone would not satisfy my longings. I would spread the Gospel in all parts of the earth, even to the farthest isles. I would be a missionary, but not for a few years only. Were it possible, I should wish to have been one from the world's creation and to remain one till the end of time. Open, O Jesus, the Book of Life, in which are written the deeds of all Thy saints; each one of those deeds, I long to accomplish for Thee."

The Little Flower tells us that Our Lord was pleased to grant these desires; that is, He made her a martyr of love and He made her an apostle of prayer. Indeed her very vocation as a Carmelite nun required her to become an apostle and a victim for sin. Every Carmelite has a special vocation and duty of becoming a voluntary victim offered to God for the sins of mankind. Just as Christ offered himself for sin, generous souls in imitation of Him fling themselves between the sinner and the avenging wrath of God. The enormities of a proud and lustful world rise as a filthy stench to the gates of heaven. Sin is everywhere, filling the world with misery, eternity with ruined souls, and the body of Christ with reopened wounds.* "Over this whirling carnival of sin hangs the terrible wrath of God which is withheld by thousands of pure souls who have dedicated themselves as Carmelites and Poor Clares to love God and to hold back with weak but powerful hands the bolts of God's just anger. While the world dances merrily down the paths of sin, the Carmelite Sisters do penance before the crucifix. While the world banquets, they sit down to bread and water and unseasoned vegetables. When at midnight the sound of drunken revelry drowns the chiming clock, they rise from hard couches to pray God's mercy on a sinful world.

"They love Christ for the millions who hate Him. They honor Him with solemn chant for the millions who mock Him and revile Him. They offer up unceasing prayer for the millions who will not pray for themselves. And though the world never sees their faces nor knows of their existence, their prayers search the ends of the earth, snatching uncounted souls from ruin and bringing heedless wanderers safe, to God.

* Lord—"Story of the Little Flower."

"God's justice is satisfied by the sacrifice of their innocent souls and stainless bodies. They are the precious victims by which a mad world is saved from the consequences of its folly.

"Into this life, little Thérèse plunged with all the ardor of her vibrant nature. To love Christ for all the world's hatred, to sing His praises night and day, to fast and wear an iron girdle, to wash soiled clothes and scrub on bended knees, to stretch her young limbs on the planks of her tiny cell and rise at midnight blind with sleep, to keep her eyes cast down and her tongue silent—all this gladly, if she might win one soul to love her lover. She looked on herself as a little victim to be offered to God for the sins of mankind. And in the most terrible of her trials, she looked up toward God and cried, 'If I can serve Thee better in hell than in heaven, and by my eternal suffering win for Thee the love of the damned, let me suffer forever in the depths of hell. Take me as a sacrifice to win love from those who do not love Thee!'

"Fired from the start with a splendid ambition, she set her whole soul to pray for priests. In her burned the zeal of an apostle; but as she was too weak, she thought, too insignificant to win souls herself, she dedicated herself to winning courage and strength and zeal and stainless purity for the soldiers of the King. Her sacrifice and prayer would make her an apostle of apostles. She would be a little sister of God's missionaries."

The Little Flower had, like every Carmelite Sister, proclaimed at her Profession, "I have come to save souls and especially to pray for Priests." After quoting these words in her Autobiography, the Little Flower adds, "Our Lord made me understand that it was by the cross He would give me souls. The more I met with crosses, the stronger grew my attraction to suffering."

It should be recorded that not only as a nun, but as a mere child, Thérèse was already filled with a desire to save souls. One Sunday at Mass, before she entered the convent, a photograph representing our Savior on the cross, partly slipped out of her prayer book just far enough to let her see Our Lord's hand pierced and bleeding. A sudden grief and resolution came to her. It grieved her to the heart to see the Precious Blood falling to the ground with no one eager to gather it as it fell, and she resolved to remain in spirit under the Cross that she might collect this Blood shed for man's salvation and pour it forth upon souls.

From that day the dying cry of Jesus, "I thirst," re-echoed continuously in her heart, enkindling there a vehement zeal unknown to her before. She longed to quench the thirst of her Beloved. She, too, was consumed with desire for souls, and was eager to save them from everlasting flames at any cost.

Soon afterwards she heard of a notorious criminal who had been condemned to death and who had determined to go to the gallows impenitent, without confessing his sins. To obtain his conversion, Thérèse made use of every imaginable spiritual means. Her prayers and many little sacrifices were rewarded, for the man repented before death, and Thérèse was overjoyed. After that singular grace, her desire to save souls grew stronger every day. "One thing only is necessary here on earth," she declared, "to love Jesus and gain souls for Him, that they, too, may love Him."

For souls then, for the souls of sinners, for the souls of pagans, for the souls of priests who were laboring to convert the sinful and the unbelieving, she offered all the little mortifications of her little way, all her prayers, all her sorrows. Since her sorrows thus offered were winning souls to God, crosses were at once sweet and bitter, at once painful and full of joy. All her merits were spent on souls. "Were I to live to be eighty, I should always be poor, because I cannot economize. All my earnings are immediately spent on the ransom of souls."

The Little Flower—A Seraph of Love

A Seraph is an angel of the highest order; the word is derived from a Hebrew verb meaning "to burn." When therefore we call the Little Flower a seraph of love, we mean to express the thought that her soul was almost superhuman, almost angelic in its burning love of God. The marvelous purity of the Little Flower's love of God is a revelation even to those most intimately acquainted with the lives of the saints. In her Autobiography she expresses her burning love of God in ways more striking, more beautiful, and more tender than any other saint ever expressed Love of God. She writes, "God in His infinite goodness has given me a clear insight into the deep mysteries of love, and if I could only express what I know, you would hear heavenly music; but alas, I can only stammer like a child." She does not stammer; she makes heavenly music; let us listen and say whether we have ever heard such music before.

"If, supposing the impossible," she said, "God Himself could not see my good actions I would not be troubled. I love Him so much I would like to give Him joy without His knowing who gave it." Did ever a saint utter sentiments like these? "When He sees the gifts being made," she argued, "He is obliged, as it were, to make a return. I should wish to spare Him the trouble." This is love which is indeed a thing for angels to wonder at.

She loved Jesus too much even to think of a reward for her life of heroic devotion to Him. "My Jesus, Thou knowest I do not serve Thee for sake of reward, but solely out of love, and a desire to win Thee souls."

How delightful to God must have been this love of His Little Flower who never thought of self, never considered the reward, never desired any merits but thought only of the satisfaction she could give to her beloved. She thought only of the satisfaction she could give to her beloved. Let us glean from her Autobiography a few examples of these sublime dispositions of her heart.

A novice said to her, "You are right, Sister; henceforth I shall not let others see my troubles; henceforth my tears will be for God alone."

"Tears for God!" ejaculated Thérèse in her loving way, "That must not be. Far less to Him than to creatures ought you to show a mournful face. It is for us to console Our Lord, and not for Him to console us. We must learn to hide our troubles from Him and to tell Him daily that we are happy to suffer for Him."

In the following passage she reveals the same disposition; she thought only of Jesus: "Far from feeling consoled I went through my retreat in a state of utter spiritual desolation—seemingly abandoned by God. Jesus slept in my barque, as was His wont. But how rarely will souls allow Him to sleep in peace! Wearied with making continual advances, our good Master readily avails Himself of the repose I offer Him, and probably will sleep on till my great and everlasting retreat; this, however, rather rejoices than grieves me."

It rejoices her because, as she writes elsewhere, "I love Him so much I am always content with whatever He sends me. I love all that He does." What a marvelously pure and unselfish love! It matters not whether He sends a rose or a cross, she loves all He does. The one wish of her heart is to give Him pleasure. In her solicitude for Our Lord she goes back through the centuries and tells us that had she been on the ship which carried the apostles, when the sea threatened to overwhelm it and Christ slept on quietly amid the tossing billows and the lashing waves, she would have taken good care not to have awakened Him. Under no circumstances would she have anticipated by even one single instant that moment of time which Jesus might choose to awake and quiet the storm. For to have done so would have been to depart though ever so little, from her own little way which she has told us is the way of spiritual childhood, the way of trust and absolute self-surrender. Is there love more perfect than this?

The same perfect love looking only to the pleasure of her Lover is manifested in her words, "I would not choose to die rather than live, and if God were to offer me my choice, I would not make one; I only Wish what He wishes; it is what He wills that I love." It is manifested again in this little poem which the Little Flower inscribed to our Blessed Lady:

> All, all that He has granted me, Oh!
> Tell Him He may take it!

> Tell Him, dear Mother, He may do whate'er
> > He please with me;
> That He may bruise my heart today, and make it
> > sore, and break it,
> So only through Eternity
> > my eyes His Face may see!

Still other passages in which may be heard the heavenly music of her language of love are these: "I will that creatures should possess not a single atom of my love. I wish to give all to Jesus. I desire no sensible consolation in loving. Provided Jesus feel my love, that is enough for me. Oh! to love Him and to make Him loved . . . how sweet it is! . . . I have but one wish, one desire: to love Jesus above everything else, to love Him to excess, even unto folly. Yes, it is love that draws me . . . O Jesus, I beg Thee only for love without limits and without bounds. Would, O my Jesus, that for Thy love I could be a martyr! Oh, give me martyrdom of soul or martyrdom of body, or rather give me both!"

"Never shall it be said that a woman in the world did more for her husband than I for my Beloved." Accordingly she sought little opportunities of giving pleasure to Jesus. She gave Him a smile, a pleasant word when inclined to be silent or to show fatigue. And when she could find no such opportunities for little attentions, she would tell Him again and again that she loved Him. Two nights before she died[*] the infirmarian looking in upon the Little Flower during the night, found her with hands joined and eyes raised to heaven and asked, "What are you doing? You ought to try and get some sleep." "I cannot, Sister, I am suffering too much; so I pray." "And what do you say to Jesus?" "I say nothing—I love Him!"

She wasn't saying anything to Him; she was just loving Him. And she died loving Him, with these words of love upon her lips: "O! . . . I love Him! . . . My God, . . . I . . . love . . . Thee!"

---

[*] The Little Flower died on September 30, 1897.

The Little Flower's "Little Way"

To outline the life of St. Thérèse without saying a few words on her little way would be to leave even the shortest sketch incomplete. This little way is the secret of that mysterious power which comes forth from every page of her Autobiography and which has won the love of millions of human hearts.

Jesus taught her a little way to heaven, a way that may be followed by all little souls, a way that will lead little souls to great sanctity, a way which may be embraced by anyone and every one precisely because it is a little way, in which there is nothing extraordinary, nothing complicated, nothing to discourage little souls.

Her little way has been variously termed: Her little way of spiritual childhood; her little way of love; her little way of humility; her little way of confidence in God; her little way of abandonment and self-surrender. Of these terms the first is the most comprehensive because the phrase "spiritual childhood" includes humility, simplicity, love and confidence, all of which are characteristic of childhood, all elements of Thérèse's little way, all virtues which blossomed full in her childlike soul.

Her little way is not an entirely new one. It was taught by Our Lord in the words, "Unless you become as little children you shall not enter into the kingdom of heaven." It was practiced by Him, by Joseph and Mary, by countless souls all down through the centuries. But Our Lord deigned to reveal it in all its beauty to little Thérèse, who made it peculiarly her own and interpreted it, under His inspiration, with unparalleled skill and incomparable charm. She has become, under God's direction and providence, the modern apostle of that little way. She is God's messenger to the twentieth century; her message is her way of spiritual childhood, and her credentials are contained in these words of the Vicar of Christ: "There is a call to the Faithful of every nation, no matter what may be their age, sex, or state of life, to enter whole-heartedly into the 'little way' which led Sister Thérèse of the Child Jesus to the summit of heroic virtue."

Elsewhere Pius XI says of the Little Way of Thérèse, "Here, then, is a way which, without giving to everyone assurance of reaching the heights to which God has led Thérèse, is not only possible, but easy for all. As St. Augustine remarks, not everyone can preach and perform great works, but who is there that cannot pray, humble himself, and love?"

Her Own Description of Her Little Way— Her Mission to Souls

What then, in the Little Flower's own words, is her little way? One evening, in the closing days of her life, when Mother Agnes of Jesus went to the infirmary, Sister Thérèse welcomed her with an extraordinary expression of joy: "Mother!" she said, "some notes from a distant concert have just reached my ears, and there has come to me the thought that soon I shall be listening to the sweet melodies of paradise. This thought, however, gave me only a moment's joy, for one hope alone makes my heart beat fast—the love I shall receive and the love I shall be able to give! I feel that my mission is soon to begin—to make others love God as I love Him . . . to teach souls my little way. I WILL SPEND MY HEAVEN IN DOING GOOD UPON EARTH. This is not impossible, for the angels keep watch over us while they enjoy the Beatific Vision. No, there cannot be rest for me till the end of the world—till the angel shall have said: 'Time is no more.' Then I shall take my rest, then I shall be able to rejoice, because the number of the elect will be complete."

"And what is the little way that you would teach?" asked Mother Agnes of Jesus.

"IT IS THE WAY OF SPIRITUAL CHILDHOOD, THE WAY OF TRUST AND ABSOLUTE SELF-SURRENDER. I want to point out to souls the means that I have always found so completely successful, to tell them there is only one thing to do here below—to offer Our Lord the flowers of little sacrifices and win Him by our caresses. That is how I have won Him, and that is why I shall be made so welcome by Him."

The Little Flower then was conscious of her own mission given her by God to teach other souls her little way. She calls her little way "the way of spiritual childhood, trust and absolute self-surrender."

Other passages in which she amplifies this definition should be quoted: "You see, Mother, that I am but a very little soul, who can offer to God only very little things. It still happens that I frequently miss the opportunity of welcoming these little sacrifices which bring so much peace; but I am not discouraged—I bear the loss of a little peace and I try to be more watchful in the future." Little sacrifices, then, little acts of self denial, are part of her little way.

Again she writes: "Jesus deigns to point out to me the only way which leads to love's divine furnace, and that way is self-surrender; it is the confidence of the little child who sleeps without fear in its father's arms." Confidence in God and absolute trust in Him, it appears, are likewise constituents of her little way.

We may conclude, therefore, from her own pronouncements, that her little way consists of the practice of Spiritual childhood, in the cultivation of a childlike spirit, in simplicity and humility, in holy abandonment, in confidence and trust in God, and in the practice of little mortifications.

Of these various departments of her little way concrete examples should be given here so that others may learn to follow in the way of her to whom was given by God the mission of preaching His little way to the modern world.

Her Humility

Of this constituent of her little way a beautiful example has already been given in the Prelude to Her Life Story quoted on page 4. Another passage redolent of humility follows: "You know, Mother, that I have always desired to become a saint, but in comparing myself with the saints I have ever felt that I am as far removed from them as a grain of sand trampled underfoot by the passerby is from the mountains whose summit is lost in the clouds."

"Instead of feeling discouraged by such reflections, I concluded that God would not inspire a wish which could not be realized, and that in spite of my littleness, I might aim at being a saint. 'It is impossible,' I said, 'for me to become great, so I must bear with myself and my many imperfections; but I will seek out a means of reaching heaven by a little way—very short, very straight, and entirely new. We live in an age of inventions: there are now lifts which save us the trouble of climbing the stairs. I will try to find a lift by which I may be raised unto God, for I am too small to climb the steep stairway of perfection'."

The very name which Thérèse gave herself, The Little Flower, demonstrates her humility. She was not, in her own estimation, a stalwart oak in God's kingdom but just a little flower in God's garden.

Her Littleness and Childlike Spirit

The fundamental disposition of the life of spiritual childhood (which is but another name for humility of heart) consists in recognizing our weakness and in seeking and loving a state of littleness and weakness. The Little Flower's childlike spirit is illustrated by the passages given under the preceding heading, humility, and by the following passages: "In Holy Scriptures I came across these words uttered by Eternal Wisdom itself, 'Whosoever is a little one, let him come to Me.' I therefore drew near to God, feeling sure I had discovered what I sought. But wishing further to know what He would do to the little one, I continued my search and this is what I found, 'You shall be carried at the breasts and upon the knees; as one whom the mother caresseth, so will I comfort you.'

"Never have I been consoled by words more tender and more sweet. O Jesus! Thy arms, then, are the lift which must raise me even unto heaven. To reach heaven I need not become great; on the contrary, I must remain little, I must become even smaller than I am."

Again she writes, "What pleases Jesus in my little soul is to see me love my littleness and to see my blind trust in His mercy.

Because I was little and weak Jesus stooped down to me and tenderly instructed me in the secrets of His love. It was Jesus who did all in me, and I—I did nothing but be little and weak."

This state of spiritual littleness is always possible at any age and in all positions of life. As Thérèse remarks, "it is quite possible to remain little even in filling the most important office, and even on attaining extreme old age. If I lived eighty years and filled all offices, I should, I feel certain, be quite as little at the time of my death as I am today."

Examples of Her Little Sacrifices

In the Little Flower's Autobiography we read: "I resolved to give myself up more than ever to a serious and mortified life. When I say mortified, I do not speak of the penances of the saints. Far from resembling these beautiful souls who from their childhood practiced all sorts of macerations, I made mine consist entirely in breaking my will, checking a word of retort, rendering little services to those around me without attracting notice, and a thousand other things of this sort."

Although her two beloved sisters were in the convent with the Little Flower, their presence afforded the young postulant many occasions for repressing her affection—a form of self-denial most keenly felt. The rules of solitude and silence were strictly observed and she saw her sisters only at recreation. Had she been less mortified she might often have sat beside them, but no one could remark in her any special affection for them, since by preference she sought the company of those religious who were least agreeable to her. Of the repression of her desires to be with Pauline, who was for a time her Mother Superior, the Little Flower writes: "I remember when I was a postulant there were times when I was so violently tempted to seek my own satisfaction by having a word with you, that I was obliged to hurry past your cell and cling to the banisters to keep myself from turning in. Many were the permissions I wanted to ask, and pretexts for yielding to my natural affection suggested themselves in hundreds. How glad I am that from the beginning I learned to practice self-denial!"

Certain dishes were especially distasteful to her but the sisters tried in vain to discover the dishes Thérèse preferred. The kitchen sisters, too, finding her easy to please, invariably served to her whatever was left, and it was only during her last illness, when she was put under obedience to say what disagreed with her, that her mortifications came to light.

The care of the aged invalid Sister St. Peter, who was impossible to please, was entrusted to the Little Flower. "It cost me a great effort to offer my services," writes Thérèse, "but I was unwilling to lose such a golden opportunity, remembering Our Lord's own words, 'As long as you did it to one of these My least brethren, you did it to Me.' First her stool had to be moved and carried in a particular way, without the least hurry, and then began the journey. Supporting the poor old sister by her girdle, I tried to acquit myself of the task as gently as I could; if by some mischance she stumbled, I was told I was going too fast and that she would certainly fall; when I tried to lead her more slowly she would say, 'Where are you? . . . I don't feel your hand . . . You are letting go your hold . . . I am going to fall . . . I was right when I said you were too young to take care of me'."

"A long time has elapsed since all this happened, but Our Lord allows the memory of it to linger with me like a perfume from heaven. One cold winter's evening, when I was humbly leading Sister St. Peter, there suddenly fell on my ears the harmonious strains of distant music. A picture rose before me of a richly furnished room, brilliantly lighted and decorated, and full of elegantly dressed young girls conversing together as is the way of the world. Then I turned to the poor invalid; instead of sweet music, I heard her complaints; instead of rich gilding I saw the bare brick of our cloister, scarcely visible in the dim, flickering light.

"The contrast thrilled me, and Our Lord, so illumined my soul with the rays of His truth, in the light of which the pleasures of the world are but darkness, that not for a thousand years of such worldly delights would I have bartered the ten minutes spent in my act of charity."

The Little Flower practiced other penances such as these: to refrain from turning around and silencing with a look a sister near her in chapel who fidgeted incessantly during meditation; to refrain from drawing back and wiping her face when a sister, while washing the linen, continually sprinkled her face with dirty soapsuds; to treat a sister who was particularly disagreeable to her with such gentleness that one day she said to the Little Flower, "Sister Thérèse, tell me now what it is that attracts you to me so strongly? I never meet you without being welcomed with your most gracious smile!" "Ah! what attracted me was Jesus hidden in the depths of her soul, Jesus who makes sweet even that which is most bitter."

Only a very few of her little mortifications have been described here, but those few will suffice to suggest a method of daily self-denial which is at hand to every one.

Her Childlike Confidence in God

The confidence of the Little Flower in God and in the Mercy of God may perhaps best be illustrated by the following words of the Little Flower: "What offends Jesus, what wounds Him to the heart is a lack of confidence. Never can we have too much confidence in the good God—He is so good. It is not because I have been preserved from mortal sin that I mount to God on the wings of trust and love. Nay, I feel that I should not lose a whit of my confidence, even had I on my conscience every crime that it is possible to commit. With a heart that sorrow had broken, I should throw myself into my Savior's arms. I know that the prodigal child is dear to Him; I have heard His words to Mary Magdalen, to the adulteress, to the Samaritan woman. No one can frighten me, for in so far as His love and mercy are concerned I know what to rely upon. I know that all that multitude of sins would disappear in the twinkling of an eye, even as a drop of water cast into a flaming furnace."

Confidence was the Little Flower's key to the greatest treasures of God. From her place in heaven she admonishes both just and sinners: Trust in God, if you desire many and great graces.

Her Abandonment and Self-Surrender

This virtue has already been partly illustrated in these passages given under the caption, "The Little Flower – seraph of love;" "What He chooses for me is what pleases me most. I love all that He does." Again she exclaims: "My God, one thing alone do I fear and that is to retain my own will. Take Thou my will, for I choose all that Thou willest."

She could find no better way of illustrating her little way of abandonment and self-surrender than by asserting that we should have all the trust of a little child who sleeps in his father's arms without fear of the present or of the future. In one of her poems she expresses her holy abandonment:

> My heaven is—to feel in me the likeness
> Of the God of power who created me;
> My heaven is—to stay forever in His presence,
> To call Him Father—just His child to be;
> Safe in His Arms divine, near to His Sacred Face,
> Resting upon His heart, of the storm I have no fear;
> Abandonment complete, this is my only law—
> Behold my heaven here!

The purest disinterestedness appears to be the distinctive mark of her abandonment. This it is that is most prominent in her words, as also in the comparisons she employs to explain her thought. In truth she desires but one thing: that is, to be in the hands of the Child Jesus as a little toy, but a toy of no value, that He can throw on the ground, toss about, pierce, leave in a corner, or else press to His Heart, if it so please Him. For she desires no other joy but that of making Him smile. Or again, what she wishes to be is a rose that sheds its petals beneath the feet of Jesus, one that is treated without care, forgotten, thrown at the mercy of the wind. He may trample it underfoot, He may crush it; that does not matter, provided only it soothe at least His last steps on Calvary!

It goes without saying that preferences of a personal nature would be incompatible with such a degree of abandonment. And so Saint Thérèse, in what concerned herself, made it a rule not to be occupied with any particular desires. Indifferent to life or death, although her heart told her that death was the more enviable portion, she abstained from choosing. She left that care to her Father in heaven. "What He chooses for me," she said, "is what pleases me most. I LOVE ALL THAT HE DOES."

Her Simplicity

Simplicity excludes all that savors of duplicity. Simplicity is one of the most fascinating characteristics of childhood, which impresses on the slightest movements of the little one, on its every word, on all its ways, that stamp of uprightness and candor which renders it so lovable in our eyes.

St. Thérèse was a perfect model of this beautiful and lovable simplicity. In her little way everything is ordinary; everything happens in the very simplest way. There was nothing complex in her little way; it was simple. It is the property of simplicity to go straight to its end; in the spiritual life the end is God. Thérèse proposed God as the direct end of all her actions. She had but one constant preoccupation: to please the Good God. Her direct way to God was by love and therefore in her eyes all was reduced to love. "I know of one means only by which to arrive at perfection: Love. Let us love, since our hearts were made for nothing else." Nothing could be more touching nor more beautiful in its simplicity than her answer to the question addressed to her on her death bed: "What do you say to Jesus?"

"I say nothing: I just LOVE Him."

Love of God is the simple secret of the simplicity of Thérèse.

The Little Flower in death:
"I will spend my heaven doing good on earth."

Part Three

Beatification, Canonization, and Shower of Roses

Beatification and Canonization

The Little Flower was declared "Blessed" by Pope Pius XI in 1923. She was canonized by the same pontiff on May 17, 1925, to the great joy of uncounted multitudes who from every quarter of the world had sent touching and innumerable supplications begging the Holy See to raise to the honors of the altar the humble little Carmelite who had been dead but twenty-eight years.

Her Shower of Roses

The extraordinary abundance of favors attributed to the intercession of her who is now known as "everybody's Little Flower" proves that she had a divine mission to perform, for God does not lavish His miracles without weighty reason. A miracle is the letter of recommendation that God gives His messengers to accredit them with men. The Little Flower's life and little way, therefore, come to us stamped with the seal of the approval of the Vicars of Christ, as we have seen, and with the seal of Almighty God, for miracles are His seal.

More marvelous than her miracles is her foreknowledge and prediction, while she was still alive, that she would heap the world high with wonders. "I will spend my heaven in doing good upon earth," she said. "I shall let fall from heaven a shower of roses. My work begins after my death." And how marvelously have her prophecies already been fulfilled! She has drawn thousands of little souls to her. She, who in life was not known five miles from her Lisieux convent, in death is known and honored by multitudes throughout the world by thousands of members of her Society all over distant America, by thousands who so crowd her National Shrine in Chicago every Tuesday that the attention of the whole city is attracted and even protestants ask, "May non-catholics go in to see little Thérèse?"—meaning her shrine. Her society in America promises to become one of the largest religious organizations in the history of the Church in America, a grand national Society which by its members alone serves already to attract public attention to the Little Flower and to her little way.

To the members of the Society of the Little Flower, to all her lovers, Thérèse is not dead; she lives. She is alive to them all. They open their arms to receive her roses—roses of healing, roses of financial assistance, roses of relief from trouble and trial, roses of greater love of God, of strength against temptation, roses of the gift of prayer, roses of the virtues of humility, simplicity and purity. The roses drop and are caught by millions all over the world, by thousands of the members of her Society here in America.*

Already five volumes, called "The Shower of Roses," have been printed to record some of her spiritual and material favors. Every day the Chicago Carmelite Fathers in charge of the Society of the Little Flower receive from all parts of the United States and Canada acknowledgment of favors attributed to the Little Flower's intercession. Pius XI says authoritatively of her shower of roses, "We have invoked her as our advocate and our patron because of the rain of roses which, as she promised, she does not cease to pour down upon men."

---

* Those who wish information concerning conditions for membership in the Society of the Little Flower can visit www.littleflower.org. All members of the society and their intentions are automatically remembered in all the Masses and Devotions of the Perpetual Novena at the National Shrine of the Little Flower in the Carmelite church of St. Clara, Chicago.

The nuns of Lisieux said to the Little Flower during her last illness, "You will look down upon us from the heights of heaven, will you not, Sister?" "No," she replied, "I will come down."

She has indeed "come down" not once but, upon the testimony of most reliable witnesses, hundreds and hundreds of times; always simple, always sweet, always doing good. She has come down* not always, however, letting herself be seen, to bring to earth the gifts of the good God. It has been easy to recognize her, for she still has her own particular way of doing good; even in her way of scattering wide her shower of roses we recognize the lovable simplicity of her childlike soul.

May she "come down" to all our readers, doing good to them, teaching them her little way, leading them finally, according to her promise, before the throne of the Blessed Trinity as a legion of little victims worthy of the merciful, boundless love of the good God.

---

* To a nun in France the Little Flower appeared and made known that the surest way to her favor was to labor to make her better known. One of the ways of making her better known is by becoming a promoter of the society of the Little Flower; other souls are thereby made acquainted with the Little Flower and her little way.

The Living Sisters of the Little Flower

Saint Thérèse of the Child Jesus, surrounded by her sisters.
Top: Pauline, Sr. Agnes of Jesus.
To her right: Marie, Sr. Marie of the Sacred Heart.
To her left: Léonie, Sr. Frances Thérèse.
Bottom, to the right of the saint: Céline, Sr. Geneviève of the Holy Face.
To her left: her cousin, Marie Guérin, Sr. Marie of the Eucharist.

Chapter One

Description of Lisieux, of the Little Flower's Convent and of the Personal Appearance of the Little Flower's Sisters

Since, my dear friends, you are all so eager to hear the account of my visits with the Little Flower's sisters, I shall, without any preliminary other than to say that I am glad to be back home* and to see you all, plunge directly into the narrative of my visit to the home of the Little Flower.

As most of you know, the Little Flower, St. Thérèse, has four living sisters. They are: Pauline, the eldest, Marie, Céline and Léonie. The first three are Carmelite nuns living now in the same convent in which the Little Flower lived and died. Pauline's name in religion is Mother Agnes of Jesus. Marie's name in religion is Sister Mary of the Sacred Heart and Céline's name is Sister Genevieve of the Holy Face. Those are the three sisters of the Little Flower who are Carmelite nuns. The fourth sister, Léonie, called in religion Sister Frances, is a Visitation nun who lives in a convent at Caen, not far from Lisieux.

While in France I interviewed at length all four of these living sisters of our little saint and they sent to you messages, which shall be delivered in the course of the novena, but in order that we may proceed in an orderly manner, let us begin this afternoon by a brief description of Lisieux.

---

* Father Dolan, upon his arrival in New York from France, rushed from the pier to the train and arrived in Chicago at the National Shrine just in time to deliver this first discourse at the opening service of the May novena during which all these talks were given. (Editor's Note.)

The town in which the Little Flower lived and died, Lisieux, is an old Normandy town with a history that dates back to the time of its conquest by Julius Caesar in the year 57 before Christ. It is located in the fresh and fertile valley of the Touques River, about half way between Cherbourg and Paris. The journey to Lisieux is supremely delightful. The train passes along interminable apple orchards which when I was there were in full bloom, and apple blossom time in Normandy affords views that are not soon to be forgotten. The Little Flower tells us in her Autobiography that the wooded hillsides on each side of the valley in which Lisieux is situated afforded her many delights on her afternoon walks with her father before she shut herself up in the convent, from the garden of which she could gain a view of but a tiny corner of God's sky.

Although Lisieux is charmingly situated, the town itself is not beautiful. On the contrary, Lisieux would be ugly if it were not picturesque. Its buildings are old and crumbling. Its streets are extremely narrow, so narrow that one might walk in the middle of the street and stretch out his arms and touch the buildings on each side of the street. No one but a saint, no one but a saint as attractive as the Little Flower, could have made that little old town known in all the corners of the world.

Before I went to Lisieux, I imagined that I would find the convent, in which the Little Flower lived and died, situated in the outskirts of the city, perhaps on a wooded hillside in a rural or semi-rural district.

But instead, I found her convent situated in the very center of the city; quite near the station, on a little side street, and although the chapel which adjoins the convent is very beautiful, the convent itself is an old brick building, dilapidated in the extreme.

As I walked those narrow streets that first day and gazed upon that dilapidated convent, the wonder of the Little Flower's story burst upon me with new force. What a marvel it was and is that anyone, anyone, living in that ancient convent, on a side street of an obscure Normandy town, should become known the world over! What a marvel it is! Thirty years ago, who, viewing that ancient convent on that side street, would have imagined that a girl-nun living there would, in a few short years, attract the attention of the world, and not only its attention but also the love of millions of every age and sex and race and condition in life? What a manifestation of God's power the Little Flower's story is! Queens born in palaces in the time of the Little Flower have died and even their names have been forgotten, but the name of the Little Flower shut up in that obscure Carmelite cloistered convent at the age of fifteen and dying at the tender age of twenty-four, when most people are beginning their life work, her name by God's power has been blown to the most remote villages of the earth. What a manifestation of God's power! He wanted a messenger and He selected Thérèse of Lisieux, and behold today, even humanly speaking, there is no glory like unto hers—no glory equal to that of this young and humble Carmelite nun. Whose name is on so many lips today? What hero's portrait is so rapidly diffused and so widely multiplied as the photograph of the Little Flower? Her picture looks down from the walls of millions of homes. What would Lisieux be today without the Little Flower? It would be as it was before her coming, unknown and unnoticed; but since her coming and because of her, Lisieux has become a world-city. Just as we speak of Teresa of Avila and Francis of Assisi, so now we speak of Thérèse of Lisieux and undoubtedly all down through the ages Lisieux will be hailed as one of the holy cities of humanity.

That first day, my dear friends, as I walked those narrow streets there was one thought that returned again and again to my mind, namely: "Saint Thérèse once walked these streets; the Little Flower as a girl once walked these very streets." With that thought those ugly little byways took on beauty and charm and even glory—I was walking on holy ground, upon ground sanctified by the frequent presence of the Little Flower.

I sought to find a hotel at a point that would be very near to the convent of the Little Flower, but I could find none near enough to suit me. However, directly across the road from the convent of the Little Flower there was a little inn which was licensed only for invalids. But before I had left America for France I had broken my ankle and I was still on crutches when I reached Lisieux. Consequently I was an invalid, disabled, and I was therefore entitled to and given a room in that inn. From my room I could have tossed a coin to the roof of the cell in which the Little Flower lived.

By the way, my crutches occasioned an interesting experience. The first day I wanted, of course, to see everything in the little town and I hobbled about on crutches, attracting no particular attention, as everyone who saw me thought I was like thousands of others who had come there to be cured by the relics of the Little Flower. But the time had come that night to put aside the crutches, and consequently the next morning when I appeared without crutches, immediately the rumor went abroad that I had been cured by the Little Flower. In spite of repeated denials the rumor persisted and as I passed through the streets towards the end of the week I could hear, "There he goes!" "There he is—the American priest that was miraculously cured by the relics of the Little Flower." This mistaken supposition did not have consequences that were at all unhappy because everywhere I went, people were anxious to wait on me and to do me favors and to talk to me, which was just what I wanted.

A word now about the life of the sisters in the Carmelite convent in order that my narrative may be clear, as it is unfolded, to all. The Carmelite sisters live under the most rigorous of all the rules of religious orders. Their life is one of absolute obedience and of prayer, and mortification. Their humiliations and mortifications and prayers they offer in atonement for your sins and mine. They offer their prayers and mortifications in atonement for the sins of the world. One of their greatest mortifications is what is known as absolute cloister; that is, once they enter the convent they never again reach the street. Once the door of the convent closes upon them, it closes upon them forever. Carmelite sisters are never transferred from one convent to another, and never under any imaginable pretense are they allowed to leave the convent. Once they have taken their vows they never again see their friends or relatives. Their friends and relatives, if there is sufficient reason and after a long interval, may come and visit them in the parlor, but they do not see the sister with whom they are visiting, nor does the sister see them. The parlor is divided into two sections, interior and exterior, by a solid wall which is called a grille. In this grille there is a bamboo panel through which voices may penetrate so that, for instance, when the Little Flower's father came to visit her in the parlor he talked with her, but he did not see her, nor did she see him. They talked through the grille. No one ever sees the Carmelite sisters except under the most unusual circumstances such as, for instance, when it is necessary to call a physician or nurse in extreme cases. Although almost no one ever sees the sisters of the Little Flower, still by a strange coincidence I am able to tell you this evening just what the appearance of the three Carmelite sisters of the Little Flower is today. That extraordinary coincidence was this: You may know that when a bone is broken it is kept in a cast and after the cast has been put aside massage is necessary. While in Lisieux, therefore, I sought a masseur and found that the only people who gave massage in Lisieux were the nuns of the Miséricorde Hospital. They are what we would call in this country "visiting nurses." So I called one of them and one Sister Agatha came, and fortunately for me, Sister Agatha a few months before had nursed one of the Little Flower's sisters, Marie, through a serious illness. She had been day and night at the bedside of Marie and had seen and talked not only with Marie but also many times with Pauline and Céline, the other two sisters of the Little Flower. Moreover, she was most willing to answer the questions I was eager to ask her.

I said to her, "Sister, what does Pauline look like?"

Sister Agatha answered: "Pauline is very short; she is extremely thin, and dark and her most distinguished characteristic is large, luminous, black eyes." She continued, "She is so small and short and thin that no one in Lisieux ever calls her 'Mother Agnes'; they call her 'The Little Mother,' even as the Little Flower called Pauline, [Ma petite mere]: 'My Little Mother', because Pauline was indeed the second mother of the Little Flower: her own mother died when she (the Little Flower) was four years old, and from then on Pauline was the mother of little Thérèse."

I said to Sister Agatha, "What does Céline look like?"

She answered, "Céline is not dark, but fair. She has blue eyes and even in her old age resembles the pictures that you see of the Little Flower."

"And," I said, "Marie? What does she look like?"

"Marie," said Sister Agatha, "is the stoutest and the jolliest of the three. She is dark like Pauline and has black eyes but they are not as large or as luminous as those of Pauline."

I asked her, "Which is the prettiest?"

She answered without any hesitation, "Céline, because she resembles the Little Flower."

"Which is the holiest?" I asked.

She answered again without any hesitation, "Pauline."

I said, "Sister, what makes you think so?"

She replied, "Because Pauline it was who formed the character of the Little Flower and therefore she must be the most holy."

So you see, my dear friends, how this chance meeting with Sister Agatha resulted in this intimate and interesting information concerning the Little Flower's sisters; information probably not obtainable from anyone in the world today except Sister Agatha. Tomorrow I shall tell you of my visit with the first of these sisters, Pauline.

Chapter Two

First Visit with Pauline

Today, my dear friends, I wish to speak to you of one who is to me and undoubtedly to you and to all lovers of the Little Flower, one of the most interesting persons in all this world. I speak of Pauline, Mother Agnes of Jesus, the beloved sister and second mother of Saint Thérèse.

One afternoon during my stay at Lisieux, after having said Mass in the morning at the tomb of the Little Flower and after having told her before the Mass, "Do what you will with this Mass, but remember, I want to talk with your sister, Pauline, today," I went over to the Carmelite Convent and pulled the bell cord at the street entrance. One of the sisters, the sister portress, came.

I said, "Sister, may I speak with Mother Agnes?"

The sister answered, "Mother Agnes does not come to the parlor." She pointed to a placard which read: "The pilgrims are requested not to ask to talk to the sisters of the Little Flower because they will be obliged to refuse to do so. The Little Flower will reward the pilgrims for this sacrifice of leaving her sisters to their life of prayer and solitude."

Nevertheless I said to the sister, "As a special favor would you take my card to Mother Agnes? I have received several letters from her in America and I am a director of The Little Flower Society in America, the largest organization in the world in honor of Saint Thérèse. Perhaps on this account Mother Agnes will see me."

"Very well, Father," said the sister, "I will take your card to her," and opening the door to the parlor, she asked me to have a seat.

You may imagine with what mingled feelings of trepidation and hopeful anticipation I waited before that grille, in that bare Carmelite convent parlor. Would she come? Was I to have the privilege of speaking with the Little Flower's sister or was I to be cruelly disappointed? I was more nervous and excited by far while waiting for Pauline than I was in Rome while waiting to be introduced unto the immediate presence of the Pope. Finally, I heard a door open behind the grille, but there were no footsteps, and then without any warning there came the customary greeting of the Carmelite sisters, "Deo Gratias"—Latin for "Thanks be to God."

But what a voice! So soft, so fresh, so musical, an angelic voice! But none of those adjectives give you any idea of the quality of that heavenly voice. I knew it must be Pauline because I had read of her voice. St. Thérèse in her Autobiography tells us how she, The Little Flower, loved the voice of her sister Pauline and so I said, "Is it Pauline?"

Again came that heavenly voice saying "Oui, mon Père, c'est Pauline" (Yes, Father, it is Pauline).

Then I became tongue-tied for a moment; I passed into a temporary trance when I realized that I was in the immediate presence of the beloved sister and second mother of Saint Thérèse! There rushed into my mind a flood of memories, memories of her association with the Little Flower. For instance, in a flash, there came that scene at the Little Flower's mother's deathbed. Around her bed were kneeling all her daughters, including the Little Flower, and when the last moment came and the Little Flower's mother was able no longer to speak, she took Pauline's hand and then pointed to her daughters about the bed; then she raised Pauline's hand reverently to her lips and kissed it with respect. By the gesture she meant to indicate that Pauline was now the mother of the now motherless children and the kiss signified the maternal authority with which she thereby vested Pauline.

There then before me, behind that grille, was Pauline, the mother of the Martin household throughout the girlhood of the Little Flower. There was that stern but devoted and affectionate teacher of the Little Flower who demanded perfect lessons from her every morning under the penalty of refusing her permission to take her usual walk with her father.

I recalled an incident of the Little Flower's girlhood which has always interested me and which illustrates Pauline's character. One hot summer's afternoon, Thérèse, returning from a long walk with her father, ran to Pauline saying, "Oh, Pauline, if you only knew how thirsty I am."

Pauline, thinking to teach the little girl a lesson in sacrifice, said, "Could you not bear the thirst, Thérèse, and offer it up for some poor sinner?"

The Little Flower looked up with her great eyes at her sister a moment and then said, "Oui, Pauline" (Yes, Pauline), heaving at the same time a great sigh which indicated the magnitude of the sacrifice.

Pauline soon relented and brought a refreshing drink to her little sister, but the Little Flower was scandalized and refused it, saying, "Oh no; take the drink and abandon the poor sinner? Oh, no."

Pauline explained that having accepted the sacrifice Thérèse had the merit of it and that now she must add to that merit the merit of obedience. Such was the beautiful training the Little Flower received from Pauline.

There before me was the sister who assigned the household tasks to the Little Flower. One of these duties was to answer the bell, which the Little Flower delighted to do, especially on Mondays when the poor of the town came to the Martin gate to ask for alms. The Little Flower would scamper across the lawn to the gate at the wall which surrounds the Martin home and then report the visitor's message to Pauline. On one occasion the Little Flower returned and said, "Oh, Pauline, it is a little lady with two tiny, tiny babies; what can I give them?" On another occasion when she had given some alms she returned all radiant with joy and said, "Oh, Pauline, the poor man said, 'God will bless you, my little miss.'"

There before me was Pauline who prepared the Little Flower for her first confession and to whom the Little Flower always went thereafter for counsel in her examination of conscience—if we can understand what the examination of conscience of a saint must be—the examination of conscience of one who could say just before she died, "From the age of three I never gave God aught but love."

Pauline was loved so tenderly by Thérèse that when Pauline left the Little Flower to become a Carmelite nun, the Little Flower was so grief stricken that she was seized with that mysterious illness of her girlhood which almost resulted in her death.

It was Pauline, who as the second mother of the Little Flower, Mother Superior of the convent, commanded St. Thérèse to write her Autobiography. It was to Pauline that Thérèse wrote most of her touching, affectionate and highly spiritualized letters.

Then, too, I thought in a flash, it was Pauline to whom Céline, her other sister, referred towards the end of the Little Flower's life when she (Céline) said one night, "Thérèse, your last loving look must not be for me, nor for Marie, but for Pauline." And it was Pauline who was with the Little Flower that last night when the sudden change for the worse came and Pauline it was who rang the bell summoning the sisters of the community to the bedside of the dying saint.

These were the memories that crowded into my mind as I found myself abruptly in the presence of the beloved sister of the Little Flower. No wonder I couldn't speak for a moment.

Then I found myself and said, "Mother, I can not tell you how happy I am to have the privilege of speaking with the sister and second mother of St. Thérèse."

Again that heavenly voice, "I am pleased, Father, that you are pleased, because I have heard that you have done much in America to promote devotion to the Little Flower."

"Yes, perhaps," I said, "Mother, but this visit more than repays anything I have done or will do."

"You know, Father, I could not come to talk to you as an individual priest. Our rule, as you know, forbids all unnecessary conversation, but I have come to you because you are the director of the Society in honor of the Little Flower* of which I have heard so much." Then she proceeded to ask many questions concerning the society in America—What was its membership? She asked me questions concerning the shrine in Chicago, the national headquarters of the Society of the Little Flower, and she asked for a photograph of the overflowing crowds at the shrine on Tuesdays. I promised to send her the photograph, which, by the way, I have done.

Then there followed some conversation which is relatively unimportant, and then I asked her permission to ask some questions. She assented and I asked, "Mother, during the lifetime of the Little Flower, did the sisters of her community look upon her as a saint?"

She answered, "No, Father, they looked upon her as a perfect religious but I do not think that they regarded her as a future canonized saint."

"But, Mother," I asked, "did they not notice anything extraordinary about her?"

"Oh, yes," she said, "they knew that she was no ordinary sister; she was so infinitely sweet and gentle that they all knew she was perfect in the practice of all virtues."

"But you, Mother," I said, "you, who were her second mother, who were the recipient of all her confidences, did you not know that God had marked her for a special mission?"

"Yes, Father, I knew; I knew all along that my little sister was no ordinary perfect religious; I knew all along that God had conferred upon my little sister His rarest and choicest graces, and especially toward the end when she began to utter her prophecies—'My work will begin after my death'—'I will

---

* Those who wish information concerning the spiritual privileges of membership in the Society of the Little Flower can visit www.littleflower.org.

spend my heaven in doing good upon earth'—'I shall let fall from heaven a shower of roses'—then I knew that her words had been inspired from on high and from then on no words escaped her lips but that I made a careful record of them in writing. I knew it then but I know it now more clearly than then that God had marked her for a special mission to the modern world."

The time is up now and I have not yet completed our narrative nor have I delivered the message Pauline sent, one to the men and one to the women. Those messages I will deliver tomorrow when we will complete this unfinished narrative of my interview with the sister of the Little Flower.

Chapter Three

First Visit with Pauline—Continued

We were forced to stop yesterday before I had completed my story of my interview with Pauline, the sister and second mother of the Little Flower. In order that you might appreciate the thrill of the interview, I tried yesterday to explain how close and intimate was the union between Thérèse and Pauline, but today we may add by way of preliminary a few more facts which will serve to illustrate their intimacy.

No one understood the Little Flower as well as Pauline. No one, not even her father, I think, contributed so much to the formation of the Little Flower's character. To realize this, just consider that the Little Flower's mother died when Thérèse was four years old and from that time on Pauline was more than a mother to St. Thérèse, more than a mother because for several years the Little Flower was too frail to be sent out to school and during that time Pauline was her only teacher. Then later in the Carmelite Convent, Pauline was the Little Flower's Mother Superior and therefore, the religious mother of the Little Flower also, and it was to Pauline, as her religious superior, that the Little Flower first confided her promises—"I will spend my heaven in doing good upon earth. . . . After my death I will let fall a shower of roses." Pauline knew the Little Flower so well that when at nine years of age the Little Flower expressed a desire eventually to enter a convent, Pauline knew that it was no passing childish fancy but a real vocation, and therefore she encouraged the Little

Flower, although another sister, Marie, tried to discourage Thérèse. It was Pauline, too, who did not a little to remove the obstacles in the way of the Little Flower's entrance to the convent at the age of fifteen.

Then here is another fact that will illustrate the tenderness of the Little Flower's attachment to Pauline. After Pauline had left for the Carmelite Convent, the Little Flower as a consequence had fallen seriously ill, and while she was still confined to her bed, the day on which Pauline would take the veil was approaching. That day would ordinarily be a joyous day for the entire Martin family because on that day, since the vows had not been taken, relatives could not only talk with but actually see for the last time the sisters who were taking the veil. The family of the Little Flower carefully refrained from speaking of the coming event in the hearing of the Little Flower because they feared to aggravate her illness by exciting regrets that she could not seize this last opportunity of seeing Pauline. But the Little Flower needed no reminder; she surprised the entire family one day by declaring from her sick bed that they would be able to attend the ceremony, and as a matter of fact she was able to go and she tells us in her own words, "When the glorious day came I was able to leave my bed and to go to the convent where, after the ceremony, once again I had the happiness of embracing Pauline, my little mother, of sitting on her knee and receiving her caresses and hiding my little head beneath her new white veil."

Let us continue then, my dear friends, the account of my conversation with the beloved sister of St. Thérèse. We stopped yesterday at Pauline's answer to my question, "Did the sisters or did you recognize the Little Flower during her life time as a saint."

Next I asked her whether there was anyone who saw in the Little Flower as a girl such signs of sanctity that would lead him to guess that she might one day be a saint.

She answered, "Well, Father, you know that the very nature of her little way would preclude anything that would be very ostentatious but, nevertheless, there were some people who guessed and declared her sanctity," and then she told me the following anecdotes:

One day in the Little Flower's girlhood a pious old lady who had observed the Little Flower closely in church with Pauline and who had seen, during the procession, the Little Flower's great eyes in ecstasy in the presence of the Blessed Sacrament said to Pauline as they left the church, "That little sister of yours is an angel. I will be very much surprised if she stays long on this earth, but if she lives, mark my words, you will see that she will be spoken of some day as a saint."

Another time in the Little Flower's girlhood an old laborer who came to work at the Little Flower's home insisted when he was leaving that Pauline give him a lock of the Little Flower's hair, which he said he would hold precious for it would one day be the relic of a saint.

"Often," Pauline said, "when I was on the streets of the town with Little Thérèse, the passers-by would turn fascinated to look long at the Little Flower, not so much because of her physical beauty but because of the celestial charm that seemed to radiate from her person."

Pauline said too that the doctor who attended the Little Flower towards the end of her life said one day to Pauline, "Oh, you do not know how much she suffers; never in all my experience have I seen anyone suffer so much or with such expression of supernatural joy." Then he added positively, "C'est un ange"—"she is an angel."

The chaplain, Pauline said, who came to hear the Little Flower's last confession was tremendously impressed to see her so beautiful and even transfigured in the midst of her excruciating pains. He looked upon her with the greatest reverence and later declared that he entered the infirmary as if it were a sanctuary, and he said to Pauline as he left, "Quel ange! (What an angel!) She is absolutely confirmed in the grace of God."

These then are some of the recognitions of the Little Flower's sanctity from those who knew her when she was alive.

Then I asked Mother Agnes to settle a much disputed question, namely: the question of the color of the Little Flower's eyes.

"Her eyes," said Pauline, "were not exactly blue but bluish." She used a French word which signifies a color between green and blue, although she said that those who did not observe closely thought her eyes were blue. "She was tall," Pauline, said, "her hair was blond, her complexion lily-like. She had a small mouth and fine regular features and she walked with a certain dignity which was at once simple and majestic. But," she said, "the most remarkable feature of her appearance was a certain expression on her countenance, an expression of charm and serenity and heavenly peace, which impressed all even from her girlhood." By the way, all the others with whom I talked who had known the Little Flower as a girl spoke of this charming, peaceful expression.

Then I asked Pauline for a message to the members of the Little Flower Society. She thought a while then asked, "Would they really be interested in a message from me?"

I said, "Of course they would be, Mother; they would be tremendously interested."

"I do not know what to say," she answered, "could you tell them that I will pray especially for them."

I said, "No, Mother, they already know that you Carmelite sisters pray for all the world."

"But I will pray particularly for them, the members of the society."

"But could you not send them some more personal message, something that will be less general and more concrete, some spiritual counsel or advice?"

Then there was a pause and then she said and I was careful to write each word, "Tell the ladies of the Little Flower Society of America that if they would please the Little Flower and win her favor, they must not follow the fashion when the fashion demands immodest or indecent dress."

I thanked Mother Agnes and then said to her, "That is a message, Mother, for only part of the society because a large proportion of the Little Flower Society consists of men. Would you send a message also to men?"

That amused her. "I," she said, "a cloistered nun, send a message to the men?" Then she laughed. It was a laugh such as I imagine the Little Flower's must have been—soft and musical and whole-hearted, although restrained. The Little Flower would probably have been similarly amused if during her lifetime she had been asked to send a message to the men of distant America.

But I was quite insistent and so after a long pause there came Pauline's message to the men. "Tell the men of the Society of the Little Flower that if they would please St. Thérèse and win her favor, they must hold themselves aloof from all that is low and base and ignoble and go to Holy Communion frequently."

I left the Carmelite Convent that afternoon walking on air, for I had talked nearly an hour with the beloved sister of the Little Flower. Later on I had a second interview with her during which she gave me the precious relics of which you have all heard. Tomorrow I will tell you of that interview and of how I persuaded her to let me talk also with the other two sisters of St. Thérèse, Marie and Céline.

Thérèse and sisters, with Mother Marie de Gonzague

Chapter Four

The Second Visit with Pauline

Last night, my dear friends, I completed the story of my first visit with the sister of the Little Flower, Pauline.

For many reasons I wanted a second interview with her and I wanted, of course, also to talk with her other two Carmelite sisters, Marie and Céline, who, you remember, are sisters in the same convent in which the Little Flower lived. I knew that that would be very difficult and consequently I planned a little strategy.

After my visit with Pauline I waited ten days in Lisieux and in that time I made three powerful friends. One was the sisters' Chaplain. The second was the famous Pierre, the guardian of the Little Flower's tomb. He had been miraculously cured years ago, by the intercession of the Little Flower, of an illness that was thought to be incurable and he has since been the guardian of her tomb. No one is closer to the Little Flower's sisters than Pierre, because he performs all their errands for them and has absolute charge of the chapel and of the tomb. The third friend was one Mademoiselle Violette, the guardian of the Little Flower's home in which she lived throughout her girlhood. Mademoiselle Violette is a sister of one of the Little Flower's novices, Sister Mary of the Trinity, who is still living in the Carmel of Lisieux. I couldn't have chosen more powerful friends, and I needed them in order to obtain what I wanted from Pauline.

When after the ten days I judged the time to be opportune, I wrote a letter to Mother Agnes, Pauline, asking three favors. The first was this: I asked her to give not to me personally but to the American National Shrine in Chicago, to be the property of the society of the Little Flower, the rarest of all Little Flower relics, namely, a portion of her flesh.*

I knew that there were three such relics and that all of them were at Lisieux, and I asked her in the letter if it were really necessary for all three to remain there, and if one could not come to America to inspire devotion similar to that which one witnesses at her tomb.

Secondly, I asked her to loan to the Society of the Little Flower, for the Eucharistic Congress, the picture of the Little Flower painted by her own sister, Céline, the picture to be exhibited throughout the congress at the National Shrine in Chicago.

Thirdly, I asked her to give permission to Marie and Céline to come to the parlor so that I might visit with them. I told her that I knew I was asking a great deal, but that I was emboldened by the thought that I was not asking for myself but for the lovers of the Little Flower in America, in order that their devotion to her might be intensified by the relics and painting and by the accounts of the talks with her own sisters.

I told her that when I said Mass that morning at the Little Flower's tomb, I asked the Little Flower to inspire Pauline to grant to me all three of these favors, and that I would await her reply with the greatest anxiety at the little inn across the street from the convent, the little inn at which I was staying.

Before sending the letter, I mobilized my three friends, the sisters' Chaplain, Pierre and Mademoiselle Violette, and asked them all to go to the convent and in some way get word to

---

* The Little Flower's body, as she prophesied, was reduced to dust with this exception: that when her body was exhumed, a very small portion of her flesh was found clinging to her habit. It is about this rare relic that Father Dolan speaks here. (Editor's Note.)

Mother Agnes, Pauline, asking her as a favor to them to grant the requests which would be contained in a letter she would receive that morning.

After they had all been to the parlor, I said to Pierre, "Pierre, will you take this letter and see that it reaches Pauline immediately?"

Pierre agreed readily, and he was as anxious about the result as I was.

The letter was delivered to Mother Agnes about ten o'clock one Tuesday morning. You may imagine with what anxiety and suspense I awaited the answer. I waited for more than two hours—two of the longest hours I ever spent. I had played my last card—there was nothing else to be done. Would I succeed or would I fail?

I waited at the window of the little inn across the street from the convent, because I knew that Pauline's answer would be delivered by the Sister Portress, and from the window I could see the Sister Portress if she left the convent on any errand. She did leave the convent two or three times, but did not come in my direction. Finally, about 12:15 or 12:30, the landlady insisted that I go downstairs and eat. I was scarcely seated in the dining room when the Sister Portress entered the inn looking for "Pere Dolan, the American Carmelite Priest." She did not have to look long, for I saw her first, and was at her side in a jiffy.

She said, "Voulez vous, mon Pere, venir au parloir a une heure parler avec Mere Agnes?" which means, "Would Father please come to the parlor at one o'clock to speak with Mother Agnes?"

Would I? I certainly would, I told her, although I regretted I could not say in French, "I hope to tell you I will."

I made for the door with the sister, but she said, "You need not come now, Father, you have nearly half an hour."

I replied, "I know it, Sister, but I am going to the tomb of the Little Flower first, to ask the intercession of the Little Flower, that Pauline may grant the requests I have asked. You may tell

Mother Agnes that, if you wish; tell her that I have gone to the tomb to speak to the Little Flower before I go to speak with her."

At the appointed hour, I again pulled the bell cord at the street entrance, and this time without any question or delay I was admitted to the parlor before the grille, and after a short delay I again heard the door open and again the celestial voice of Pauline, saying, "Deo Gratias"—"Thanks be to God."

I echoed sincerely, "Thanks be to God."

Without any preliminary, she said, "Father, I have received your letter, and here is the relic," and she turned the little revolving door in the grille. When it had been turned, I found on it a box, in which was the relic of the Little Flower, a portion of her flesh, which I had hardly dared to hope to obtain. It was enclosed in a magnificent reliquary made by Pauline's own hands. I then noticed there was a second relic—several generous locks of the Little Flower's hair.

Thinking that there was a mistake, I said, "Mother, there are two relics here."

Pauline answered, "Yes, you said in your letter you were not asking for anything for yourself, so the relic of the flesh is for the shrine, and the locks of hair are for you."

Of course I could not thank her. I was not able—but I am sure she understood.

I told her that I would not keep it for myself but would place it in the reliquary with the other relics, which I did later on, and it is with those relics you have been blessed each evening.

She then said that she would be glad to lend us the painting*; so the second request was granted, but she made no mention of the third request and talked as if the interview were closed. Of course, I was greatly disturbed. I did not want to mention the request after having written it, and I temporized, but to no avail.

Finally I had to say, "Mother, you have not mentioned the third request."

---

* Pauline has since graciously donated the picture permanently to the Little Flower Society.

"You mean about speaking with Marie and Céline?"

"Yes, Mother," I answered.

"But that is not necessary, Father," she replied, "and, besides, you have been so greatly favored already."

"I know, Mother," I said, "and I do not want you to think I am ungrateful, but I cannot return to America without having interviewed Marie and Céline when I came especially to gather firsthand information."

"I myself can give you all the information you want concerning Marie and Céline," countered, Pauline; "and, besides, they are very busy and then, as you know, the Carmelite rule forbids me to give them permission to come to the parlor except on urgent business."

"This is urgent, is it not, Mother?" I asked, "when one comes all the way from America expressly to speak with them." I argued that if they were to come to the parlor for only a short time, it would not materially interfere with their work or with their recollection.

I continued, "I asked that third request in the Little Flower's name, and I do not think you will refuse anything asked in her name. If it is not convenient for you to permit me to interview them this afternoon, then please let them come tomorrow afternoon or later."

"When are you going to leave Lisieux?" Pauline asked.

"That, Mother, depends on you," I answered. "I cannot leave until I have spoken with Marie and Céline."

She laughed and said, "Suppose I refuse?"

"Well, then, Mother," I said, "I will come back again in a few days and ask again, on the chance that you may have relented."

"Suppose I refuse again?" she said.

"Well, I understand, Mother, that the bishop of the diocese has the power to grant such permission, and I have a letter granting me an audience with him on Friday. If you refuse me, I shall have to go to him, but I am sure you will give in before that."

"You are certainly very persevering, Father," she said.

"Yes," I said, "but so was the Little Flower. You remember, Mother, that she broke all the rules of the Vatican when she spoke to the Holy Father about her vocation during a public audience. You remember that on another occasion when with Marie she was walking the streets of Lisieux and she wanted to go to Holy Communion before the age established, she saw the Bishop and wanted to speak to him then and there on the street about advancing the date of her first Holy Communion. Perseverance, then, is not such a bad trait, is it?"

She laughed and said, "What time is it, Father?"

I looked at my watch and answered, "Ten minutes after two."

"Wait a moment," she said and was gone.

In an incredibly short time the door behind the grille again opened and I heard Pauline's voice saying, "Here, Father, is Marie, and here is Céline."*

Of that interview with Marie and Céline I shall have to tell you tomorrow evening.

---

* Father Dolan's plan of concluding his talks at a climax, resulted at the end of this talk in very audible sighs of disappointment from the throng in the church. They had been spellbound during the narrative and he himself could not repress a smile as he left the pulpit and heard the disappointed sighs of his audience at his abrupt conclusion. The story he told was by many called "a serial." He himself disclaims any merit for the intense interest displayed and explains that it was their love of the Little Flower that caused such unprecedented interest in these talks about the saint's sisters. (Editor's Note.)

Chapter Five
The Visits with Marie and Céline

Yesterday, my dear friends, we were speaking of my second visit with Pauline, Mother Agnes of Jesus, the sister of the Little Flower, and we had come to that point at which Pauline brought the other two sisters of the Little Flower to the grille, saying, "Here, Father, is Marie—and here is Céline."

In order that you may understand and appreciate, my dear friends, the solemnity of that moment, consider that scene in the Carmelite convent parlor before the grille. On one side of the grille, one who had been reading and preaching about the Little Flower for years; and on the other side, three of the sisters of that saint. Except at Lisieux one could not enjoy a similar experience the world over today and it will probably be centuries before it will be possible to speak with one, to say nothing of three sisters of a canonized saint, because ordinarily the process of canonization is so slow that the relatives of a saint are dead long before the saint is canonized.

In order to enter into my feelings at that moment, consider the intimacy of the union between St. Thérèse and these three sisters of the Little Flower. Their father in referring to or speaking to his daughters always used the following titles: Marie he always referred to as "Marie, my diamond;" Léonie, was always "My good Léonie;" Céline, "My intrepid one;" Pauline, "My precious pearl;" and Thérèse, "My little queen." And there before me at one time, were three of the five daughters of this magnificent christian man!

A reproduction of a painting done by Céline in 1894, of the Blessed Virgin Mary and the Divine Infant.

Although I had prepared carefully what I would say to them, I did not for the moment know how to begin because again a throng of memories of their associations with the Little Flower rushed through my mind.

There before me was Marie to whom the Little Flower said one Christmas eve before the midnight Mass, at a time when the Little Flower was too young to receive Holy Communion, "Marie, if you will only help me, I have a plan by which I, too, tonight may receive the Little Jesus: If you will only take me with you to the midnight Mass and let me kneel at your side, I would hide close to you at the Communion rail and I am so tiny that no one will notice me," and her face shone with eager desire as she unfolded her plan, and then her eyes saddened as her sister explained that her desire could not then be realized.

There before me was Marie, who has been a witness to the transfiguration of the countenance of the Little Flower when in her girlhood during a serious illness, the statue of the Blessed Virgin became animated and smiled upon the Little Flower, curing her instantly when all thought that she was dying. It was Marie who, too, during the last illness of the Little Flower saw her bestow such a look of love upon that same statue that, remembering the former miracle, Marie said, "Thérèse, what do you see?" And Thérèse said, "Never has the statue of Our Lady seemed so lovely, but today, Marie, it is the statue, whereas the other time, as you know well, it was not the statue, but our Blessed Lady herself who smiled on me." It was to Marie that the Little Flower addressed that letter which contains one of the most beautiful passages ever written concerning our Blessed Mother. These are the words of that letter, "Often, Marie, I say to our Blessed Mother, 'Sometimes, oh cherished Mother, I think that I am more fortunate than you, because I have you for Mother, and you have, not like me, the Blessed Virgin to love.'" Was there ever love of our Blessed Lady more beautifully expressed, except it might be in that other passage of the Little Flower's writings in which she says, addressing her words to the Blessed Virgin, "If I were

Queen of Heaven and thou Thérèse, I would still wish to be Thérèse in order that I might see thee Queen of Heaven."

And then besides Marie, there before me was Céline; Céline, whom the Little Flower called "The little companion of my infancy, the sweet echo of my soul." Céline it was who throughout the Little Flower's girlhood roomed with Saint Thérèse in a little room off the larger bedroom occupied by their older sisters, Marie and Pauline. It was in this larger room on Marie's bureau that the Little Flower erected her little shrine to Mary. It was with Céline that Thérèse spent all her holidays playing in the garden their religious games, playing at Mass and at Benediction. When the family moved from Alençon to Lisieux, Marie wrote to one of her friends in Alençon, "We are finally settled in Lisieux in a home charmingly situated with a large garden wherein Céline and Thérèse can play their games."

Their games, however, were not always religious in character because both the Little Flower and Céline were, of course, human. One day, for instance, the Little Flower, tiring of playing with her dolls, gave all her dolls to Céline, who arranged the dolls in a row on the lawn in the garden and then played at school, with Céline as the teacher, the dolls as pupils and the Little Flower as an interested spectator. The Little Flower greeted the instructions of her sister with great delight, laughing heartily at her sister as she gave the dolls lessons in geography and spelling, but she laughed heartiest when at the end Céline said, "I am going to reward the highest pupil," and selecting one doll she embraced it saying, "Now, little one, as your reward you may kiss your teacher."

It was Céline who was the companion of the Little Flower during the well known pilgrimage to Rome. The little girls, Céline and Thérèse, were the most daring members of the pilgrimage. What they wanted to do, they did, regardless of rules and regulations. For instance, at Rome in the Coliseum they wished to stand at the very spot on which the early Christian martyrs had died. The spot was surrounded by a barricade, because excavations were being made there at that time. But the Little Flower observed that she and Céline were tiny enough to slip under the barricade, and said to Céline, "Come, follow me." The two little girls then slipped under the barricade and disregarding the warnings of the guard calling loudly to them to return, they scrambled over the ruins to the spot they sought and kneeling they pressed their lips to the dust once reddened by the blood of the early martyrs. Thérèse said afterwards, "Papa did not have the heart to scold us. I could even see that he was proud of the daring that we had displayed."

Here, then, before me was this companion of the Little Flower's infancy, Céline, and just as she had been the roommate of Thérèse in their girlhood, so during the Little Flower's last illness Céline had the consolation of being given a room just off the infirmary and of being appointed assistant infirmarian. That room she never left except to attend services at the chapel at which time Pauline, the other sister of the Little Flower, relieved her. It was Céline who was always on the alert, when the fever was at its height, to place a morsel of refreshing ice upon the lips of the Little Flower. For that service, Céline was rewarded by one of the last loving looks of Saint Thérèse and by one of her last celestial smiles.

These, then, were the thoughts that passed in a flash through my mind as I was abruptly introduced into the presence of all three of the sisters of our little saint and I didn't know whether to talk first with Céline or with Marie. In my excitement I said, "Céline, will you please say something?"

Céline, who was the most timid of the three, evidently did not know where to begin, either, because, there was a momentary pause and I heard some one prompt her in a whisper behind the grille and then came Céline's voice, not as remarkable as Pauline's but still an unusually beautiful voice, saying, "Our Mother tells us, Father, that your work in America is to promote devotion to the Little Flower."

I said, "Yes, Sister, that is my work."

"What a beautiful mission! Be sure, Father, that we will all pray for the success of your work and for the members of the Little Flower Society."

I thanked her and said, "I want to tell you how very happy I am to have the privilege of speaking with the Little Flower's sister whom she called 'The little companion of her infancy, the sweet echo of her soul.'" As soon as I said this, I heard confusedly surprised comment on the part of all three behind the grille that one coming from distant America should be familiar with those favorite names of the Little Flower for Céline.

Then thinking that I should not neglect Marie, and knowing that I could again turn to Céline, I said something that is awkward enough in English and worse in French, "Now, may I hear Marie's voice; where is Marie?"

"Here I am, Father," said Marie, who was the jolliest of the three and of whose good nature I will give you some examples later on.

I said, "Your Mother Superior is very kind, Sister, to allow me to talk with you both."

"Oh, she is always kind," said Marie, whose voice is quite ordinary. "She is always kind and besides," she said, "we are glad to be united because we are not often together like this, because we must imitate the example of the Little Flower and bestow ourselves during recreation upon the other sisters of the community rather than upon each other. Besides you will be able to do your work better now, will you not, now that you have spoken to the sisters of the Little Flower?"

"I certainly will, Sister," I answered, "for I can imagine nothing so inspiring as these interviews with the sisters of a saint."

Then followed some talk which is of relative unimportance and then I asked their permission to ask some questions. For instance, I asked Céline concerning an incident which has always interested me. It occurred at the time of the Roman pilgrimage. On the train in the compartment with Céline and Thérèse and their father, there was an old fellow who marred the joy of the journey by constantly complaining and finding fault and making disparaging remarks about the scenery about which the girls were so enthusiastic. He kept up his grumbling so long that finally the Little Flower declared roundly, "Why in the world didn't he stay home?"

I asked Céline whether the old fellow overheard this remark of Saint Thérèse.

She was shocked that I would think for a moment that he did. "Oh, no," Céline answered, "Thérèse was most careful that he should not overhear. She whispered that remark to me." Céline added that a few moments after making the remark the Little Flower said to Céline, "What an interesting study this world is, when one is about to leave the world!"

Then I asked Marie concerning an incident which happened on the last night that the Little Flower lived. The story had been told to me by Sister Agatha and I wished to verify it. The story was that Marie had been with the Little Flower all during that last night and about midnight Marie gave to the Little Flower a glass of water which Thérèse was able merely to sip, very slowly, on account of her extreme weakness. In the meantime Marie, fatigued by many nights of watching, fell asleep and the Little Flower, rather than disturb her sister, held the glass, in spite of her weakness, for several hours.

So I said to Marie, "Is it true that you fell asleep that last night?" She didn't understand and I was asked to explain further, and as I unfolded the story, there was a sudden chorus of "oui's" from the other side of the grille, "yes, yes, yes, it was true, the Little Flower was so thoughtful of others even to the end that she did hold the glass for several hours in spite of her weakness in order not to disturb Marie."

"But, Father," said Marie, "how did you know that story? I do not remember telling it to anyone."

"You must have told someone, Sister," I answered, "because I have heard it," and I left the mystery unsolved because I did not wish to betray the confidence of Sister Agatha.

Then I asked if they would send a message to the members of the Little Flower Society and to all lovers of the Little Flower in America.

At this request I heard Pauline say to her sisters, "Now you'll have to put on your thinking caps. Now it is your turn; I had my turn the other day."

There was quite a long pause and then came the message of Céline. Céline said, "Tell the members of the Little Flower Society in America that they should not only admire but also imitate the Little Flower."

My dear friends, there is great danger in merely admiring the Little Flower, in seeing in her only what is sentimental and attractive and not seeing what is solid and spiritual. There is great danger in seeing only her roses and not her cross. You will notice, for instance, that the statues of the Little Flower represent the Little Flower indeed carrying roses, but we should also notice the cross beneath the roses; the symbolism being that she bore her cross so resignedly, so cheerfully that it was for her a cross of roses, the roses being the smiles with which she greeted the trials that God sent her. That is in part what Céline means in saying "Tell them not only to admire but also to imitate the Little Flower." We must imitate her in her patience, in her resignation to the will of God in the most severe sufferings and trials.

Then came Marie's message which was exactly what we would expect from one who had witnessed the transfiguration of the countenance of the Little Flower by the smile of the Blessed Virgin. "Tell the members of the Little Flower Society in America, Father," said Marie, "that they never need fear losing their souls if they imitate Saint Thérèse in her love of our Blessed Mother."

Then I told the sisters that I had a little picture with me, which was my favorite picture of Saint Thérèse and asked if they would write a little message on it and sign their names to it so that I might have as a souvenir of my visit with her sisters. They agreed; so I placed the picture in the little revolving door of the grille and when it reached the other side, I heard one of the sisters, I do not know which one, I think it was Marie, say, "Oh, it is my favorite picture, too."

Just then the bell rang out from the chapel summoning the sisters to vespers. Pauline explained that they could not write me the message then but would write and sign it later and send it to the inn where I was staying, which they did do, and those signatures of the Little Flower's sisters may now be seen in a little glass case at the Shrine.

The sisters then said farewell and then, to my great embarrassment, they knelt and asked my blessing! My blessing! I felt like a hypocrite in giving it, when it should rather be I who should kneel for their blessing.

Then as I rose to leave the parlor, there came Pauline's memorable last words, "Be assured, Father, that we will pray for the members of the Little Flower Society and for your work." And then she added beautifully, "And I myself shall daily ask my little sainted sister to have you always under her sweet protection." Certainly if she had been asked beforehand, she could not have chosen more inspiring words with which to terminate these thrilling interviews with the sisters of Saint Thérèse.

I shall tell you tomorrow evening of my visit with Léonie, the fourth sister of the Little Flower, who is a Visitation nun in a convent not far from Lisieux.

Léonie in 1915.

Chapter Six

The Visit with Léonie

I have told you, my dear friends, almost all that transpired during my two interviews with Pauline and Marie and Céline, the three Carmelite sisters of the Little Flower. Having talked with three of her sisters I resolved to try also to talk with the fourth, Léonie, who is a Visitation nun in a convent at Caen, which is about a three hours' journey from Lisieux. Accordingly, we set out one morning in a so-called automobile, bumping and rattling over the ruts of the French dirt roads to Caen. We did not notice the discomforts, however, because the ride was through the rolling country of beautiful upper Normandy with superb vistas at every turn of the road.

Arriving at Caen I immediately set out to find the Visitation Convent. No one seemed to know the location of the convent until finally two French priests approached and I asked them to be directed to the Visitation Convent. One of them said, "Why, it is right here, Father, and we are going there ourselves to see the Mother Superior on business."

"What good fortune," I thought, "I can perhaps persuade these priests to take me with them and if they will do so, since they have business with the Mother Superior, I will be certain then to see the Mother Superior and will be able to present my request." I am sure that I would not have been admitted into the presence of the Mother Superior had I not met these French priests. To see a sister it is necessary to get the permission of the Mother Superior, and, if there is anything difficult, it is to see the Mother Superior of a French convent, especially when one is not known, and I was not known at all at Caen as I had been at Lisieux.

I explained to the French priests that I was an American priest who had come to Caen solely to see the sister of the Little Flower, Léonie, and I asked them to take me with them to the parlor without announcing me so that after they had finished their business, I might present my request to the Mother Superior. At first they protested that that wasn't the correct or regular thing to do and that by so doing they might incur the displeasure of the Mother Superior. But finally they consented and we rang the bell and the Sister Portress answered. The French priests were evidently well known because we were admitted to the parlor without any question.

The Visitation rule is not as strict as the Carmelite rule nor is their cloister so absolute. The parlor in the Visitation Convent differs from the Carmelite Convent parlor in this: that although there is a grille, the grille is not a solid wall as it is in the Carmelite Convent, but is composed of a series of iron bars heavily curtained. When a sister comes to the parlor that curtain may be and is pulled back, so that one can see the sister with whom he is talking. That arrangement of course pleased me, because I knew then that if Léonie came to the parlor I could not only talk with her but also see her.

After we had waited some few minutes, the curtain was pulled back and there was the Mother Superior. The French priests transacted their business, introduced me and left.

I immediately asked the Mother Superior to see Léonie. She explained that that was "impossible." But I had become accustomed to the word "impossible" by this time and was not greatly disturbed.

I showed her the picture I had on which was the message signed by Marie and Céline and Pauline and argued that it would be incomplete without the signature of Léonie, the fourth sister.

She agreed that it would be incomplete but proposed this plan: "I will take the picture up to Léonie and have her sign it and then I will bring it down to you again."

I said, "But, Mother, that will never do; I want to talk with her myself."

"Impossible," she declared, "Léonie is the busiest of all the sisters and besides, as you know, I could not permit her to come to the parlor except on urgent business."

"But, Mother," I pleaded, "couldn't an exception be made in favor of one who has come to this town exclusively to see Léonie?"

She asked, "Haven't you seen the Cathedral?" (The Cathedral is the ordinary magnet which brings people to Caen, as it is one of the architectural gems of France.)

"No, Mother," I answered, "I haven't seen the Cathedral and do not intend to see it; I came here solely to see Léonie."

Then she asked, "When are you going to leave Caen?"

My reply to a similar question to Pauline had worked so well that I thought I would try it again and answered, "I don't know, Mother; that depends on you—I must see Léonie before I go."

That didn't amuse her at all, as it did Pauline. She failed to smile and maintained still that it was impossible for me to see Léonie. I pleaded but to no avail, and I was afraid for a while that I was going to lose out. However, she couldn't put me out. The only way of getting rid of me was to leave, and she was too polite to leave, and I was impolite enough to stay.

Finally I actually begged. I told her that I would get down on my knees, if necessary, in order to speak with Léonie for three minutes.

At this plea she began to thaw and said, "We are not as stingy as that. If she comes to the parlor you may talk with her as long as you wish. Just wait and I'll see," and she left the parlor.

In a few moments an elderly sister entered the parlor. It never occurred to me that it might be Léonie, but I inquired her name and to my great surprise, I found it was Léonie. We are inclined to think of the Little Flower's sisters as being of the same age as she was when she died, twenty-four, but they were all older than she and she has been dead for twenty-nine years. Léonie is sixty-one years of age now. She is thin and short and dark and her face, at least when it is in repose, is not especially attractive or distinguished. In fact the personal appearance of Léonie would be disappointing were it not for three redeeming features—bright, black eyes full of kindness and amiability, a most attractive and pleasing smile, and a most courteous and charming manner. It was easy to understand why the Little Flower's father always called Léonie "My good Léonie." She was goodness and kindness itself, and throughout the interview there was always that willing readiness to do everything she was asked.

I explained my work in America, and she was most interested and asked many questions about the Little Flower Society. She asked its age and its membership, and she was very pleased when I told her that although the Society was only eighteen months old it had nearly 200,000 members in every part of the United States and Canada. She was very much interested in the account I gave of the services at the American National Shrine in Chicago every Tuesday throughout the year, seven services each Tuesday afternoon and evening for the benefit of the crowds that wait their turn outside the church in any and all weather in order to attend the devotions of the perpetual novena of Tuesdays.

Léonie was highly pleased with the design of our reliquary which I showed her, the reliquary being in the form of a golden rose branch, each rose of which contains one of the five major relics of the Little Flower. I asked her if she would autograph the picture which had already been autographed by her three sisters. She agreed and I passed the picture to her through the bars of the grille and when she returned the picture she gave me with it a little relic of the Little Flower.

Then, knowing that she had been present in the Little Flower's girlhood when Saint Thérèse was miraculously cured by the smiling statue of the Blessed Virgin, I said to her, "Sister, did you see that smiling vision of our Blessed Mother when Thérèse was cured?"

"No," she answered.

"But you were in the room with her, were you not?" I questioned.

"Yes," she replied, "but I saw nothing. Marie saw everything because she was kneeling at the head of the bed near the Little Flower, whereas I was kneeling at the foot of the Little Flower and Thérèse had taken such a sudden change for the worse that I, thinking that she was dying, buried my head in the bedclothes, weeping and praying at the same time, and so I saw nothing until we all saw a few moments later that she had been instantly cured."

Then I said to her, "Sister, are you not lonely here sometimes in this convent so far from your other sisters?"

She answered, "No, Father, I am where God wants me to be and I wouldn't be imitating my little sainted sister if I were to be sad in doing God's will. Of course, all who leave home are a little lonely sometimes, n'est-ce pas, Father, but it is necessary to smile, n'est-ce pas? And the Little Flower helps me to smile."

I said, "But, Sister, do you not regret sometimes that you did not enter the Carmelite Convent instead of the Visitation Convent? It seems to me that if I had a sister who had become a saint and who had made a convent famous for its sanctity and had three sisters in that convent, I would regret that in my youth I had not entered that convent. Do you not feel that way?"

"No, Father, I have no such regrets because I had no vocation to the Carmelite Convent but to the Visitation rule and instead of regrets I have nothing but gratitude to God for having given me my Visitation vocation which I love."

I then said, "I suppose, Sister, that the Little Flower bestows many favors upon you, her sister."

"Yes," she answered, "many, many favors." And then, with a twinkle in her eyes, she added by way of a "comeback" to my doubts about her happiness in the Visitation Convent, "And not the least of the favors she gives me, Father, is to preserve my love for my Visitation vocation." All this was said with the most charming gentleness and with that ever-present exquisite smile which gave her some resemblance to the Little Flower in spite of her advanced age of sixty-one.

I then asked her to write a little message, a little spiritual bouquet, in her own hand writing, as a souvenir of my interview of a sister of the Little Flower. She readily agreed and asking the loan of my fountain pen, wrote as follows: "I shall daily ask my little sainted sister, Saint Thérèse of the Child Jesus, to bless your mission of promoting devotion to her amongst the Americans." She signed her religious name, which is "Sister François Thérèse," and under it, at my request, she wrote her family name, "Marie Léonie Martin."

Then I asked her would she send a message to the members of the Little Flower Society in America and to all lovers of the Little Flower. Unlike the other three sisters, she didn't hesitate a moment. She must have been asked similar questions before, because immediately she said, "Give them this message, Father: tell them that if we would please the Little Flower we must be humble as she was, and we will be humble if we will repeat frequently every day the ejaculation, 'Jesus, meek and humble of heart, make my heart like unto Thine.'"

The Little Flower's sister's message to us, my dear friends, will bear many a meditation and much pondering. Let us heed that message; we may indeed be sure that we will not be proud or haughty, if we say frequently every day, "Jesus, meek and humble of heart, make my heart like unto thine."

Léonie had nothing more to say that is important and I left the Visitation Convent with a prayer of thanksgiving in my heart to the Little Flower for having made it possible for me to talk at length with all four of her sisters.

Tomorrow, my dear friends, I will tell you of the very interesting visit I had with the only living cousin and playmate of the Little Flower.

Left: Zélie Guérin (Martin) before her marriage.
Right: Louise Guérin, before her entrance into the
Convent of the Visitation at Mans.
Center: Isidore Guérin, the father of Marie and Jeanne.

Chapter Seven

The Visit with Jeanne Guérin, the Little Flower's Cousin and Playmate

Today, my dear friends, I want to tell you of my visit with the only living cousin of the Little Flower, Jeanne Guérin. Guérin was the maiden name of the Little Flower's mother, and Jeanne Guérin was the daughter of the Little Flower's mother's brother. The Little Flower's mother's brother had two daughters, Marie and Jeanne. Marie became a Carmelite nun and died some years ago, and Jeanne is the lady of whom we are speaking today.

Jeanne Guérin was not only the Little Flower's cousin, but also her schoolmate. When the Little Flower became strong enough to be sent out to the Benedictine school which was some distance from the Little Flower's home, the following arrangement was made: Thérèse with one of the servants of her father's household was to walk every morning from her home to her uncle's pharmacy, and there she would be joined by her two cousins, Jeanne and Marie Guérin, and then all three little girls were to set out together for the school. So the lady of whom we are speaking today was one of the girls who walked with the Little Flower every morning and every evening to and from school.

By the way, I also visited the servant who accompanied the Little Flower every morning as far as the Little Flower's uncle's drug store, and she told me the following interesting anecdote which illustrates the girlhood character of the Little Flower. She said that one morning when she and the Little Flower were passing along the street, the Little Flower overheard, for the first time probably in her life, profanity on the part of some workmen and after murmuring a little ejaculatory prayer, the Little Flower turned to the servant and said, "You know we must not judge the hearts of these poor men. They haven't had the graces nor the training that we have received and God knows that, and perhaps they are more to be pitied than to be blamed." You see, my dear friends, how early in life the Little Flower began to practice the virtue of charity towards others, the virtue of charity which she later so developed that its perfection dazzles all who read her life.

To return to the Little Flower's cousin: Jeanne Guérin was not only her cousin and schoolmate but also her playmate, for Jeanne's father, the Little Flower's uncle, had a summer home at the seashore near Deauville and during vacation the Little Flower played daily along the seashore with her two cousins, Marie and Jeanne.

As a preliminary to our account of my visit with the cousin of the Little Flower, I wish to read to you a short passage of the Little Flower's Autobiography in which she refers to this cousin. I read it not only because it refers to the lady of whom we are speaking today, but also because of the beauty of the latter part of the passage which illustrates the ardor of the Little Flower's love of God. This is the passage: "Eight days after I had taken the veil, my cousin, Jeanne Guérin, to whom I had always been very devoted, was married to Dr. La Neele, and at her next visit to me I heard of all the little attentions she lavished on her husband. I was greatly impressed and I determined that it should never be said that a woman in the world did more for her husband than I for my Beloved. Filled with fresh ardor, I strove with increased earnestness to please my heavenly Spouse, the King of Kings, who had deigned to honor me by a divine alliance."

My visit with the Little Flower's cousin came about in this way. One day I said to my friend Pierre, the guardian of the Little Flower's tomb, "Pierre, are there any of the Little Flower's relatives besides her sisters who are still living here?"

He answered, "Yes, Jeanne Guérin."

"Do you know her?" I asked.

"Oh, yes," he answered, "we are great friends."

"Would you come with me to see her and introduce me?" I asked.

Pierre, who is a saint and amiability itself, readily agreed.

Accordingly that afternoon Pierre and I set out for the Little Flower's cousin's home which is not far from the convent. A maid answered our ring and we were admitted. All the rooms on the first floor of the Little Flower's cousin's home open off a long corridor which leads from the door to the beautiful garden, a glimpse of which we could catch as we were conducted down the corridor to one of the parlors. The parlor was magnificently furnished and carpeted; exquisite paintings hung from the walls, and I was quite surprised to find such luxury and artistic beauty in a home of that little Normandy town.

While we were waiting I whispered to Pierre: "What a contrast, Pierre, between the surroundings of the two cousins and playmates. For Jeanne Guérin, all this luxury; for the Little Flower, the narrow and bare cell of the Carmelite convent."

"Yes," said Pierre, "but now the Little Flower possesses all the riches of God's palace in heaven."

"But," I said, "so will Jeanne possess that kingdom some day."

"Yes," admitted Pierre, "but her place will not be so high in heaven as the Little Flower's."

"Is she not good then; has her wealth made her proud and haughty?" I asked.

"Oh, no," said Pierre, "she is very amiable and very humble, as you shall see. And," he added, "there is no one in Lisieux more charitable to the poor."

Looking out the window we saw walking slowly in the garden an old lady accompanied by a little girl.

"There she is," said Pierre, "the lady is the Little Flower's cousin."

"Who is the girl?" I asked.

"She is an orphan which the Little Flower's cousin adopted after her husband died," he answered.

The maid just then approached the lady and announced us, and at that, the lady walked rapidly into the house. She didn't come to the parlor though, and I wondered why not. Pierre said that his guess was that she had gone upstairs to sit before a mirror a while before she came to see the visitors. After a while she came in and apologized for the delay saying that she hadn't expected visitors and that therefore she had to dress up a little before coming into the parlor. So Pierre's guess was correct.

She was a charming lady, about sixty, I should say, thin and short, hair just beginning to gray, bright eyes, no wrinkles and red cheeks as have all the old women of Normandy I saw. She was dressed in black. Her manner was delightful and cordial in the extreme. She greeted Pierre, who introduced me as the director of the Little Flower Society, whose work was to promote devotion to the Little Flower in America.

"'What a beautiful mission," she said, using, strangely enough, the same expression that Céline had used.

I told her that I came not only out of curiosity to see the Little Flower's cousin and playmate but to ask some questions about the Little Flower and gather first-hand information for a book I was writing, and I told her that to that end I had already interviewed the Little Flower's sisters.

"Oh, if you have seen them," she said, "they have told you all. I think I could add nothing, but I will answer any questions you may want to ask."

"Of course," I said, "you often played with the Little Flower when you were girls?"

"Oh, yes, hundreds of times," she said, "out there, in that garden," pointing out the window.

"Did she ever lose her temper?" I asked.

"Never," she answered, "not once as long as I knew I her, although as a little girl of three before she came to Lisieux, it is said that she knew well how to display temper." The Little Flower confesses these infantile fits of temper in her own Autobiography. They all happened before the time which she terms her conversion, her conversion at the age of four.

"Did the Little Flower play as ardently and wholeheartedly as other children?" I asked.

"Of course, I was older than the Little Flower and it was my sister Marie who played with her more than I, but I would say that the Little Flower did not care a great deal to play as other girls would and neither did my sister Marie."

"But," I said, "what did they do then, in the garden if they didn't play?"

"Oh," she said, "they played, but their games were religious in character. They played at hermit and at Mass, benediction, vespers and so on."

"But were they always so serious and solemn in their play?"

"Oh," she said, "they were never long-faced even while they were playing those religious games. They were always very joyous. The Little Flower never seemed sad. My father used to call her his little ray of sunshine. And it was an experience," she added, "to see her smile. I have never seen such a charming smile. But nevertheless she was always very thoughtful. Everyone remarked how absorbed in thought she always seemed to be."

"You went to school every day with the Little Flower," I said, "and do you remember anything that happened on your way to and from school with her that is worth recording?"

She thought a while and said, "Well, yes, this is an amusing incident I remember," and then she told a story which the Little Flower herself tells in her own Autobiography and with which therefore I was familiar, although of course I didn't say so. The story, however, is worth retelling.

Her story was, "One day we were returning from school and Marie and the Little Flower were walking ahead of me and a girl who was walking with me, and it seems that Marie and the Little Flower decided not to wait until they arrived home to play at hermit but to begin then on the street to imitate the modesty of the hermits by casting down their eyes. 'You lead me,' said the Little Flower to Marie. 'I am going to close my eyes.' 'I am going to close mine too,' said Marie. So they joined hands and walked along together with their eyes closed, the blind leading the blind. But unhappily they hadn't proceeded far when they bumped into a stand in front of a fruit store and scattered the merchandise all over the street and the proprietor dashed out in a fury and the little girls took to their heels, with their eyes wide open then in order to put on full speed."

During the remainder of my visit the Little Flower's cousin didn't tell me a great deal that isn't generally known about the Little Flower.

I said, "I suppose the Little Flower does a great deal for you, her cousin and schoolmate."

"She gives me many, many favors," said Jeanne, "but she doesn't give the members of her family the material favors she gives to other people. She sends them instead spiritual favors. For instance she has given me wealth which I do not enjoy because my sister is dead and my husband gone. I have had to adopt a little orphan for company in this big house in my old age. But she has given me what is greater than material favors, namely the grace to live as she did, not so much for this world as for the next, and therefore I am happy and spiritually secure and so I couldn't ask for more from my little sainted cousin than she has given me. Besides, since she has been dead, she seems to be very close to me and that is one of my greatest consolations."

Then I asked her to sign her name to a little card or picture of the Little Flower which I had with me and she wrote: "Asking not to be forgotten in your Mass and in the prayers of the members of the Little Flower Society in America. (Signed) Jeanne Guérin."

As we left the house Pierre said, "Was I not right, Father, is she not humble and amiable and gentle?"

"Yes, Pierre," I said, "she is charming. She is all that we would expect in the cousin and playmate of the Little Flower."

Tomorrow our subject will be my visit with one of the Little Flower's teachers, Sister Francis de Sales.

Chapter Eight

The Visit with Sister Francis de Sales, the Little Flower's Teacher

Tonight, my dear friends, our subject is my visit with Sister Francis de Sales, a Benedictine nun who was the Little Flower's teacher for five years and who prepared her for her first holy Communion.

The interview with the Little Flower's teacher came about in this way: I inquired if any of the Benedictine nuns who taught the Little Flower were still living, and I was told that there was one, Sister Francis de Sales, who was now old and feeble but with whom, perhaps, I could secure an interview.

So I went up to the Benedictine school which the Little Flower attended for five years, from the age of eight to the age of thirteen, from 1881 to 1886. In the chapel of the school there is a placard at the Communion rail which reads: "Thérèse Martin made her first Communion at this communion rail on May 8, 1884." There is also in the school a little oratory in which are preserved many interesting souvenirs of the Little Flower, for instance, her first Communion veil, some of her school books, one of her compositions, a crucifix which the Little Flower brought from Rome to her catechism teacher, Sister Francis de Sales, and also the desk which she used and on which she had engraved with a pen knife not her own initials but the initials of the Blessed Virgin.

After viewing these souvenirs I asked the Sister Portress to see Sister Francis de Sales. I was told that she hadn't been well and was extremely feeble in her advanced age, but that perhaps she would come to the parlor. I was taken to the parlor and asked to have a seat before the grille. In a few moments the curtain of the grille was pulled back and there was the teacher of the Little Flower. She was indeed old and feeble but she was nevertheless most agreeable and willing to talk. She is now eighty years old and was in the neighborhood of forty when she taught the Little Flower.

I had pencil and paper with me to jot down her answers to my questions. I said to her first, "Sister, will you please talk slowly, because my French isn't all that it should be."

She answered, "I have to talk slowly, Father, because I haven't many teeth left." And she didn't have many, either.

Then I asked her, "Did you find the Little Flower, when she was in your classes, an ordinary pupil?"

"In some ways, yes, she was ordinary, but in other ways she was most extraordinary. First, she was extraordinarily intelligent. She was very talented and precocious, and when she first came to us, at the age of eight, she was placed in a class which contained pupils who were all from four to six years older than she, and amongst these, some, of course, at first surpassed her, but very soon she took her place as leader of her class. Sometimes by way of a rare exception she obtained marks that were not the highest. At such times the little girl was inconsolable, not because of personal pride but because she couldn't bear the thought that in the evening her father would have less pleasure than usual in looking over her marks. Then, too, she was extraordinarily obedient, scrupulously faithful to the minutest particulars of the rules of the school. And then again she was extraordinarily pious; her heart and mind were always on God and she always wanted to talk of God and of the saints."

"Did you think that she would one day be a saint, Sister?"

"Oh, no, one doesn't guess that of a girl eight or nine years old. It was evident to all of us however, that she had never lost her baptismal innocence. I remember that one of the sisters said to me one day: 'Did you notice the angelic expression on the countenance of Thérèse Martin? One sees other children with features as fine, but this child has heaven in her eyes.' We knew, Father, that we had a little treasure in Thérèse Martin, but we didn't estimate her at that time at her true worth."

"Would you tell me something, Sister, about her life in school?"

"Well," she said, "she didn't care much to play with the others on the playground. She preferred the garden with its birds and flowers to the playground and preferred the chapel to the garden. Often during recreation she would go to one of the sisters to talk of convent life or to seek religious counsel and advice. I remember once she astonished me during recreation by asking me, 'Sister, how does one make a meditation?' A meditation is an advanced form of mental prayer practiced by nuns and priests and religious, and it is of course most extraordinary that a little girl of nine should ask how to make a meditation.

"She almost always took the prizes offered for academic excellence, especially in her favorite subjects, Church history and catechism. She was so perfect in catechism and showed such a sure knowledge of spiritual things and asked so many questions about subtle religious problems that the Chaplain of the school used to call her 'his little doctor of theology'—his little doctor of theology at nine or ten years of age. 'She seemed endowed with a marvelous intuition,' he said, 'for things pertaining to the spiritual world.'"

"Did the other pupils like her, Sister? Was she popular?"

"With the sisters, yes, she was a general favorite, but with the pupils, no. They were jealous of her intellectual superiority and outside the classroom they made her pay in a thousand little ways for her little classroom triumphs. Secondly, the fact that she was never punished because she was never disobedient prevented popularity. This immunity from punishment acted as kind of a barrier between her and the others who were punished frequently."

"Then again, Father," she continued, "as in all schools the world over, then as well as now, some pupils were always ready to take advantage of the momentary absence of the teacher to create general disorder. Thérèse had been taught at home that although such misconduct was not gravely sinful, God would be more pleased if pupils were to be strictly obedient, not to avoid punishment, not to win the favor of their teachers, but to please Him. She therefore in the midst of disorder in the classroom or corridors was always silent, and her silence, noticed of course by the others, was a rebuke to the disturbers and brought upon her head their displeasure. And even children," Sister Francis de Sales went on, "do not tolerate rebukes, even though silent, from one of their companions."

The Little Flower's obedience therefore, her desire to please God in all things was one of the causes of her unpopularity.

"Again," the sister said, "Thérèse didn't like games. In fact, she was too frail to play as strenuously as the others, and when she did play, she tells us herself, 'I was useless,' and the others took full opportunity on the playground to make fun of the awkwardness and lack of skill of her who put them all to shame in the classroom. The result of all this was a mutual coolness between her and the others which obliged her to spend her recreations apart from the animated and noisy groups of other children. At such times she would often be found studying her catechism because although she grasped its doctrine with remarkable facility, the literal answers of the catechism she always found difficult to memorize."

But with the Little Flower's affectionate nature it was necessary for her to have some friends, and she did have two friends, little serious-minded girls like herself. Of the shipwreck of one of these friendships she tells us in this passage of her Autobiography: "Just about this time I chose as friends two little girls of my own age. It happened that for some reason one of them had to remain at home for several months. While she was away, I thought of her very often, and upon her return I showed great pleasure at seeing her again.

All I met with, however, was a glance of indifference—my friendship was not appreciated. I felt this very keenly and I no longer sought an affection which had proved so inconstant. Nevertheless, I still love my little school friend and I pray for her; God has given me a faithful heart and when once I love, I love forever. I am most thankful to Our Lord that He has allowed me to find only bitterness in earthly friendships. With a heart such as mine I should so easily have been taken captive and had my wings clipped. How then should I have been able 'to fly away and be at rest?'* How can a heart given up to human affection be closely united to God? It appears to me impossible. I have seen so many souls who, having been allured like poor moths by this treacherous light, fly into the flame and burn their wings, then return injured to Our Lord, the Divine Fire which burns and does not consume."

So you see, my dear friends, the Little Flower was one of those rare souls of whom God seems to be jealous. He demanded her whole heart; He wished that she would not give even one small corner of it to creatures.

It was therefore the Little Flower's successes in school, the fact that she was never punished, her inability to play, and the jealousy of her companions which were the causes of her unpopularity. "Although," Sister Francis hastened to add, "the Little Flower was always gentle, kind and most patient with her companions, who, except those who were utterly blinded by jealousy, couldn't help but like her a little and in their hearts admire her and guess her worth."

Then I said, "Sister, do you remember anything that happened in the classroom while you were teaching the Little Flower that is worth recording?"

She thought a moment and then told this interesting story: One day she, Sister Francis de Sales, had been explaining to the class the fate of those little children who die without baptism. Throughout the entire explanation there was an expression of extreme puzzlement on the Little Flower's countenance.

---

* Psalm LIV. 7.

Finally Thérèse raised her hand and said, "Sister, does God not love all souls?"

"Yes, my child," the sister replied.

"Does He not love the souls of little children?"

"Yes."

"Well then, how can He punish them; they never did any wrong; they never committed any sins themselves."

The sister explained that God did not punish them, that they enjoyed a state of happiness far beyond any experienced here on earth. Their only deprivation was the deprivation of the vision of God. They could not see God.

But the Little Flower was not yet satisfied, and after a moment's thought she declared, "Well, if I were God, Sister, I would let the little children see me at least once."

Later on, of course, the Little Flower understood better this mystery of God's dealings with little children who die without baptism. But you see, my dear friends, how early in life the Little Flower began to give signs of her mission of teaching the mercy and goodness of God. Even as a child, she could not understand how any bounds could be set to God's goodness and mercy. And this same little girl who in the classroom puzzled over God's apparent harshness to unbaptized children, later taught millions by the beautiful comparisons and by the poetical language of her Autobiography, the illimitable mercy and goodness of God.

I had asked so many questions that the aged Sister Francis was perceptibly tiring and so I asked no more questions that day, but at this juncture I thanked and bade farewell to the sister who had given me such a complete and vivid picture of the Little Flower's school life.

In these little talks I have given about my visits with those who knew St. Thérèse, I have left it to you to draw your own lessons and your own practical applications. The stories of the Little Flower's childhood told by her sisters, and retold to you during the week in these talks ought to cause parents to realize the value of home influence and to resolve to give their children similar training. The narratives of the Little Flower's love of the Blessed Sacrament ought to occasion resolutions to be more devoted to the Blessed Sacrament, the secret of her sanctity and the support of our own virtue. Other stories told of her love of our Blessed Mother and her thoughtfulness of others, of her charity, undoubtedly occasioned resolutions which the Little Flower will help you always to keep.

All have doubtless been led during the week to see and to admire the sweetness, the charm and the beauty of the Little Flower's life—charm and beauty which like the perfume of roses cannot be resisted. Each one has been led to contrast the beauty of her life with the comparative ugliness of his own and then naturally came the resolution to uproot from the garden of our lives all the weeds we find there and to make that garden, by frequent Communion, persevering prayer and persistent effort to imitate the Little Flower's virtues, a garden of roses.

That the Little Flower may bestow upon each of you the rose you most need, whether it be greater humility, greater love of God, greater prayerfulness, greater purity, greater charity, greater love of Mary or greater love of Our Lord in the Blessed Sacrament, is my prayer.

Thérèse at the foot of Pope Leo XIII.

Chapter Nine

An Audience with the Holy Father Concerning the Little Flower

A year ago, last May 17th, our Holy Father assembled the court of the Vatican in St. Peter's Cathedral and there solemnly declared the Little Flower to be a saint.

It is a happy coincidence, my dear friends, that today on the first anniversary of that canonization of the Little Flower, I should be speaking to you of an audience with that same Holy Father—an audience during which he spoke almost exclusively of the Little Flower.

My first morning in Rome last April I went to St. Peter's to say Mass at the tomb of Saint Peter whose body lies under the peerless dome, upon which are written, in letters of the gold, the words: "Thou art Peter and upon this rock I will build my Church." After the Mass I went to the Vatican to ask an audience, which was arranged for the next day.

The next morning I passed through the famous Vatican bronze doors, at which are posted the Swiss guards in their picturesque uniforms, and was escorted up interminable marble staircases, across the inner court of the Vatican and into an immense marble hall upon the walls of which hung some of the world's most famous tapestries and paintings. About a hundred people were waiting there, and I began to fear that, instead of the private audience which had been promised me, I was to have a public audience in which I could not speak to the Holy Father. But in due time the Papal Chamberlain appeared and summoned me and without speaking a word conducted me along many, many corridors lined with papal guards until finally he broke his silence, saying, "We are now approaching the apartments of the Holy Father." We continued on past the Noble Guard in their glorious uniforms up to the very door leading to the rooms of the Pope. There he bade me wait, he entered the Pope's room, returned in a few moments and said, "The Holy Father will now receive you." He then led the way into the very presence of the Pope.

What an experience! There all clothed in white sat Christ's Vicar on earth, the successor of Saint Peter to whom Our Lord had said, "Thou art Peter and upon this rock I will build my Church. I will give to thee the keys of the Kingdom of Heaven."

I knelt and kissed the Holy Father's ring. The papal chamberlain introduced me and then left me alone with the most exalted personage in the world, Christ's representative on earth, the infallible head of the one true Church, the spiritual monarch whose dominion is world wide, that king who rules spiritually over 300,000,000 of souls, left me alone with the most exalted of all lovers of the Little Flower, with him who had beatified her in 1923 and canonized her in 1925.

The Holy Father waited for me to speak. I said, "Holy Father, may I say a word."

"You may say many words," he answered with a kindly smile. The Holy Father looks exactly like his pictures except that he looks very tired. I would say his most distinguished characteristic is an exquisite mildness and gentleness of manner—the manner of one who bears a heavy burden but who bears it without complaint and with infinite patience.

I said, "Holy Father, I have come to Rome to ask your blessing upon my particular work."

"What is that work?" he said slowly and rather indifferently, I thought.

"My work is to promote in America devotion to Saint Thérèse."

Immediately he brightened and said, "What a very beautiful mission!" and from then on his attention and interest were much more marked.

I said, "There are thousands in America, Holy Father, whose special affection you have won chiefly because of what you have done for Saint Thérèse."

He smiled and said, "We call her in Europe, Little Thérèsee, but in America you call her (and then he used his only words of English, speaking with a slight accent), the Little Flower."

"But," I said, "there are other thousands in America, Your Holiness, who know her only by name and hence my mission of going from city to city and from church to church speaking of her and of her Little Way. I have come to ask your blessing upon that work."

"Oh," said the Pope, "not one but three blessings are necessary, one for the success of your work," and here he made the sign of the cross and gave me his ring to kiss; "the second for yourself that you may have the strength and the health and the holiness to do your work," and then again he made the sign of the cross; "the third for the people to whom you speak, that they may listen with those good dispositions that are essential if your words are to bear fruit," and again the sign of the cross and the ring.

I thanked him and then asked him if he would not send to the members of the Little Flower Society in America his special personal blessing and empower me to give it in his name upon the close of novenas in honor of Saint Thérèse. He granted me that permission, confirmed later by a letter from the Papal Secretary of State, Cardinal Gasparri, and that blessing will be bestowed after the sermon.

Then I told the Holy Father about the crucifix made from the Little Flower's rose bush* and given to the American National Shrine, and I asked him to indulgence the crucifix so that the people of the National Shrine might gain an indulgence of 300 days every time they venerated it.

---

* See page 118-119 for explanation of the Crucifix made from the Little Flower's rose bush.

The Holy Father told me to put my request in writing and let it pass through the regular channels and that when it came he would approve it. The indulgence has since been received from Rome from the Sacred Congregation.

Then I asked him if he would not send a message to the members of the Little Flower Society in America and to all lovers of the Little Flower.

He answered, "Tell them that all should study carefully and imitate closely the humble life and the little way of Saint Thérèse, who is an exquisite miniature of perfect holiness." High praise, indeed, from the Vicar of Christ—"An exquisite miniature of perfect holiness."

Then I asked the Holy Father if he would explain what he meant in his sermon on May 17th, on the occasion of her canonization, when he called her in that sermon his "Guiding Star."

He answered, his face all aglow with enthusiasm, "That is just what she is, my guiding star. Whenever I have a problem that is particularly difficult and which I can not solve, I take it to her and she always immediately clarifies and solves it for me."

Then the Holy Father said, "Again, Father, my blessing upon you and, your work, and may Saint Thérèse bless both you and it." Then came his last words, so soft and beautiful in Italian, "Addio, caro padre, addio," "Goodbye, dear Father, goodbye." With these affectionate words of the Holy Father ringing in my ears I left the presence of the Holy Father.

That same Holy Father, my dear friends, on May 17th last year, moving amid scenes of surpassing splendor in St. Peter's, that world cathedral, solemnly enrolled the name of the Little Flower upon the register of the saints, calling her on that occasion his "advocate," his "patron," calling her his "guiding* star" and his "refuge in difficulty."

What a marvel it is that this young and humble Carmelite nun should win such titles from the Vicar of Christ! What a marvel it is that this little girl nun of Normandy should be called the "Guiding Star" of the successor of St. Peter, the great

Pope of Rome! And what a privilege it is and what an honor that this little girl saint who spends her heaven doing good upon earth should have chosen to take up her abode amongst us at this, her American National Shrine! What an honor that she should have chosen to bring here to our Shrine every possible relic of her most pure body and every portable souvenir of her earthly life! Having brought these relics and souvenirs she will surely bring us also her smile and her shower of roses.

"Saint Thérèse," we say to you today, "by reason of all these, your precious relics, you are surely here amongst us today. You are here smiling down upon us tenderly from your shrine. You are here and we hail your smiling presence and we greet you for the Little Queen that you are, and we say to you, Little Queen, Queen of the roses, pray for us today. Help us to heed the message of the Holy Father, 'To study and imitate your Little Way,' help us to heed the messages of your sisters, 'To imitate your humility,' 'To hold ourselves aloof from all that is low and base and ignoble and immodest,' help us 'to imitate you in your love of our Blessed Mother and in your love of Our Lord in the Blessed Sacrament,' and we ask you, our dear little guardian, in the words of your sister, Pauline, to keep us always 'under your sweet protection.'"

Pierre and Father Dolan in the cemetery before the admirable Little Flower statue, which marks the spot where her body formerly lay.

Chapter Ten

Pierre, the Little Flower's Sacristan and Guardian of her Tomb

Tonight, my dear friends, I wish to tell you of Pierre, the Little Flower's sacristan, the guardian of the Little Flower's tomb and the custodian of her chapel at Lisieux. Nowhere in the world, I think, could there be found a man more sincerely and completely given over to devotion to the Little Flower, and excepting my interviews with the Little Flower's sister, I enjoyed my interview with Pierre most.

Pierre Derrien is his full name, although no one in Lisieux ever calls him "Monsieur Derrien" but it is always, in referring to him, "Pierre," and in talking to him, "my good Pierre." When you go to Lisieux you will see in cassock and surplice darting here and there and everywhere about the chapel, lighting the candles for the various Masses, supplying the vestments to the priests, as one after one they say Mass at the tomb, changing the wine and water always at the exact time, a little, short, pleasant looking man with black hair, bright eyes and a great mustache, his lips always ready for a smile in spite of his serious demeanor. "To go quickly and to return soon" seems to be his motto. He is the first one in the chapel in the morning and he is the last one to leave the tomb in the evening. Throughout the day he bestows the most charming courtesy upon the most humble of the pilgrims, answering their incessant questions always with remarkable patience. When he speaks of the Little Flower it is always "notre petite Thérèse", "our little Thérèse". When he speaks of Pauline, the

Mother Superior of the convent, it is always "notre Mère," "our Mother", as if he were himself a novice and she his superior. It was Pierre who prepared the 160 Masses said in the chapel on the day of the Little Flower's Beatification. It was Pierre to whom Cardinal Vico referred when, after observing the efficiency of the little man in serving so many priests at once, the Cardinal said, "Voilà un sacristain qui a de la tête," "There is a sacristan who has a head."

In 1904, Pierre was stricken with a grave malady and had been abandoned by the doctors. In his extremity he implored the intercession of the Little Flower. To his joy he was immediately cured and he immediately undertook a journey to Lisieux to thank his patron. He prayed long at the tomb to her and then called at the convent to report his cure to Mother Agnes. Later on he made a pilgrimage alone to Rome and begged a private audience with the Holy Father, who was then Pius X. Surely the Little Flower was with him, for this poor little Breton, a lone pilgrim without any sponsor, obtained the private audience with the Holy Father. Pius X, taking the head of the kneeling Pierre between his hands, said to him with his paternal smile, "You have the faith, my son, and the good God will bless you."

Pierre had scarcely returned to his native town in Brittany when Pauline, who had been much impressed by the touching devotion exhibited by Pierre to the Little Flower, sent him a letter in which she offered him the enviable post of guardian of the Little Flower's tomb. Pierre could not contain himself with delight. From then on, he told me, he has not had an unhappy moment.

"What could make me happier," he said, "than to be permitted by the Little Flower's own sister to watch at the tomb of little Thérèse, to keep her grave in order and to see that fresh flowers are always placed upon it."

Then later, when the Little Flower's body, before her beatification. was removed from the cemetery to the church, Pierre was made the sacristan of the chapel in addition to retaining his post as guardian of the Little Flower's tomb. No one could possibly fulfill the duties of sacristan and guardian with more faithfulness and exactitude than Pierre, and the Little Flower's sisters, recognizing fully his efficiency and his work, took him into their confidence, made him their familiar, always referring to him as "the good Pierre," so that Pierre is as much a part of the Lisieux Carmel as one of the altars.

Because of his remarkable, childlike devotion to the Little Flower, Pierre was given the honor of being chosen as the banner bearer for the pilgrimage from Lisieux which went to Rome for the Beatification of the Little Flower. During the public audience with the Holy Father given to the Lisieux pilgrimage, Pierre called out to the Pope as the latter walked past, "Très-Saint Père, Voulez-vous bénir ma bannière," "Most Holy Father, would you please bless my banner?"

The Holy Father glanced up astonished at this unwonted interruption, and then seeing the pleading eyes of the kneeling Pierre, walked over to him, fingered the banner admiringly and said, "What a beautiful banner!" and blessed both the banner and Pierre, giving his hand to Pierre to kiss.

Pierre by reason of his audacity, became immediately famous upon his return to Lisieux, but Pierre, discussing the incident, always dismissed it lightly, saying, "It was the Little Thérèse who inspired the Holy Father."

I had read an account of this incident in a French book and had seen in the same book Pierre's picture, and therefore when I entered the Lisieux chapel to say Mass my first morning, I recognized Pierre and said to him in the sacristy before I vested, "You are Pierre, are you not?"

He looked at me surprised and answered "Yes, Father, but I do not remember having met you before."

"No, you never met me, Pierre," I said, "I am from America, from Chicago."

"And you know me?" he exclaimed, wonderingly.

"Yes, Pierre," I answered, "I know you. You're the man who said to the Holy Father at the beatification audience in

Rome, 'Holy Father, will you bless my banner?' You see I know all about you. I, from distant America, am acquainted with Pierre of Lisieux. You see you are a famous man, Pierre."

Pierre beamed his pleasure and from that moment we were great friends. He served my Mass and bestowed every possible attention upon me after Mass. How long was I going to be at Lisieux? . . . Well, I could say Mass at any altar I chose; at the altar of the tomb every morning if I wished, and anything that he could do for me while he was there he would be proud to do.

"Well, Pierre," I said, "I could have no better guide to the Little Flower's tomb in the cemetery than you, who were guardian of her tomb for so long. Could you arrange to be my guide to the cemetery?"

Of course he could, and that afternoon Pierre and I visited the cemetery which is a considerable distance from the town. As we walked along the road to the cemetery, Pierre said, "Four times a day for fifteen years, Father, I walked this road while the Little Flower's body was still in the cemetery."

He took me first to the tomb of the parents of the Little Flower. After the death of Mr. Martin, Mr. Guérin, the Little Flower's mother's brother, brought the body of the Little Flower's mother from Alençon to Lisieux, and the father and mother were buried together under a plain but massive headstone on which is inscribed "La Famille Martin," "The Martin Family" and underneath that there are written in French these words: "The race of the just shall be blessed." We knelt reverently at the tomb for several moments, but I could not bring myself to pray for, but rather to, that saintly couple.

We passed on then to the tomb of the Little Flower and after our prayers there Pierre told me many stories of his experiences at the tomb during all the years when the Little Flower's body was there. A magnificent new monument to the Little Flower, the one which Léonie's godmother, Madam Tifenne, claims is the best likeness of any to the Little Flower, has been erected at the place that once was her tomb.

Later Pierre was my guardian during my first visit to the Little Flower's home and, as you have read, accompanied me at my visit to the home of Jeanne Guérin.

One day Pierre took me into the sacristy at Carmel after Mass and said, "Father, I will show you something that few see," and laying his hands on his lips to signal silence, he conducted me past the little door, now sealed and inscribed: "At this door the Little Flower left her father after the last farewell embrace before she passed through this door to make her entrance into Carmel." On we went until we were in the inner sacristy which is separated by a thin wall from the actual cloistered Carmel. In the wall there is a large revolving door which Pierre turned.

"I turn this every morning, Father, before Mass, because the Sister Sacristan in the interior sacristy prepares the chalice for the priest who says the community Mass for the sisters in the morning. Before Mass I enter here, turn the door, and I find there on the slide the Chalice already prepared by the Sister Sacristan of the convent. As you know, Father, the Little Flower was for a long time the Sister Sacristan of the convent and mille, mille fois, a thousand, thousand times, she put her hand where my hand is now. You may put your hand there too, Father," he said, after kissing the handle of the revolving door. I placed my hand there and following Pierre's example, kissed it reverently.

Pierre said, "Father, I have a souvenir of the Little Flower which this afternoon I wish to show you. It is absolutely unique in the world. There is no other memento like it. I call it my inestimable treasure. I would not part with it for all the world. It is my most precious possession."

"What is it, Pierre?" I said, very much interested.

"Be patient, Father and, this afternoon at two, I will call for you at the inn and shall take you to my little room and show it to you."

My curiosity was of course greatly aroused but I asked no more questions. That afternoon Pierre appeared and brought me over to his little room near the sacristy. On the way he said: "I suppose, Father, you have been making a thousand guesses as to my treasure."

I said, "Yes, Pierre."

"Well, Father, you will see it in a moment. You know," he said, "in the lifetime of the Little Flower there was in the convent garden a rose bush. This rose bush grew in the grotto of the garden and beneath the rose bush the Little Flower often went each day to pray to our Blessed Mother in the grotto. From this rose bush she daily culled the roses for her statue to the Infant Jesus. When the convent chapel was enlarged after her death to accommodate the throngs of pilgrims the rose bush was uprooted. I begged Mother Agnes to give the rose bush to me. 'What will you do with it, my good Pierre,' said Mother Agnes. 'Leave that to me, Mother. When I am finished I will show it to you,' I replied. 'Well,' said Mother Agnes, 'I know no one who would appreciate this precious souvenir of the Little Flower more than you, Pierre, so you may have it.' Of course," continued Pierre, "I was overjoyed. I set to work immediately and with the greatest pains and after several months of work interrupted by my daily duties, I finished my treasure which I hold so precious and which in a moment you will see."

Arriving at his little room, Pierre opened the door and the most conspicuous object in the room was a magnificent crucifix, an immense "Calvaire" or "Calvary," as they call it in French.

"There is my treasure," said Pierre, pointing to the Crucifix. Before it several vigil lights were burning and before it also there was a prie dieu, and beside it Pierre knelt, motioning to me to kneel on the prie dieu itself.

After our little prayer, Pierre explained to me in great detail the difficulties that he had had in making the crucifix entirely out of the wood of the rose tree.

I followed his explanation admiringly and Pierre said, "I can see, Father, that you envy me the possession of my treasure."

"Yes indeed, Pierre, I do envy you," I said.

"You know, Father," he declared proudly, "The Little Flower's body now lies in the exact spot where this rose tree once grew, and of course that circumstance increases the worth of my treasure. I must show you the letter of congratulation the sisters of the convent sent me after they had seen the Calvaire."

He then showed me a note in Marie's handwriting which read as follows: "My good Pierre: We cannot get over your magnificent crucifix, for we never imagined that you could make anything as beautiful and as artistic from the rose bush. Our Reverend Mother told me to compliment you also for her. The entire community has admired your masterpiece very much and cannot imagine how you were able to make this crucifix from the trunk of the rose tree, but our Little Flower always acts thus toward us. That she may continue to bless you is our prayer. (Signed) Sister Mary of the Sacred Heart."

"Céline, too," said Pierre, "One day at the grille added her word of praise for my crucifix, praise which I valued particularly because she is an artist herself and loves artistic and original objects. She called my Calvaire 'Wonderful', 'Merveilleux'."

Pierre then proceeded to show me some of his other souvenirs, a piece of the coffin in which the Little Flower's body lay, some of the earth from her grave, a piece of the carpet on which she stood when she took her vows and a piece of the silk and silver band which bound the remains of the Little Flower when they were transferred from the cemetery to the church, also a piece of the bridal gown she wore when she went up to take her vows, all relics which had been given to him personally by the Little Flower's sisters.

After having allowed me to inspect closely and handle these precious relics Pierre said, "I see that you love our little saint much and it would be great pleasure to me if you would accept these little relics for your American National Shrine."

I was dumbfounded for I had not expected any such generosity. I thanked Pierre as best I could.

"Indeed I would like to do more for you, Father, if I could. It is too bad there is only one crucifix made from the rose bush for I would surely give you one if I had two."

"Is there only one, Pierre?"

"Of course," he said, "Father, only one. I used all the rose tree for my crucifix with the exception of parts of a few little branches from which the sisters of the Little Flower made souvenir objects which they themselves keep and hold precious."

During the remainder of my stay in Lisieux I saw much of Pierre. Every day we took a little walk together. Every morning he served my Mass. Frequently in the evening he accepted my invitation to have supper with me in the little inn at which I was staying.

One night he brought over to me a little poem, which he called "A little story of the crucifix obtained from the rose tree which grew in the convent of Lisieux and beneath which Thérèse of the Child Jesus often went to pray and to cull the roses for her Little Jesus."

The first verse of the poem translated into prose reads: "The rose bush (rosier), from which my beautiful rose-cross is made, once covered with its branches Mary Immaculate in her grotto of Carmel. Under the branches of my rose-cross, often in times past, Sister Thérèse knelt whispering the Ave Maria. Now her holy body rests where once my rose bush grew."

Several verses of the poem end with these words: "Pour tout le monde je ne donnerais mon rosier, mon beau calvaire",— "For all the world I would not part with my rose-tree, my beautiful crucifix."

On another occasion he said to me, "Father, perhaps you would like to see little notes that I have received at one time or another from one or the other of the sisters of the Little Flower," and he gave me these little notes which throw some little light on the daily life of the Carmelite sisters of the Little Flower.

Finally the night before I was to leave Lisieux Pierre said to me, "Father, will you let me see again the picture of the

Shrine in America to the Little Flower, the picture of the crowds which you showed me the other night?"

Wondering why he was anxious to see the picture again I mounted to my room, secured the pictures and put them before Pierre. He looked at them long and silently and finally said, "All the crowds which come to the Shrine would be very happy if they had my crucifix, made from the rose bush, to venerate, would they not, Father?"

I answered, wonderingly, "Indeed, Pierre, the crowds would be delighted with such a treasure, with such a beautiful souvenir of the Little Flower."

"I asked the question, Father, because ever since I first saw in your eyes, in my room, how much you envied me the possession of my rose bush, I have been thinking of my crucifix and of the ultimate disposition that I will make of it. I feel that I haven't long to live and then after my death to whom would my crucifix go? I would not give it to any of my relatives because perhaps in any one of their homes it might, after a while, be placed in a corner and neglected. If I were to give it to a monastery or a convent it would serve to remind only a few of the Little Flower, because being in a private place it could not bring a great deal of honor to her. But, I said to myself, if I were to give my crucifix to the Director of her Society in America, if I were to give it to him not for himself but for the Shrine, where so many thousands come weekly to honor the Little Flower, then indeed would the crucifix be placed where the most honor would be done to it and where it would be most frequently venerated, where it would remind thousands of the love of the Little Flower for the Infant Jesus, for whose shrine she so often plucked the roses from my rose bush. But if I were to wait until my death, if I were to will the crucifix to the Shrine, perhaps through some chance it might never reach America but might be broken in transit, whereas I could trust Father Dolan, if I were to give it to him, to transport it safely to its destination. These are the thoughts, Father, that have been running through my mind, which prompted my question, which prompted my request for the pictures of the shrine and the crowds. I haven't made up my mind yet, Father, to give it to you, or rather to your shrine, because it is very difficult for me to part with my treasure with which I so often declared I would never, never part. I have decided, Father, to ask notre Mère (Pauline) whether I have her permission to give it to you. Then I shall go to the tomb and talk long tonight with the Little Flower and let you know my decision in the morning."

You may imagine, my dear friends, with what wonderment I listened to these words of Pierre. I could hardly believe my ears. I hardly dared to hope that he would eventually give me the crucifix, to possess which had been until that evening beyond my wildest dreams, but his words certainly gave me ground for hope.

"What time are you going to say Mass in the morning, Father?" asked Pierre.

"At 6:30 at Buissonnets, in the room of the Little Flower."

"When you return from Mass in the morning, Father, I shall have my decision for you. I shall let you know then definitely if I shall give the crucifix to the Shrine. I shall talk long with the Little Flower tonight."

I could hardly wait until the morning. At six o'clock as I was about to leave my room to go up to the Little Flower's home to say Mass, there came a knock at my door. When I opened the door there was a little servant girl of the inn with an envelope on which was written "To be given immediately to the American Carmelite Father, Father Dolan." Within I found this note from Pierre: "My good Father: I have decided to give you my precious and inestimable treasure which is entirely unique in the world. I am happy to give it to you. Think of me in your holy Mass this morning. Pierre."

I was in the seventh heaven of delight, of course, to know that we were to have in our Shrine in America the treasure which was exactly what Pierre called it, unique in the world. I needn't tell you how sincerely I thanked Pierre, but my delight was not unmixed with regret when I saw the expression of sadness upon the face of Pierre as he helped me arrange the crucifix in a large box to take with me to Paris that afternoon.

"Pierre," I said, "if you are going to be sad and lonely without your treasure, I'd rather leave it here."

"Father, I'm not sad, or at least if I am, or if I am a little lonesome at first, it is because I am human. But I have given the crucifix because I thought that in America it will redound most to the honor of the Little Flower. She is sure to help me to imitate her and to smile whenever I miss my treasure. I have deliberately preferred to find my happiness rather in giving the crucifix to America than to keep it myself. I assure you that my permanent emotion will not be sadness but gladness that the crucifix is where it is going."

That afternoon Pierre accompanied me to help with my precious package. Although every day at Lisieux had been bright and warm it was cold and raining softly as we left the inn for the station.

"It is too bad, Pierre, that after all the wonderful weather that I have had throughout my stay that the last day should be like this."

"Yes," said Pierre, with a smile, giving me the most gracious compliment I have ever received, "Oui mon père, vous partez et Lisieux pleure", "Yes, Father: you are going, and Lisieux is weeping."

The Little Flower in her youth.

Chapter Eleven

Visits to Buissonnets, the Home of the Little Flower

Tonight, my dear friends, let us visit the family home of the Little Flower in Lisieux. The Martin property there is called "Les Buissonnets," the meaning of which, as nearly as it can be translated, is "The Little Woods," the aptness of which name will become evident later on in my talk.

With Pierre I set out one morning from the Carmelite Convent chapel and traversed the narrow streets past the church of St. Jacques, then along more stony narrow lanes until suddenly we issued upon a broad boulevard along which the walk was more pleasant. Just before the boulevard reaches the outskirts of the town, Pierre directed that we should turn into a little lane which wound in and out until finally we reached the door or gate in the wall which surrounds the Martin estate. Certainly Mr. Martin could not have chosen for his home a more peaceful, nor secluded spot, because its situation on the edge of the town and the wall around it completely isolated the home.

I pressed the bell and, while waiting for an answer, remembered how often the Little Flower had scampered across the lawn to answer the bell at that same door, for that was one of the duties Pauline had once assigned to the Little Thérèse.

The door was opened for us by the caretaker, Mademoiselle Violette Castel, who is a sister of one of the Little Flower's novices, Sister Mary of the Trinity. She greeted Pierre enthusiastically and he introduced me, and on account of Pierre's presence I was given unusual liberties. Pierre asked to act as my guide and was told that the freedom of the house and gardens was his.

We entered and I paused inside the gate to drink in the full joy of my first view of the home made so familiar to me from pictures. Nothing could be more gracious and charming than the large, comely, and at once rustic and comfortable house situated in a nest of verdure, with bushes along the sides, the trees of the garden in the rear peeking their heads over the roof of the house. Before the house was a spacious and smiling lawn with trees and little garden plots here and there and the whole surrounded by a wall covered with a tapestry of ivy. Surely here was peace, no other noises ever than that of a symphony of crickets or the notes of the nightingales building their nests in the lilac hedges. No wonder that Marie wrote to her cousin when they first moved to Lisieux, "We are finally settled in Buissonnets. It is a charming home, smiling and gay, with a garden large enough for Céline and Thérèse to play their games," and no wonder that Mr. Martin called the little lane leading to Buissonnets "the road to Paradise."

Visitors are usually surprised at their first view of the exterior of the home, because it is so modern and recent looking a structure, the perfect type of a well-to-do middle class home.* Again one is reminded here of how modern and recent St. Thérèse is and of the wonder of the story of the Little Flower whose home was made a place of pilgrimage before she had been fifteen years dead.

Pierre conducted me first to the rooms of the house made interesting and sacred by the presence of the Little Flower. First he showed me the fireplace where the Little Flower used

---

* In her Autobiography the Little Flower says of Buissonnets: "Next day they took us to our new home, Les Buissonnets, and there everything proved a fresh source of delight. The trim lawn in front of the house, the garden at the back, the distant view from the large attic windows—all this appealed to my young imagination. Its situation too, was an added charm, for it stood in a quiet part of the town within easy reach of a beautiful park laid out with flowers. This pleasant abode became the scene of many joys, and of family gatherings which I can never forget."

to place her shoes at Christmas time until that Christmas of 1886 which Thérèse describes as follows: "On reaching home, after midnight Mass, I knew I should find my shoes in the chimney-corner, filled with presents, just as when I was a little child, a fact which proves that I was still treated as a baby. Papa loved to watch my enjoyment and hear my cries of delight as I drew each fresh surprise from the magic shoes, and his pleasure added considerably to mine.

"But the hour had come when Our Lord desired to free me from the failings of my childhood, and take from me even its innocent pleasures. He permitted that Papa, instead of indulging me in his usual way, should feel annoyed, and as I went upstairs I overheard him say: 'All this is far too babyish for a big girl like Thérèse, and I hope this is the last time it will happen.' These words cut me to the very heart, and Céline, knowing how sensitive I was, whispered: 'Don't go down just yet, you would only cry if you looked at your presents before Papa.' But Thérèse was no longer the same—Jesus had transformed her. Choking back my tears, I ran down to the dining room, and making every effort to still the throbbing of my heart, I picked up my shoes and gaily drew out the presents one by one, looking all the time as happy as a queen. Papa joined in the laughter and there no longer appeared on his face the least sign of vexation."

Next we went to the dining room so often mentioned in the Little Flower's Autobiography and mentioned in the passage just quoted. The dining room is kept locked and pilgrims view it through a glass window which has been placed in the wall and upon which is written in French this notice: "This dining room and its furniture, round table and chairs, are preserved exactly as they were in the lifetime of the Little Flower. It is here too that on the eve of her departure for the Carmelite Convent, St. Thérèse sat for the last time at the family repast."

Pilgrims have not been allowed for some years to enter the dining room because some unscrupulous relic hunters had begun to cut off bits of the upholstery of the chairs. But Pierre asked Mlle. Violette for the key and we entered. Of course I was overjoyed at this privilege and examined every corner of the room and looked long at all the pictures, and sat in all the chairs and tried Pierre's patience, I am sure, by keeping him waiting so long. I asked him to request for me from Mlle. Violette the privilege of being admitted to the room often during my stay. Pierre obtained the privilege and I often sat in the dining room, out of the sight of other pilgrims, and read there from the Autobiography of the Little Flower such passages as this: "Monday, April 9, 1888—Feast of the Annunciation was the day chosen for me to enter Carmel. On the day we all gathered round the table where I was to take my place for the last time, and as if to increase the pain of parting—for farewells are in themselves heart-rending—I heard the tenderest expressions of affection, just when I should have most liked to have been forgotten."

You may imagine how much vividness the Little Flower's words have when read in the very spot she is describing. Later I became great friends with Mlle. Violette, who assiststed at my Mass many mornings in the Little Flower's room upstairs, and she permitted me to be photographed at the famous round table in the dining room and after Mass on the day of my departure she said with a smile, "Father, I have a surprise in store for you; you may have your coffee this morning on the round table."

This was beyond my wildest dreams and as I breakfasted there, I said to myself, "If only some one of my brother priests could peek in the window and see me now."

Then we went upstairs to visit the room of the Little Flower, the room in which she had been miraculously cured by the smiling vision of the Blessed Virgin! There at first I saw everything in a haze, so powerful was the impression made by the memories called forth at my entrance into that room sanctified over and over again because in it the Little Flower had read, studied, slept, played and prayed. There at night prayers the Little Flower had often knelt beside her beloved father, learning from his countenance how the saints pray. There Pauline had often put the Little Thérèse to bed, the little girl at such times invariably asking, "Have I been good today? Is God pleased with me? Will the angels watch over me?" and as the Little Flower says: "The answer was always 'Yes,' otherwise I should have spent the whole night in tears. After these questions my sisters kissed me, and little Thérèse was left alone in the dark."*

When I came out of the daze and was able intelligently to grasp details, I was given one thrill after another. A plate on the door read: "This is the room where the child Thérèse stricken with a grave malady was favored by the smile of the Queen of Heaven."* The altar in the room, the placard read, marks the exact spot where once stood the bed on which Thérèse lay when the vision of Mary came. Near the altar is a replica of the statue of the Blessed Virgin that had become animated and smiled on Thérèse, and on the pedestal of the statue* are written these words of the Little Flower, describing the miraculous animation of the statue: "La Sainte Verge s'est avancée vers moi et m'a souri", "The Blessed Virgin advanced toward me and smiled upon me."

So powerful was the influence that this room of the Little Flower had upon me that I said Mass there far more frequently than I said Mass at her tomb. Mlle. Violette would admit me at 6:30 each morning, serve my Mass, give me a cup of coffee, and then the freedom of the Little Flower's home and gardens was mine two hours before the doors were opened to the public. She allowed me to have photographs taken everywhere as the illustrations will show.

In the corner of the Little Flower's room there is another window cut in the wall through which pilgrims may see the

---

* Autobiography, Chapter II.
* "Chambre où Thérèse enfant atteinte d'une grave maladie fut favorisée d'un sourire de la Reine du ciel."
* The original is now in the chapel of the tomb of the Little Flower.

Little Flower's father's bedroom, and a placard reads: "The furniture is exactly as it was left at his death, and the lamps on the mantle were those that were used for the family repast on the night of the first Holy Communion of the little saint."*

From Mlle. Violette, Pierre secured the key for this room too, and I made the same minute inspection and similar meditations as in the dining room downstairs.

Then in another room which had been Pauline's, the toys of the Little Flower are assembled behind glass. There are dolls and checkerboards, picture books, a goldfish bowl, a bird cage, a hamper for use on her fishing trips with her father, a toy boat called "Abandon," a book of the Sunday epistles and gospels, her skipping rope, her geography, her crucifix, her desk, her chair and her prayer book opened to the "examination of conscience," little housekeeping sets of stoves and tables and dishes and finally tiny models of everything used at Mass and Benediction and a tiny altar on which to say the make-believe sacrifice. You may imagine how vivid were the memories of the Little Flower recalled by these toys.

Then we climbed another flight of stairs to the "Belvédère", a large room with great windows all along one side. This was the playroom of the Little Flower on rainy days when she couldn't go into the garden. In this room also Mr. Martin assembled his daughters for his daily spiritual lecture. Some of his prayer-like writings in his own hand are framed and hang from the walls of the "Belvédire", and since they illustrate the character of the saintly father, I will read free translations of two of these which I copied during one of my many hours in that room: "O Holy Roman Catholic Church, Mother of Churches and of all the faithful, church chosen by God to unite all his children in innermost bonds of the same charity, may we always from our hearts hold to that unity."

---

* "La chambre du père de St. Thérèse avec les mêmes meubles. Les lampes qui sont sur la cheminée ont servi le soir de las première Communion de la petite sainte pour le repas familial."

Another reads: "Most men trouble themselves with many things as if they had still several centuries to live. They are ever seeking the prizes of this world, doing nothing to render themselves immortal. God laughs at such bustle, for He knows the moment in which He will choose that all worldly things shall vanish for them. Let us be more wise than the majority of men and place our hope and trust in God, who alone is unchanging, and eternity, which alone is lasting."

Then we went out of the door at the rear of the house into the pretty garden and strolled about the paths where the Little Flower and her sisters, particularly Céline, so often ran and played. There in the garden is a magnificent group of statuary marking the spot where Thérèse asked her father's permission to enter Carmel. The statuary represents Thérèse in the act of making her request. The group is artistic in the extreme, Pierre said that for a long time he could not look at it without tears, for on the Little Flower's face there is an expression of anxiety and eagerness that her request be granted and at the same time there is written on her countenance pity and pain for the very human sorrow she knew her "King" was feeling at the prospect of permanent separation from her, his "little queen." On Mr. Martin's face there is the natural agony which would be felt by a father who had lost his wife and three of whose daughters had already left him for the convent and who now is asked to consent to part with his favorite whom he so adored. But the father's eyes are raised toward heaven to gather strength for the sacrifice which he knew well God was asking him and there is therefore in his eyes, predominating over the pain, resignation and even gratitude that God should honor him by asking the loan of all his daughters.

The group in white marble is indeed a masterpiece and many a time I tried, as I looked at it, to reconstruct in imagination the actual scene it depicts. The request was made on Pentecost Sunday after Thérèse and her father had returned from vespers. The sun was just setting and Thérèse and her father were walking arm and arm along the paths of the garden, as the birds in the trees all about them sang, like an evening prayer, their adieu to the dying day. The noble countenance of Mr. Martin beamed with the serenity of his saintly thoughts. Gently, her eyes swimming with tears, Thérèse without speaking led him to a little garden seat.

He looked at her with touching tenderness and then drawing her close to him he said: "What's the trouble, my little queen, tell me; confide to me your trouble."

Between her tears, Thérèse sobbed her secret—she felt herself called to Carmel and she wished to go soon, very soon.

The first blow was a cruel one for the poor father. Must he then live henceforth in a desert, in an empty house, he himself abandoned in his old age to the care of hired servants? Like his Saviour on the eve of His sacrifice, the father felt his heart break with grief and he would weep. But that grief was but, for an instant, a tribute to weak human nature. An instant more and the grand christian recovered. He asked her reasons, her motives, holding her the while closely in his embrace. Now more sure of herself, Thérèse explained, and then the father, satisfied that her decision was well founded, plucked a white flower from the lawn and gave it to his child telling her that the tiny white flower was the symbol of the virginial purity which she wished to consecrate to God and for which consecration she had his consent. The heart of the father and of the daughter were henceforth fused, united in aspiration for the same ideal, and Mr. Martin was henceforth active in clearing away the obstacles in the way of his little queen's entrance to Carmel.*

Not the least interesting of all the souvenirs of St. Thérèse at Buissonnets is the little grotto of the Little Flower in a niche in the wall in the garden. There is preserved (reconstructed by her sisters) one of the altars that the little girl erected and called "marvellous" in reporting her achievement to her father.

---

* Mr. Martin made several journeys to arrange audiences with the bishop of the diocese for Thérèse, so that she might present her plea, sponsored by her father, for entrance into the convent before the canonical age.

"Everything about the shrine is authentic," reads an inscription on the wall, "the statue of the Blessed Virgin and of St. Joseph are the same ones once placed in the grotto by the Little Flower herself."

Thanks to the kindness of Mlle. Violette, many an afternoon after the doors had been closed to pilgrims, I strolled about the garden alone or lolled on the lawn luxuriating in the memories that the sacred place called forth. At one time I could almost hear in fancy the patter of the footsteps of the Little Flower as she ran up the gravel path, after completing her shrine, to call her father or Pauline to see her marvellous altar. At other times I would take out my copy of the Autobiography and read my favorite passages in the very places to which those passages had reference. For instance, if the passage concerned the Little Flower's first Communion feast or the evening games of the family, I would go to the dining room; if it told of the smile of the Blessed Virgin, I would mount to the Little Flower's room; or if of her vocation I would go to the garden to read the passage before the marble group.

All this was for me, as indeed it would be for anyone, an unending joy, and when the time came to leave, departure was difficult. After Mass and breakfast at the round table, I bade farewell that last morning to Mlle. Violette and started down the path to the gate. I paused once to look around once more at the place I so loved and again I continued on my way; once again I turned to get a last look at the hallowed home. I reached the door and opened it but I could not but turn to look again and this time Mlle. Violette, who understood the faltering, called out, "Never mind, Father, you'll be back again some time soon." I waved and said to myself, "Yes, God willing," and then I walked with a heavy heart down the lane, which was not for me that day "the road to paradise".

Louis Martin surrounded by his family, one year before his death. From left to right: Marie Guérin; Léonie; Celine, near her venerable father; M. Guérin; Madame Guérin; a friend. Rear: the Martin servants.

Chapter Twelve

Visits at Alençon, the Birthplace of the Little Flower

A tedious journey by train which contrasted sharply with the beautiful ride from Paris to Lisieux brought me to Alençon one day from Paris. I sought out immediately the Martin home in which the Little Flower was born.* It was easily found on one of the main streets, No. 42 Rue Saint-Blaise. The house, though neat and cozy, was most simple and plain, not at all as large or imposing as the Little Flower's home at Lisieux. The Alençon house has no front lawn or garden surrounding it; it sets immediately upon the street and one steps from the sidewalk into the front parlor.

I rang the bell and it was answered by the caretaker, the famous Mrs. Grant. Mrs. Grant is the wife of one of the Little Flower's first and most noted converts, the Rev. Mr. Grant, who before his conversion was a United Free church minister of Lochranza in Arran in Scotland. The story of his conversion by the intercession of the Little Flower is a very beautiful one and may be read in the Autobiography. When the Grants after their conversion were driven out of their native town in Scotland, they came to Lisieux on a pilgrimage and just at the time of their arrival Pauline, the Little Flower's sister, was looking for some couple to act as guardians of the Little Flower's birthplace in Alençon. The Grants received the

---

* Because the Little Flower's family moved from Alençon to Lisieux when the Little Flower was only three years old, Alençon is not of course as well known to those interested in the Little Flower as Lisieux.

commission and always attributed to the intercession of the Little Flower their position in her home, where they were so happy and contented.*

Mrs. Grant answered the bell, and it was of course for me a delightful meeting. From my boyhood I had read of her as one of the Little Flower's earliest converts, and my meeting with her brought me, it seemed, very near to the Little Flower herself, for her conversion took place only about thirteen years after the Little Flower's death.

She is a delightful little old lady with gray hair and a pleasant, smiling countenance. I have met many people whose affection for the Little Flower was most edifying, but excepting Pierre, I have never met anyone who seemed to radiate quite so much love for the Little Flower as Mrs. Grant. She didn't say how much she loved our little saint, but I didn't have to be told—her eyes when speaking of the Little Flower, the tone of her voice when discussing her, told me the degree of her affection. Trust too, without bounds, has Mrs. Grant in St. Thérèse. For instance, she told me that she has a strong hope that the Little Flower will convert the entire village in which she and her husband formerly lived. "Because," she said, "when I last visited Lochranza where we had been driven out upon announcing our conversion and where on a former visit I was greeted with jibes and jeers, I was treated with courtesy and respect and even kindness. So will you join me, Father, and have the members of the Little Flower Society in America join me in praying to the Little Flower for the conversion of my town and of my country."

I would have liked to talk indefinitely with Mrs. Grant. She was so refreshing, so edifying in her manner, in her speech, in her appearance, that it was not difficult to guess that this little old lady who thanks the Little Flower in every breath she draws for the privileges of being the guardian of the Little Flower's birthplace, is indeed very close to the Little

---

* Mr. Grant died in the house privileged to be the birthplace of the Little Flower in July, 1917.

Flower and has absorbed much of the Little Flower's own gentleness, amiability and spirituality. Indeed, I think, my dear friends, that the reason why these Little Flower devotions here at the national shrine every Tuesday attract such throngs is that the Little Flower lovers feel that they are better in every way for their brief contact at the Shrine every Tuesday with all that concerns the Little Flower. Familiarity with her, constant devotion to her, frequent visits to her shrine and relics will serve to do for us in some degree what similar intimacy has done for Mrs. Grant.

Mrs. Grant took me first, of course, to the little chapel which is the room in which the Little Flower was born. The room in which the Little Flower was born! What thoughts crowded into my mind as after our prayers we stood there in the little chapel room and read the inscription: "In this room, January 2nd, 1873, Thérèse Martin, now St. Thérèse of the Child Jesus, was born." How much or how little did the Little Flower's mother guess that night of the future of that little newborn girl? You probably know that when, two days after birth, the Little Flower was brought back from the baptismal font of the Church to that room, the Little Flower's mother in nursing her child thought she discerned a halo radiating divinely from the little one's forehead, and once too the father in singing to the little one a few days after her birth thought for a moment that he heard the little one also feebly sing. Whether or not she did so sing, the presage would be verified, for that soul that had just made its appearance into the Martin home became indeed one of the world's sweetest singers, singing God's mercy and goodness so sweetly that all the world has paused to listen.*

I tried as I stood there in that room to imagine the expression on the Little Flower's father's countenance as he bent over the baby in that room to learn if he had really been

---

* "I will sing, I will always sing even if I must gather my roses in the very midst of thorns and the longer and sharper the thorns the sweeter shall be my song." Autobiography of the Little Flower.

mistaken in fancying that he heard the little one softly singing. I conjectured that he would on that occasion have offered up a prayer to God to make his little child a saint. I thought while I was standing there, too, of much that I had so recently heard of the Little Flower's saintly mother, who never ruled the household at Lisieux, but who died in the same room in which I was standing, the room in which the Little Flower was born. On another occasion I will tell you of the many anecdotes of the Little Flower's mother that I heard from authentic sources while I was in France and which because they throw so much new light on the saint's mother will not only be interesting but extremely beneficial especially to mothers, of whom thousands in America are trying to fashion their households as much as possible after the Little Flower's family home as their model.

Leaving the chapel I stood at the head of the stairs with Mrs. Grant and said to her, "Is this the staircase which the Little Flower used to mount calling out at each step 'Mama, Mama' and refusing to mount until she heard the mother's 'Yes, darling' in answer?"

"Yes, Father, indeed it is the very same," replied Mrs. Grant. "I often think of that incident as I mount these stairs," and then she added, "The staircase has never been altered nor touched."

"What a patient and model mother Mrs. Martin must have been," I said.

"Oh, yes, Father, I often think that someone should write a book about the Little Flower's mother. What a wonderful amount of good it would do if all mothers could know intimately the mother of the Little Flower."

"I had already half determined to write such a book," I said, "and now I have decided. If you will agree to pray that it will do the good that you have just prophesied for it, I will write the book and call it simply 'The Little Flower's Mother'."

Mrs. Grant agreed and the book will soon be forthcoming.

Mrs. Grant and I talked further then about the Little Flower's mother, and before I left the house that first day I went back to the chapel to say another prayer, this time not for, but to the Little Flower's mother, who most certainly is in heaven and who probably had not a little to do by her prayers and sacrifices with the Little Flower's climb or rather flight to the heights of holiness. I shall develop that thought more at length in the promised book, "The Little Flower's Mother."

I asked Mrs. Grant's permission to say Mass in the morning in the chapel of the room in which the Little Flower was born and in which her mother died. Permission was readily granted, but Mrs. Grant asked me to make the hour as late as possible, "For," she said, "there is a dear old lady, a Madame Tifenne, who is Léonie's godmother and a very intimate friend of the Little Flower's family, who loves to hear Mass in that little chapel upstairs, and she cannot come early because she is past eighty now and has to walk a considerable distance. She would love to attend your Mass because we have so few American priests who come here, and Madam Tifenne loves to come here especially when the Masses are said by priests who come all the way from America to honor the little girl she knew so well."

"You say she is an intimate friend of the Little Flower's family and knew the Little Flower?" I asked.

"Yes, Father, and once the Little Flower slept in her home. She treats that bedroom, which the Little Flower used, like a chapel."

"Well, I'll be delighted to say Mass as late as is necessary to accommodate Madam Tifenne," I said, "But I must make one condition, Mrs. Grant, namely, that you tell me her address and allow me to go to her and to say that you sent me and to ask her at what hour she wishes the Mass said. That, you know, will give me another opportunity of speaking to one who had known the Little Flower and that is one reason why I came to Alençon, to collect all the firsthand information I could concerning the Little Flower."

Mrs. Grant smilingly gave the address and I went speedily off to see Madam Tifenne, but before I left Mrs. Grant posed with me for her picture at the door of the Little Flower's home.

I immediately sought out Madam Tifenne's address, No. 4 Place de Plenitre. The maid who answered the bell answered that Madam Tifenne was not in but that she expected her at any moment. The words were scarcely out of her mouth when she saw Madam Tifenne just turning the corner towards her home. She walked so spryly that I could hardly believe that it was the same lady of whom Mrs. Grant had spoken, for Mrs. Grant had said, you remember, that Madam Tifenne was over eighty years old. She came up quickly, a little, short, agile, bright eyed, red cheeked Normandy lady, and she was all courtesy and kindness when I announced that I had come from Mrs. Grant to say that I would say Mass in the Little Flower's little room in the morning at any hour which would be convenient for her.

The hour was settled and I asked to see the room in which the Little Flower had slept. She conducted me upstairs and proudly pointed to the room, kneeling as she entered to say a little prayer, and of course I did the same. After our prayer, I asked Madam Tifenne under what circumstances the Little Flower had occupied that room.

"Just before she entered the convent," she replied, "the Little Flower came to Alençon to bid goodbye to the Alençon friends and relatives of the family. I, as the godmother of Léonie and intimate friend of the family, had the honor of entertaining Thérèse and her father and this was the room which Thérèse occupied, and of course," Madame explained, "I allow no one now to occupy this room."

The room was small and simply furnished, and over the bed which stands in the corner, hangs a picture of the Little Flower, and beneath the picture there is a little stand on which a vigil light burns and where fresh flowers are always kept.

Madam then conducted me to the parlor where we sat and talked for an hour about the Little Flower whom Madam Tifenne always called, not St. Thérèse or the Little Flower, but, with simple familiarity, "Thérèse." She explained too that she was never able to call the other sisters of the Little Flower by their religious names but referred to them as "Pauline," "Céline," "Marie" and "Léonie" and she added that once when she had apologized for that habit, Pauline said to her, "Who has a better right to refer to us by our family names? You are one of the family."

"Madam," I said, "are the pictures of the Little Flower faithful likenesses of her as you knew her?"

"No," she declared, "they flatter her."

"Do you mean that the Little Flower was not beautiful?" I asked.

"No," she said, "I do not think that I would call her beautiful; not more beautiful than hundreds of other girls one sees, at least as regards her features. But there was a most unusual arresting and charming expression on her countenance, an expression of placidity which we always remarked from her earliest childhood, and her eyes—her eyes were very beautiful, large and mystic, as it were. By mystic I mean that her eyes always seemed to be looking into the next world. I remember that often while we had company, Thérèse would be sitting in this very parlor as a little girl seemingly attentive, but if one looked into her eyes one would see that her thoughts were far away."

"I do not understand, Madam," I said, "how you can maintain that the pictures of the Little Flower flatter her, because her sister Céline is the artist who painted the pictures of the Little Flower that are in general circulation."

"Well, Céline," declared Madam Tifenne, "idealized her then; she idealized her."

"Well, did you ever see a picture of the Little Flower that you thought was a faithful likeness, Madam?" I asked.

"Yes," she said, "there is one. It is the face on the marble statue of the Little Flower that has been erected over her tomb in the cemetery at Lisieux. That is a faithful likeness and if you wish to know how much I like that statue ask Mrs. Grant."

The next morning I did ask Mrs. Grant and she told me first that she herself could never understand the emphatic declarations of Madame Tifenne that the pictures of the Little Flower flattered her, "because," said Mrs. Grant, "Céline was the author of those pictures and her sister, Céline, if anyone, ought to know the appearance of the Little Flower, especially since the Little Flower declared before her death she would be nearer to Céline in death than she was in life. But," continued Mrs. Grant, "the enthusiasm of Madam Tifenne for the statue of the Little Flower in the cemetery was certainly pathetic. When she saw it for the first time, she was with me. We were walking down the gravel road of the cemetery and had just turned the corner toward the Little Flower's tomb when Madam Tifenne caught sight of the new statue and exclaimed, 'Oh, c'est elle! c'est elle! It is she! It is she!' and the tears ran down her cheeks as approaching nearer she continued to cry, 'c'est elle! c'est elle!'"*

I then asked Madam Tifenne, "Did you ever think for a moment, when you knew the Little Flower as a girl, that she would ever become a saint?"

"Oh, no," she laughed, "I never dreamt that Thérèse would become a saint. I looked upon her merely as an unusually good little girl. I was not surprised at her goodness because both her mother and her father were saints—saints," she repeated. "C'etait une famille vraiment patriarchale", she declared, that is, "It was a truly patriarchal family." She paused before the adjective "patriarchal," which was the best word that she could find in her vocabulary to characterize her admiration for the goodness of the Martin family.

Madam Tifenne then described at some length the Little Flower's father and mother. What she told me of her mother will be reserved for another occasion. She said that the

---

* In 1915 an Ecclesiastical tribunal appointed by the Bishop of Lisieux after a most minute examination of the different photographs of the Little Flower that had been preserved in the archives of the Carmelite convent at Lisieux, formulated this conclusion about the exactitude of the portraits of the saint: "The oval portrait or bust of the saint (placed as a frontispiece to this book), is a most conscientious and careful likeness to the different photographs of St. Thérèse that are extant."

holiness of the Little Flower's father was generally recognized by the common people of Alençon. So widespread was this recognition that there was in general circulation throughout the town a play on words which had reference to his goodness. "It seems," she said, "that every one knew that the sole passion of Mr. Martin was to fish. He loved to fish and the word in French for fisherman [pêcheur] also means 'sinner', so that often we would say of Mr. Martin: 'Saint Martin; Martin [pécheur] (that is 'Saint Martin, Martin the sinner' or if you choose, 'Martin the fisherman.')"

Madam Tifenne talked on and I hung on her every word. The greatest thrill of the interview came when she told me that she, the lady talking to me, had been present at the first Communion of the Little Flower and was present also at the First Communion feast at the Martin home in the evening. The Little Flower gives a whole chapter in the Autobiography to her First Holy Communion and many pages to her First Holy Communion day. You can imagine therefore the thrill of sitting there listening to one who had been actually present at the scene which the Little Flower describes in part as follows: "At last there dawned the most beautiful day of all the days of my life, of which I remember even the smallest detail of those sacred hours, the joyful awakening, the reverent and tender embraces of my school teachers and older companions, the room filled with snow-white frocks where each child was dressed in turn. . . . How sweet was the first embrace of Jesus! It was indeed an embrace of love. I felt that I was loved and I said 'I love Thee and I give myself to Thee forever.' Jesus asked nothing of me and claimed no sacrifice. For a long time He and little Thérèse had known and understood one another. That day our meeting was more than simple recognition. It was perfect union. We were no longer two. . . . How could our darling mother's absence grieve me when heaven itself dwelt in my soul? In receiving the visit of Jesus I received one from her as well. . . . I was not indifferent to the feast prepared at home and I was charmed with the watch presented to me by Papa, but my joy was a tranquil joy. No exterior thing could interfere with the inward peace of my soul."

Madam Tifenne then went on and reconstructed for me all those scenes of that first Holy Communion day. She described, for instance, the tranquil joy of the little girl, evident to all and edifying all; she described the Little Flower's enthusiasm when her father presented the watch which was his first Holy Communion gift to her. But Madam Tifenne's description, thrilling as it was to hear, could not equal the Little Flower's description of her own spiritual joy of that day, descriptions which I have read and reread many times since with more enjoyment, I think, because I had interviewed one who had been present on that occasion.

The next morning I had the happiness of giving Holy Communion at my Mass to this intimate friend of the Martin family and after the Mass Mrs. Grant and Madam Tifenne posed with me for pictures in the tiny garden of the Little Flower which is preserved in the rear of the Martin home at Alençon.

After a visit to the Church of Notre Dame in which the Little Flower was baptized,* I left Alençon well content with my visit but regretting that I had no time to have further conversation with the delightful ladies, Madam Tifenne and Mrs. Grant.

---

* The baptistry and font at which the Little Flower was baptized are preserved just as they were at the time of the saint's baptism except that there has been erected in the baptistry a magnificent altar surmounted by a beautiful statue of the Little Flower.

Chapter Thirteen

The National Shrine of the Little Flower

We have been talking for nine days of the Little Flower's sisters and relatives. What would they say or think if they could see our shrine today?* The Little Flower's sisters would feel as we do if they were here today. Our feeling is one of exultation because it is a great triumph for our little saint, a triumph because there has been completed today so superb, so magnificent a monument to her in this metropolis of distant America. The Little Flower's sisters, if present, would indeed be as proud of our shrine today as we are and would share our feelings of exultation.

But, my dear friends, I should not say, "our shrine"; it is yours. Although it was of course, very costly, it was built by you, by those hundreds of you who have given donations large and small in thanksgiving for favors received from the Little Flower. That is the first remarkable feature of the Little Flower Shrine: it is a monument to the power of the Little Flower's intercession because every dollar of its cost represents someone's thanksgiving offering to the Little Flower.

The shrine itself is built according to the traditional principle of shrines of saints in Europe around a painting of the saint in glory as its central or focal point. The chandeliers are not merely chandeliers but each is really a rose bush to symbolize her promise to let fall from heaven a shower of

---

* This talk was given on the day on which the National Shrine was completed. (Editor's Note.)

roses, and to emphasize the chief lesson she teaches, namely, love of God, the rose being for her queen of the flowers because it symbolizes the queen of the virtues, charity, love of God. The hanging rose-bushes or baskets are themselves shaped like roses. They are made of gold-plated bronze and a close view will reveal that the bronze work is all foliage; rose leaves done so delicately that one of America's most noted architects declared upon viewing the shrine, "I have never seen such magnificent bronze work. It is superb."

The outer golden bronze rose bushes, which are filled with white roses of crystal, form, you will notice, an arch which serves as an outer border to the shrine. The inner arch leads up from within the two side arches of the altar itself to culminate in the large centerpiece or glory made of golden bronze rays to symbolize light and heat, the light of inspiration and the heat of love sent forth to the world by the Little Flower.

The Little Flower herself is painted in the centerpiece in glory, in the ecstasy of her vision of God in heaven. So you see, my dear friends, we have above the altar the painting of the Little Flower, represented as she is in heaven, and below in the central arch of the altar we have the statue of the Little Flower, represented as she was on earth, and if there is any more beautiful statue of the Little Flower in Europe than the one in that arch today it could not be located by the artists whom we induced to search with us. We looked at every model of Little Flower statue in Alençon, in Lisieux, and in Paris and at Lisieux itself we found this statue of the Little Flower made after the model approved by her sisters and made under the supervision of the most skilled artists that we could find in France. I think you will all agree that the face of the statue is the most pleasing, the most winsome and the most like our ideal of the Little Flower than the faces of all the different statues we have had at various times at our shrine.

On the altar itself, supported by two angels, is the châsse or golden container for the five major relics of the Little Flower. The reliquary is in the form of a golden rose branch, each rose of which contains one of the relics. The whole constitutes the largest collection of relics in the world except those at her tomb. Two of the relics, a portion of her flesh and several generous locks of her hair, were given by her own sister, Pauline. The other three are portions of her ashes, of her bones and of the habit in which she died and was buried.

The entire shrine, counting the roses in the bronze vases in the arches, contains 578 electric roses and the beauty of this ensemble, when illuminated, you all feel and I need not therefore describe.

The bronze and electric work of the shrine, the vases, the candelabra and the reliquary were executed by the oldest and most famous firm in Europe, the house of Poussiellgue. M. Poussiellgue and his sons constitute the fourth generation who have managed this firm, which has been occupied exclusively for more than a century in furnishing shrines and the like for the most celebrated churches in Paris and Rome and other cities in Europe. There is a tradition in the family of Poussiellgue handed down by the grandfather and great grandfather of the present owner that men occupied in work such as the making of shrines and reliquaries, should not only be capable artists but religious men, men of piety and prayer. And I found that all the members of this firm are indeed of the very finest and highest type of French Catholic gentlemen and, by the way, all of them are lovers of the Little Flower. No one of us could have put into that work a more religious zeal for the Little Flower's glory than these men did, and no one in the world could have brought to this work more skill. They had to work nights to complete the Shrine before the time I was scheduled to leave Europe and the work being completed at eleven o'clock one night they set up the shrine in the studio and at that late hour assembled their families, grownups and children, and then they turned on the electricity and it was a joy to see the faces of the workmen and the artists as they listened to the delighted comments of their families upon the Little Flower's shrine upon which they worked so hard, and which they considered their masterpiece, a masterpiece which was not to be exhibited in France as their other masterpieces are but to be packed up in the morning and shipped to distant America.

It will interest you too, I am sure, to know something of the artist who painted the shrine picture of the Little Flower in glory. I had told the elder Monsieur Poussiellgue that to paint the shrine picture, I wanted not only an artist of reputation, but an artist of religious mind and heart, someone who would put into the picture not only artistic ability, but religious feeling.

Monsieur Poussiellgue said, "I know your man," and he took me to one Joseph Gerard. We found him a tall, ascetic looking, middle aged man in his garden studio in a quiet, secluded corner of Paris.

Monsieur Poussiellgue said in introducing me to the artist, "Monsieur Gerard has been decorated by the French Academy, has been awarded the Legion of Honor for distinguished bravery in the Great War and is also the president of the Holy Name Society of Paris."

The artist was much embarrassed by this summary of his fame but he became very enthusiastic when our errand was explained. He said, "I will be delighted to paint the picture of the Little Flower, my favorite saint."

He pointed to a table in the studio where there were many books and on the top of the pile was the Life of the Little Flower. He walked to the door of his studio, pointed to a window of a convent which adjoined his garden and there in the chapel of the convent, visible from the door of the studio and overlooking his garden was a statue of the Little Flower. "You see I am surrounded by her," he said.

He began a novena to the Little Flower on the morning that he started to work on his picture and the result is the work of piety and art which you see, a work produced by one who is at once a brave soldier, a great artist, a thorough Catholic gentleman and lover of the Little Flower.

That, my dear friends, is, in brief, the history of our shrine and its builders.

You know how men feel when homes they have planned have been completed. That is not our feeling nor your feeling today. It is not a feeling of proprietorship, not a feeling of personal pride, but a consciousness of privilege that the Little Flower should have chosen this church, our church, your church, as the seat of her most beautiful shrine in America. It is certainly that and we can say also, making all allowance for an inclination to be partial to ourselves, that no shrine to her in Europe can equal it; except the Lisieux chapel, and even that does not surpass it.*

There then, my dear friends, is our monument to the little girl nun of Normandy who is dead only twenty-nine years but who in that short time has already brought the world to her feet, captured the hearts and captivated the affections of millions of men and women of every race and age and condition of life; there is our monument to the little girl nun who has so won the hearts of the members of her society here in America, so showered her roses upon them that they have, in thanksgiving erected this beautiful shrine to her, their benefactor. That she will continue her benefactions, continue to shower her roses from this, her central American shrine, there can be no doubt. That we will continue to labor for her, labor to imitate her, labor to spread her devotion there is no doubt either. It will be easier now to work for her, easier to imitate her, easier to imitate the virtues that attract all to her and that make her the queen of millions of hearts; easier to do all this now that we have her enshrined in a bower worthy of her, in a rose bower worthy of a queen, in a rose bower worthy of our little queen of the roses who has done and will do so much for us all.

---

* See the foot note on page 389.

"Our Sister Is in Heaven!"

Thérèse at the age of eight, throwing flowers before the Blessed Sacrament on a feast day.

Chapter One

Holy Communion to the Sisters of St. Thérèse

Almost all of you who are assembled here, my dear friends, are aware that the Little Flower has four living sisters.* They are known to the readers of her Autobiography as Marie, Pauline, Céline and Léonie. Three of them are now Carmelite nuns living in the same convent in which the Little Flower herself lived, the Carmel of Lisieux, in upper Normandy, about half way between Cherbourg and Paris. The religious names of these Carmelite Sisters are, Mother Agnes (Pauline), Sister Mary of the Sacred Heart (Marie), and Sister Genevieve (Céline). The fourth sister, Léonie, whose name in religion is Sister Frances Thérèse, is a Visitation nun living now in the convent at Caen, about three hours journey from Lisieux.

Last year I had the privilege of visiting these four sisters of St. Thérèse, and many of you remember that I related the account of those visits here at the national shrine, and I subsequently placed the complete account in book form in "The Living Sisters of the Little Flower." Since writing that book, I have, as you know, visited the sisters of St. Thérèse again and am to begin tonight the account of that second visit with them.

---

* The chapters of this book were originally so many talks delivered by Father Dolan at the National Shrine of the Little Flower in Chicago and elsewhere, and the narratives have been preserved in their original form because it was thought that the narrative gains rather than loses interest and attractiveness in that vivid and animated form. (Editor's Note.)

I arrived at Lisieux about five o'clock one afternoon just in time for Benediction of the Blessed Sacrament sung by the sisters themselves, hidden behind the grill in the sanctuary of the chapel. If you ever go to Lisieux, do not miss that Benediction. It is an unforgettable experience. I have tried to find an adjective that would adequately describe the voices of those hidden sisters singing those ancient hymns of the Church, the "O Salutaris" and the "Tantum Ergo", and that adjective is "other-worldly." Those voices are not of this world. They come more from the soul than from the body.

Shortly after Benediction of the Blessed Sacrament, I left my seat and made for the exit of the chapel, and Pierre, the guardian of the Little Flower's tomb, literally rushed down the aisle after me. After we welcomed each other, he said to me: "Father, will you say the community Mass in the morning?"

I said, "At what time, Pierre?"

He answered, "At eight o'clock."

"That is too late, Pierre," I said. "I have a great deal to do in the morning and must say Mass earlier than that."

His face fell and he seemed puzzled.* He said, "But Mother Agnes thought that you would like to say the community Mass and give Holy Communion to the sisters."

"To what sisters?" I asked.

"To the religious, Father."

"To the sisters of Carmel, do you mean to Pauline, Marie, and Céline, and the others?"

"Yes, Father," was Pierre's smiling reply.

It took me several minutes to appreciate what a privilege was being offered me.* To give Holy Communion to the

---

* I had known that the Carmelite Sisters rose at 4:30 A.M. but did not know that they waited until the 8 o'clock Mass to receive Holy Communion. That explains why I did not immediately accept the invitation to say the 8 o'clock Mass. (Author's Note.)

* It is explained in Chapter II how Father Dolan happened to be offered this high privilege, never before enjoyed by any American priest or bishop, of saying the Community Mass for and giving Holy Communion to the sisters of the Little Flower. (Editor's Note.)

sisters of the Little Flower, to the sisters of a saint! There was little or no sleep for me that night. I was afraid that the alarm would not ring or that I would oversleep, and the result was that two hours before the time appointed, I was up and doing.

I was in the sacristy at 7:30 ready to vest for Mass. The sacristy itself is impressive; it is so immaculate, so silent, so mysterious. Just the thinnest of walls separates the inner sacristy from the cloister of Carmel. As I vested, I wondered why there was no chalice. Then a revolving door in the wall of the cloister turned and there was the chalice prepared for Mass by the sister sacristan of the convent. The office of sister sacristan, the Little Flower herself held for many years in the convent. I took great pains to find out in exactly what order the sisters came to Communion so that I would know just when I was giving Communion to the Little Flower's own sisters. I questioned the sacristan and memorized the information thus obtained.

At five minutes of eight the large chapel bell rang out and then I heard the noise of the lifting of the steel grating that covers the grill. The grating was raised in order that the sisters might see the altar during the Mass.

At eight o'clock sharp the little interior convent bell tinkled, and at that signal the server, Pierre, opened the door leading to the sanctuary and we started to the altar. As I walked, I could distinguish directly in front of me the figures of the Carmelite sisters kneeling in their places in the choir behind the open grill. "What perfection is there!" I said to myself, "What holiness! How many saints does that grille imperfectly hide. How devoutly I ought to say Mass before these sisters of a saint, who are doubtless saints themselves."

I genuflected and went up to the altar where I mechanically and somewhat distractedly unfolded the corporal, went to the missal, or Mass book, and opened it to the beautiful votive Mass of the Little Flower which Mother

---

* Rome has given Mother Agnes authority to permit the votive Mass of the Little Flower to be said there twice a month.

Agnes had authorized me to say that morning.* I offered the Mass for all the members of the Little Flower Society in America and then descending, began exultantly the prayers at the foot of the altar. The first prayer was "Confitemini Domino quoniam bonus", "Let us confess, to the Lord, that God is good." Good, indeed, I thought, to arrange all this for me.

Then came the beautiful Introit of the Little Flower's own Mass, recited in the sight and hearing of the Little Flower's own sisters, kneeling where she herself had knelt every morning during the nine years of her convent life.

The Mass went on, through the Gospel, the Offertory, the Sanctus, the Consecration, the Communion, until at last the solemn moment arrived, the moment at which I was to have the privilege, which I had never dreamt of asking, the privilege of giving Holy Communion to the sisters of a saint.

As I genuflected after my own Holy Communion, there was a stir behind the grille. It was the sisters prostrating themselves on the floor, as is their custom, to recite the Confiteor before Holy Communion. I heard the unforgettable voice of Pauline saying the first word of the prayer, "Confiteor" and then those "other-worldly" voices in that solemn, even tone complete the recitation of the prayer. I was so impressed I could hardly take the cover from the Ciborium.

As I genuflected a second time, a light flashed on the opening of the grille where the sisters were to receive Holy Communion. Then after the second "Domine Non Sum Dignus" I walked with the Blessed Sacrament, tremblingly, over to the grille.

The opening of the grille is a kind of window or panel and over this opening is an electric light and on the other side a priedieu where the sisters kneel to receive Holy Communion. Therefore I could see them all plainly as they came up one by one to receive.

The first one to come was of course the superior, Mother Agnes, Pauline, the beloved sister and second mother of the Little Flower. You may well imagine my feelings as I placed the tiny Sacred Host on the tongue of her whom you and I so revere. I felt that I was giving Holy Communion to a saint, to a saint who had made a saint. I was giving Holy Communion to her who had prepared the soil for the Little Flower, who had tenderly nurtured and watered the little bud until the rose, Thérèse, bloomed in its full spiritual beauty and heavenly charm.

How can I describe, my dear friends, what it means to give Holy Communion to a saint? Let me try by means of comparisons.

Have you ever listened to an exquisite symphony played by a perfect orchestra, sending forth music that stirred you to the very soul? Have you ever been caught by the spell of a great actor who, delivering some noble passage with his soul ablaze, rose to such heights that you too were set on fire? Have you ever listened to a great organ played by a master, pealing forth gorgeous floods of sound so that the rolling gorgeous music swept over you like a river? Combine then these three emotional experiences and you will have some idea of how it feels to give Holy Communion to Mother Agnes at that little opening in the grille.

After Mother Agnes, the next sister was the subprioress, whose name I have forgotten, and then Sister Mary of the Angels, who is the oldest sister of the convent and who therefore lived in the convent with the Little Flower during all the latter's nine years there.

Then there came the two other sisters of the Little Flower in this order, Marie and then Céline. You may well imagine with what emotion I gave our Divine Lord to these two blood sisters of the Little Flower. Then there came the fourteen other professed sisters of the convent.

Marie and Céline and Pauline, the sisters of the Little Flower, look exactly as I described them to you in the spring. Pauline is thin, short, and dark. Céline is tall, stout, and fair. Marie is the stoutest of the three, dark, and, judging from the difficulty with which she knelt and arose from her knees, she has become very feeble in her advanced age.

Their eyes were of course downcast at the moment of receiving Holy Communion, but one of the most remarkable features of their appearance and of the appearance of all of the sisters was an extraordinary expression of calm and placidity and peace on their countenances.

More remarkable was their extreme devotion at the moment of Holy Communion. I have often given Holy Communion to people whose devotion was so evident that it was more than edifying, but I have never given Holy Communion to anyone whose devotion was so impressive, so manifest as that of the sisters of the Carmel at Lisieux. It was devotion that you could almost feel. I tried to analyze it. I asked myself, "What is it in their way of receiving Holy Communion that produces so profound an impression upon me?" I couldn't analyze it at first and then it came to me; it is that expression of calm which changes ever so slightly at the moment of Holy Communion into an expression of controlled eagerness, eagerness to receive our Divine Lord. It is an expression which tells you plainly that each nun feels that this moment is the supreme moment of the day, the supreme moment of life, the moment of the coming of that heavenly Prince, to Whom they have given what? To Whom they have given themselves, body and soul. All the love of their virginal souls, in all its strength and tenderness, in all its depth and solidity, is written plainly on their countenances at the moment of Holy Communion. That is why to give Holy Communion to the nuns of Carmel is so tremendously moving an experience.

After the professed sisters, there came the novices. The professed sisters dress as we do, brown tunic, brown scapular and white cloak. The novices have the brown tunic and scapular but not the white cloak; instead they wear a white veil.

I could not help being distracted by thinking of the Little Flower as a novice as I gave Holy Communion to the novices, to these other lovely, young flowers just beginning to bloom.

The last to receive was the Novice Mistress. After she had

received Holy Communion, she remained kneeling and motionless as a sign to me that there were no more to receive.

I returned to the altar, finished the Mass and returned to the sacristy as in a dream. I felt that I had been privileged that morning to enter a corner of heaven. I felt that I have been privileged to give Holy Communion to souls as choice, as fair as any that could be found on earth, and I know that I had given Holy Communion to souls who are the choicest, fairest flowers to be found anywhere in any of God's earthly gardens. That is what the Carmel of Lisieux is, God's Garden. Whether you are on the altar saying Mass, in the chapel assisting at Mass, or talking to the nuns in their parlor you feel that you are in God's garden and you sense the perfume of that garden, the perfume of holiness, the perfume of high spirituality and the perfume of other-worldliness. That perfume of the austere heights of Carmel makes all things that are base, utterly impossible of search and all sensual allurement utterly unattractive. Everything that falls short of their high ideals seems undesirable and contemptible.

I have tried to describe to you in detail the experience that I enjoyed, in order that you too may feel its appeal, its call to a higher life, to a life more spiritual, more unworldly, more "other-worldly," a life that will imitate to some small degree the lives of these nuns of Carmel, who, treading the footsteps of the Little Flower, are living only for God.

Thérèse as St. Joan of Arc during
the prison scene of the Carmel production.

Chapter Two

What the World Does Not Know About the Little Flower

Last night we began the story of my second visit to the home of the Little Flower. I described the great privilege obtained for me by the Little Flower's sister Pauline, the privilege of saying Mass in the Little Flower's convent and of giving Holy Communion to the sisters, amongst whom were three of the sisters of St. Thérèse.

Before I proceed in our story, just let me remind you how difficult it was for me, during my first sojourn in Lisieux, to secure an audience with Pauline. You remember how I had to plead with the sister portress and, when I finally gained the presence of Pauline, how I had to beg to obtain from her permission to speak with her sisters, Marie and Céline. This time, thanks to the kindness and consideration of Mother Agnes, I had no such difficulty, as you will see.

Following the Mass, which I described to you yesterday, I spent the greater part of the morning at the tomb of the Little Flower giving thanks for the wonderful privilege that she had obtained for me. That afternoon at one o'clock I went to the convent of Carmel and asked the sister portress, who answered the bell, to speak with Mother Agnes.

The sister answered, "Mother is expecting you, Father."

She took me immediately to the parlor and gave me a seat before the grille which I have described so often in "The Living Sisters of the Little Flower."

Almost immediately, I heard Pauline's voice giving the customary greeting of the Carmelite Sisters when they enter the parlor, "Deo Gratias", "Thanks be to God."

I said, "Is it Pauline?"

"Yes, Father," she said, "It is I, but how did you know?"

"O, that's easy, Mother," I said, "your voice is not easily forgotten."

By the way, some days before I had heard an eminent French ecclesiastic turn a pretty phrase about Pauline's voice: "I have heard," he said, "the voices of all the great vocal artists. I have heard them, been thrilled by them, and forgotten them. I have heard the voice of Pauline but once and it is ringing ever since in my ears."

But to return to our story. When I said, "Your voice is not easily forgotten," she answered, "Yes, Father, but the eyes remember longer than the ears, and you saw us all this morning."

"Yes, Mother," I answered.

"And you gave us all Holy Communion." And she said this with such evident appreciation of the joy that I took in that privilege that my pleasure was doubled to hear her refer to it with such manifest understanding.

"It was you, Mother, then, who arranged that for me?"

"Yes," she said. "When your letter came announcing your coming, I wrote to the Bishop and secured his permission that you say Mass and give us Holy Communion."

"I can't thank you sufficiently, Mother," I said, "But, Mother, do you think that I could say Mass for the sisters once more and again give them Holy Communion before I leave?"

I expected a negative answer, but to my surprise she said, "You may have the privilege, Father, every morning as long as you remain here."

"I think then, Mother," I answered, "that I will remain here permanently."

She laughed at this and I went on, "I hope this time, Mother, that I can speak to you and your other sisters more often, because there are many questions I have to ask you, and Americans who love the Little Flower are hungry for information about her."

Pauline replied graciously, "Father, we are at your disposal. Come as often as you like, and as long as you have questions to ask, I or my sisters will come to answer them. You can make your own program."

I could hardly believe my ears and said so. "Mother, will you please say that again. I am not sure that I heard correctly."

She laughed and repeated the gracious invitation. And she kept her word. Counting that afternoon's visit, I spent eighteen hours in all with the sisters, visiting with them in the convent parlor before the grille, and I said their Mass and gave them Holy Communion every morning of my stay in Lisieux.

Now let me repeat some of my conversation with Pauline. One day while I was in Lisieux, in the convent parlor, I said to Mother Agnes (Pauline): "Mother, there are very few people who really understand how much the Little Flower suffered—very few who realize that she was in very truth a martyr. There is a very widespread notion that she had little or no suffering to bear. They understand her grief at the death of your mother and at the sad death of your father, and at your departure and Marie's departure for the convent, but she was always so cheerful and smiling that it is difficult for them to understand that she suffered constantly and suffered intensely. Could you give me a few concrete details of her sufferings?"

Pauline then proceeded to talk for more than a half hour of the sufferings of her little sister and she spoke of them so feelingly and so tenderly that I am sure there were tears as well in her eyes as there were in her voice. I cannot tell you all she said, today. I will not speak of her spiritual sufferings—what she suffered from aridity or spiritual dryness, from the unkindness of her first mother superior, from her inability to receive Holy Communion daily. These spiritual sufferings we less spiritual people can only with difficulty appreciate. But let me tell you what Pauline told me of some of the physical sufferings of the Little Flower, sufferings less well known.

The source of her greatest sufferings in the convent, Pauline said, was the cold. Even in winter, and even now, there is no heat in the convent there; that is one of the mortifications imposed by the rule. Only in one room, the community room, was there a tiny stove. There was no heat in her cell where she spent her nights, no heat in the chapel where she spent most of the day. Even in October and November, while I was saying Mass in the convent chapel, I had to stop during Mass and rub my hands to prevent their becoming numb, and I said to myself then, "How the frail Little Flower must have suffered from the cold as she knelt here in the chapel those long winter nights from 7:30 until eleven o'clock p.m. and those icy winter mornings from 4:30 until nine o'clock."

The Little Flower, always frail, was extremely sensible to cold. Even when she was a little girl she loved warmth. I talked, in Alençon, with a relative of the Little Flower, an old lady eighty-five years old whom the Little Flower, when a girl, once visited. The old lady told me: "I remember her first visit. She came in shivering and took off her little wraps and turned to me and said so sweetly, 'Oh, how warm it is here in your house, Madame; it is heaven'." The old lady then remarked to me "How the poor little thing must have suffered from the cold of the convent."

Pauline told me that in the winter, at eleven o'clock at night, after the long prayers in the chapel, the Little Flower would, with the other sisters, go to the community room for a moment to warm herself a little before the stove there. Then to reach her cell she had to walk a hundred yards in the cold night air under the cloisters and then climb, wearily, a steep, cold stair case and walk down along a glacial corridor to her cell which was just as icy. There she would lie down on her bed of boards and pull over her the single thin blanket allotted to her by the rule.

On her death bed it was revealed that many a winter's night she shivered and trembled the whole night long without being able to sleep at all.

Pauline said to me: "If she had only told us or her Mistress of Novices of this, she would have been given relief, for the rule is not intended to inflict such suffering. But the Little Flower wished no relief; she wished to suffer this rude mortification just as did the stronger sisters in order that she might win forgiveness for sinners. She told me of this only on her deathbed, and, to use her own words, said smilingly: 'My little Mother, I have suffered from the cold until I thought I would die of it'".

"After her first hemorrhage," Pauline said, "she made no mention of it, and the next day and on succeeding days went about her duties as usual, and, because she was always so smiling and cheerful, we never suspected the terrific strain it must have been for her in her weakened condition to scrub the staircase and corridors, and bend over the wash tub in the laundry. Then at length she collapsed and the Mother Superior commanded her to reveal her condition and then only did she tell us of her hemorrhages. I said to her reproachfully, 'O Thérèse, why did you not tell us?' She answered, with her sweet smile, 'Oh my little Mother, if you had known my condition you would have suffered too much on my account; you would have worried too much'." You see, my dear friends, it was a delicacy of her love for her sisters that led her to spare them pain by concealing her weakness and suffering. Certainly that is the perfection of thoughtfulness, the perfection of charity.

What a lesson for us there is in that anecdote! Are we careful to embrace the opportunities there are at home for the exercise of the virtue of charity? Are we, like the Little Flower, anxious to spare our loved ones pain and worry? Let us ask her to help us to imitate her in her thoughtfulness of the members of her family.

"Nevertheless," Pauline continued, "during all this time she was as usual, gay and cheerful—so much so that when she was not at recreation the sisters of the community would say with disappointment, 'We won't have occasion to laugh today. Sister Thérèse won't be here'!"

"No one, I suppose," said Pauline, "has any idea of her spiritual sufferings. God permitted that temptations against faith should come to her at the most solemn moments. For instance, when she was kneeling in the chapel trying to pour forth her soul in love for Our Lord, she would seem to hear a voice whispering out to her, 'Heaven, for which you have been striving so feverishly, all your life does not exist—God, Whom you love so ardently does not love you'."

Pauline told me of the answer that the Little Flower gave to these temptations. This was her answer: At the time when these temptations were at their height, Thérèse took the book of the gospels which she always carried near her heart and upon the flyleaf of that sacred volume she wrote with her blood the entire Credo—the entire "I believe in God"—in her own blood. That was her answer to temptations against faith: "I believe" in her own blood.

Again, my dear friends, what a lesson for us is there in this incident of the life of the Little Flower. In these days how many Catholics carelessly expose their faith to the danger of destruction by their reading and by unnecessary association with unbelievers? Let each glean his own lesson from this little saint of our own time who prized the precious jewel of faith so highly that, rather than lose or tarnish it, she was willing to write the entire Credo in her own blood.

So you see, my dear friends, that although some think the Little Flower could not have been a great saint because she did not perform great austerities, nevertheless she did have her cross and it was a constant one and a heavy one and she bore it not only patiently, but cheerfully and therein there is a lesson for us: If we love the Little Flower we must imitate her in her patient bearing of suffering and trial which God sends us. We may not be able to imitate her in bearing trial's so cheerfully that those around us do not even know that we are bearing a cross, but at least we can imitate her patience and resignation.

To know that the Little Flower suffered, to know that it was not God's plan to exempt her from the rule that He chastises those that He loves, will cause most of us to love her more than before; it will bring her closer to us.

Pauline also gave me these examples of her charity that are new. Sister Thérèse at the age of twenty had been given not the name, but the office of Novice Mistress, and one day an old and disagreeable religious said to her, "At your age, Sister, you should be learning to rule yourself rather than to be given the direction of others."

"Oh," said the Little Flower, humbly and sweetly, "You are right, my sister, I am even more imperfect and faulty than you think I am."

How typical of the Little Flower is that reply. Notice how skillfully the Little Flower avoids giving offense and how cleverly she conceals any pique which she must have felt at this ill-natured remark. "I am even more unworthy and imperfect than you think I am." How we storm and protest when someone underrates or fails to appreciate our merit. But the little saint of our own time says, for our imitation, "You are right, Sister; I am even more imperfect and unworthy than you think I am."

Pauline said that the sisters were preparing for the feast day of the Mother Superior and they brought to the Little Flower various little presents to be painted and touched up by the artistic brush of the Little Flower before being presented to the Mother Prioress. It happened that one sister, after having looked at the work the Little Flower had done for her, instead of thanking her, complained that the Little Flower had not decorated her present as prettily as that of another sister. The Little Flower made excuses for herself humbly and after the sister had gone, she turned to Pauline with a smile and said, "When we work only for God, we do not need any thanks from creatures; when we work only for Him reproaches such as those just heard are powerless to take away our peace."

Sister Thérèse, Pauline told me, was for a long time in charge of an old and invalid sister who, by her fastidiousness and complaints tried the patience of the whole community, but with her the Little Flower was never impatient. One day, instead of the Little Flower, a novice was sent to wait on the old sister, and the novice lost her patience and spoke a little sharply to the aged sister, who exclaimed to the novice: "Never, never did Sister Thérèse speak to me like that."

So you see, my dear friends, that it was in these little ways—little sacrifices, patience, charity, kindness, cheerfulness in spite of suffering in these little ways that the Little Flower was changed day by day, hour by hour, from the proud and independent Mademoiselle Thérèse Martin into Saint Thérèse of the Child Jesus. These little, but constant and incessant, mortifications were nothing short of heroic and made her not only a great saint, but a saint, as the Holy Father says, whom all the world can imitate. Surely these little acts of patience, thoughtfulness, and kindness that I have been enumerating tonight are within the power of us all.

Pauline also told me of a prophecy the Little Flower made about her Autobiography (her life written by herself). You know this life was written under obedience and the Little Flower did not know as she wrote it that it would ever be published, but later in life, just before she died, she certainly seemed to foresee how widely it would be read, because one day Pauline brought the Little Flower the manuscript and asked her to reread a passage which seemed to Pauline incomplete. Pauline left her with the manuscript and returned soon to the infirmary and found Thérèse in tears.

"You are crying!" Pauline exclaimed.

Thérèse looked up with a strange expression and said, "Indeed, my sister, these pages will do a great deal of good, they will make better known the goodness of the good God" and then she added, in a tone evidently inspired, "Yes, sister, I feel all the world will love me. All the world will love me."

It is impossible after reading these words and knowing the facts to deny that the Little Flower was given the gift of prophecy.

One day while I was visiting in the convent parlor with all three of the sisters of St. Thérèse, I asked Céline what she thought was the most beautiful sentence the Little Flower ever wrote. She answered "I can't give you one sentence. I like best two passages which reveal her love of the Blessed Virgin. First, when she said to the Blessed Virgin: 'If Thou, O Mary, wert Thérèse and if I were Queen of Heaven, I would still wish to be Thérèse that I might see thee Queen of Heaven.' Secondly, the passage in which she says, 'I love to hide my sufferings from Our Lord; to Him I love always to present a smiling countenance. But from our Blessed Mother, Céline, I hide nothing; I show her and tell her all'."

I asked Marie what passages she liked best in her sainted sister's writings and she answered: "A passage in a letter she wrote to me: 'Sometimes, Marie, I find myself saying to our Blessed Mother, "O Cherished Mother, I think that I am more fortunate than you for I have you for Mother and you have not, like me, the Blessed Virgin to love".'"

These words of the Little Flower quoted by her sisters may indeed become our own favorite passages, and if we know them and meditate upon them they cannot but produce in us a more tender devotion to our Blessed Mother.

Now, my dear friends, that is all we have time to tell you of the Little Flower today, but since it is almost Christmas Eve, I would present for your consideration one thought consistent with the occasion. Did you ever consider how appropriate it was that the Little Flower should have been given the religious name of Thérèse of the Child Jesus, the Child Jesus whose feast we are on the eve of celebrating? Pope Benedict said that if she had not chosen that name, it would have been necessary later to give it to her.

All her life she honored and practiced the virtues of the Child Jesus, littleness, humility, trust, obedience, love. Pauline gave me a little prayer to the Infant Jesus composed by the Little Flower and repeated often by her—a prayer which we may well quote here:

"O, Little Infant Jesus, my only treasure, I abandon myself to Thy divine will. I do not wish any other joy than that of making Thee smile. Impress upon my soul Thy grace and Thy childlike virtues so that, on the day of my birth in heaven, the angels and saints will recognize in me Thy little spouse, Thérèse of the Child Jesus."

Let us then, my dear friends, tonight ask the Little Flower as a Christmas gift, to teach us to love Our Lord as she loved Him. Let us ask her to give us some of her knowledge of the Infant Jesus, to teach us to understand what mean those little, but Divine hands, stretched forth from the crib.

They mean for sinners, "If you will only come to me trustfully by a good confession, all your sins will not only be forgiven but forgotten. That is a characteristic of the child, to forgive immediately and forget quickly, and that is therefore My characteristic also."

They mean for good people that Our Lord wants us to come and follow His little way of spiritual childhood by humility, simplicity, and confidence in Him.

Let us ask the Little Flower today then not only to grant us the material favors for which we have been asking her, but to give us, as her Christmas gift, the rose of some of her own tender love for the Child Jesus.

Chapter Three

New Messages from Those Whose Sister Is in Heaven

Last night I began the account of my conversations with the three Carmelite Sisters of St. Thérèse. I reported to you anecdotes of the Little Flower's life which they told me, anecdotes which hitherto had never been told for publication and which illustrated the Little Flower's thoughtfulness with others, her resignation to the Will of God, her love of suffering, her patience, her cheerfulness in physical and spiritual trials, and her charity.

Almost all the rest of our conversation was about the Little Flower's mother. Before I went to the home of St. Thérèse I knew nothing about her mother except what the Little Flower herself tells us in her Autobiography, and that is very little. I had a theory, however, that the life of the mother of a saint must be very well worth knowing, and I planned to write the life of the Little Flower's mother if I could gather sufficient information about her from her four living daughters. They were all most willing to talk of their mother and told me all that they knew of her, of her parentage, her girlhood, her maidenhood, her early married life, and of course they told me a great deal of the mother during the babyhood and girlhood of the Little Flower. Through them I also secured many of their mother's letters, letters which well illustrate her character*. One of these letters I wish to read you now as a specimen. This letter was written after the death of Mrs. Martin's daughter, the fourth Martin whom death had claimed:

"When I closed the eyes of my dear little children and prepared them for burial I was indeed grief stricken, but thanks to God's grace I have always been resigned to His will. I do not regret the pains and the sacrifices which I underwent for them. People say to me. 'It would have been much better if you had not given birth to those whom you lost so soon after their coming.' I cannot endure such sentiments. I do not find that pains and sacrifices can at all outweigh or compare with the eternal happiness of my little ones, eternal happiness which, of course, would never have been theirs had they never been born. Moreover, I have not lost them for always. Life is short and soon I shall find my little ones again, in heaven."

Surely that letter needs no comment. Its lessons are obvious. If Mr. and Mrs. Martin had been imbued with certain current views there never would have been any Little Flower, their ninth and last child.

The Little Flower's mother was indeed a very extraordinary woman. In my opinion she was herself a saint, and her holiness explains in no small degree the Little Flower's sanctity. In fact, the mother seemed to know beforehand that her little Thérèse would be a saint. Obviously, it would be impossible with the time at our disposal this week to tell you all of my conversation with the Little Flower's sisters about their mother. I have put in a book form the entire story of her life as told me by her daughters. Those interested will find the complete story in a booklet called "The Little Flower's Mother." Her life should be and will be an inspiration to all modern mothers, and the booklet also contains much new information about the Little Flower.

But let us return to my visit with Marie, Pauline, and Céline. In the course of our conversation, one day, I asked them this question: "I want to ask you whether the Little Flower ever said or wrote something which is attributed to her by rumor in the United States, a rumor for which I have never been able to find any foundation. According to the rumor she said that she would always send a cross to whomever she sent a rose. In other words, she would always send a trial whenever she granted a favor. Did she ever say that?"

They consulted one another and then Pauline, as the spokesman replied: "Neither I nor my sisters ever heard of any such statement of our sister before. We are certain that she never said or wrote anything of the kind."

Then I asked the Little Flower's sisters if they would again send messages to members of the Little Flower Society in America. You remember that during my first visit they sent messages which may well be repeated here, even though many of my readers have already read them. Their messages during the first visit were as follows:

Pauline said: "Tell the ladies of the Little Flower Society of America that if they would please the Little Flower and win her favor, they must not follow the fashion when the fashion demands immodest or indecent dress." And, "Tell the men of the Society of the Little Flower that if they would please St. Thérèse and win her favor, they must hold themselves aloof from all that is low and base and ignoble and go to Holy Communion frequently."

Marie's message was: "Tell the members of the Little Flower Society in America, Father, that they need never fear losing their souls if they imitate St. Thérèse in her love of our Blessed Mother."

Céline said: "Tell the members of the Little Flower Society in America that they should not only admire—but also imitate the Little Flower."

Léonie said: "Give them this message, Father: Tell them that if we would please the Little Flower we must be humble, as she was, and we will be humble if we will repeat frequently every day the ejaculation, 'Jesus, meek and humble of heart, make my heart like unto Thine.'"

This time they all wrote out their messages and the messages in their own handwriting are preserved now at the National Shrine and read as follows:

The message of Pauline: "I ask with all my heart that my little sainted sister shall obtain for the members of the Little Flower Society in America the grace to love the good God ardently and the grace to help make Him much loved."

The message of Marie: "I wish the dear Americans, who are devout members of the Society of my little sainted sister, may comprehend well these consoling words, which one day so long ago she wrote to me, namely, 'It is confidence, and again confidence that must lead us to God, and lead us to love Him.'"

The message of Céline: "I shall pray my little sainted sister, Thérèse, to choose for herself out of her Society in America, a legion of souls, marching in their turn along her little way, so sure of confidence in our Father in heaven."

Another day during my conversation in the parlor with the sisters of St. Thérèse, they told me of her last words to them. Let me repeat here her last words to Pauline, Marie, and Céline. The Little Flower said, "Oh my dear sisters, how happy I am. I see that I am going soon to Our Lord—I am sure of it. Do not be surprised if I do not appear to you after my death and if you see nothing extraordinary to reveal my happiness. Remember that it is my little way not to desire anything like that for you. I would wish nevertheless to have a beautiful death to give you pleasure but do not take it ill if I suffer much and if you do not see any sign of my happiness at the moment of death. Our Lord was a victim of love and see how great was His agony."

"How we will suffer after your death," said Marie.

"Oh no," replied Thérèse joyously, "You will witness my shower of roses. Farewell." And then giving a little smile to each of her sisters she lifted her crucifix and became immediately absorbed in its contemplation.

"Our Sister Is in Heaven!"

Each day as my interview with the sisters came to a close they knelt, to my great embarrassment, and asked my blessing. I determined one day to try to avoid this embarrassment and when Pauline said, "Father, will you give us your blessing?" I answered, "Are you all kneeling, Mother?"

When she answered in the affirmative, I declared, "Then, Mother, I'll kneel now with you and we'll say a prayer together that God will bless us all. That will be better than my blessing."

"As you wish, Father," she said, "But you must not hesitate to bless us. You would be depriving us of the blessing of a priest and surely you would not deprive us of that."

So I had to bless them.

Now let me describe the relics which the sisters gave not to me personally, but to the National Shrine of the Little Flower in Chicago.

The Little Flower with sisters of Lisieux, 1894.

Chapter Four

More Marvellous Relics Given to the National Shrine of the Little Flower

One of the most important parts of my mission to Lisieux was to secure more relics of the Little Flower for her National Shrine in Chicago. There we already had the largest collection of major relics of St. Thérèse in the world, except of course, at her tomb. These I secured during my first journey to the home of the Little Flower, and they had been placed in a magnificent golden reliquary which was and still is the admiration of the throngs of pilgrims who flock to the Shrine daily. Even Cardinal Dubois of Paris in visiting the Shrine expressed his astonishment that we had here more numerous and more precious relics of St. Thérèse than were to be found in any of his own churches of Paris, so near Lisieux. But we planned to devote one altar at the Shrine entirely to the relics, and there were not enough relics to fill the space at our disposal. I explained to Mother Agnes our difficulty and described the constant flow of pilgrims to our Shrine, and I set forth how greatly their devotion would be increased and how much more intimately associated with the Little Flower they would feel if at the Shrine they could look upon more personal relics, for instance objects that had belonged to the Little Flower. I asked her if it were really necessary to keep all her belongings in Lisieux; could not some of these souvenirs of her earthly life be given to her National Shrine in America, where by means of such relics devotion to her would be intensified here?

The result was beyond my fondest dreams, and I think I can describe the relics no better than I have done in a letter written from Lisieux to our Father Provincial. The letter was preserved by him and unearthed the other day, and I decided to use it in this chapter rather than write a new description of the relics. The letter is dated at Lisieux, November 9, 1926, and reads as follows:

"My dear Father Provincial:

I did not want to write you until I had all the good news together and until I actually had in my possession all the wonderful relics which the good sisters have given me. To make a long story short, I have now with me in my room, as I write, the following: (1) a photo of the Little Flower's Mother's brother, Isadore, for my next book 'The Little Flower's Mother'; (2) a photo of his wife; (3) photos of his two daughters, the Little Flower's cousins; (4) a photo of Mrs. Grant, the guardian of the Little Flower's birthplace at Alençon, and a photo of her husband; (5) (you are thinking that all that is not much, but wait) I have, in their own handwriting beautiful messages to the members of the Society from all four of the Little Flower's sisters (not verbal as before, but written messages) ; (6) I have now in my little room everything that was in the Little Flower's cell except her bed. That is, I have her chair, the only chair she ever used as a religious, and the sole ornaments of her cell, namely, two reliquaries (they look like pictures framed in wood and glass). When the sisters first spoke to me of the chair, they said that she had used it even during her last illness.* When they first showed it to me, I was so astonished that it was low that I did not say anything. The sisters waited for me to comment on it, and then Pauline said 'Are you not pleased with it, Father?' 'Yes, of course, Mother,' I answered, 'but I thought she used the chair when she was a nun; this looks like a girl's chair.' Then they explained that it was a special chair procured for her own

---

* It was in this chair that St. Thérèse made the prophecy described on page 164.

peculiar needs; that it was only in such a low chair, in a semi-reclining position, that she could find relief from pain in her last days; (7) I have one of her toys (a little tambourine, with which she used to play). All these are of course fully authenticated and sealed with the wax seal of Carmel. (8) I have all her photographs (two never before released from the convent and never published anywhere) arranged artistically by Céline and signed with Céline's name and gotten up solely for US. (9) I have a little picture of the Little Flower painted by Céline—it is about the size of a first Mass card. (10) I have the map of North America drawn by the Little Flower at 12 years and of course marked with her own handwriting—for example, 'Ètats-Unis' (United States). Isn't that a happy coincidence? I had asked them for one of her letters, but her letters were all collected for examination at Rome during the process of her canonization and they still remain in the Vatican archives. They had no letters; so instead they gave me the map (I did not even know of its existence) annotated in her own hand. (11) I have the most precious relic that remained at Lisieux to give, namely, (hold your breath) a lily made from locks of the hair of the Little Flower!!! A lily! A little flower made from the hair of the Little Flower—un petit lys! It is about half the size of this paper on which I am writing (in height) and I will get an ostensoir for it and the sisters here will arrange it in the ostensoir. (12) I have three little relics 'ex carne' (all that remains of her flesh) (Pittsburgh and Englewood Shrines will receive these). (13) I have a double relic ("ex carne et ex veste') in a silver locket which Pauline said I must not give to any shrine but keep for myself from her. The locket was hers. (14) I have precious memories of interview after interview with all the sisters. So far I have been with them eighteen hours in all, and it is useless to try now to tell you, my dear Father, about the delight of those visits and about the information obtained during them. Intimate beyond my dreams were those interviews. For instance, to give you an idea of the intimacy: When I would make too bad a break in my French, Céline and Marie would laugh like school girls (they are all very gay), and then I would pretend to be offended and appeal to Pauline, who would very seriously explain and apologize, and then I would laugh and be joined thereupon by all three. (15) I have been given the precious privilege of saying the Community Mass (not once but three times so far) and giving Holy Communion to the Little Flower's sisters!!!! As Pauline says, 'Même les évêques ne sont pas si privilégiés'. Of course I saw them all when I gave them Holy Communion. (16) I have been the messenger of Pauline to Caen (where Léonie is) and to Alençon. And at Caen I talked at great length with Léonie and was given the freedom of the convent. At Alençon I breakfasted and lunched at the Maison de St. Thérèse (her birthplace) and afterwards received the most cordial letters praising 'The Living Sisters of the Little Flower' from Madame Grant, the custodian. I had the privilege of giving the last blessing at Alençon to Madame Tiffenne, the godmother of Léonie, who is dying.

"How was all this accomplished? It is a long story and must wait until I can tell it verbally.

"I can't believe my eyes as I finger my precious relics, all stamped, sealed and authenticated. How I would like to talk with some of you about them now!

"I have a bad cold but I think I can shake it off. I have not seen the sun except twice since I landed. It has poured, not intermittently, but constantly since I set foot on French soil, and there is no such thing as a warm room. Pauline commanded me to go to bed and stay there on account of my cough, and I answered that inasmuch as I was occupied with what concerned the increasing glory of her little sister, I trusted in Thérèse to take care of me without going to bed. 'Indeed,' she replied, 'I think you are right, mon frère, she has you in her heart.' Wasn't that beautiful? You may imagine how that pleased me.

"They have simply done everything possible for me and I don't know myself why. It certainly was not all MY planning, and whatever was my planning was inspired by my little saint and protectress.

"I have not told all in this letter—the kindness I received here from everybody was astounding—simply astounding. The second visit is worth a million times as much as the first.

"One of the lay sisters of the convent said to me yesterday, 'The sisters of our little saint have treated you like a brother.' I do not deserve it but indeed they have. I'll write again soon . . . ."

Like sand in the hourglass of life, the precious God-given time here on earth slips away.

Chapter Five

The Little Flower's Last Letter

Let me tell you something of my visit with the Little Flower's fourth sister, Léonie. She is a Visitation nun, you remember, in the convent at Caen, a city about three hours' journey from the Little Flower's convent.

Many of you remember probably the difficulty I had at my first visit there in persuading the Mother Superior of the Visitation convent to allow me to speak with Léonie. You remember that she all but ejected me from the parlor before she suddenly and unaccountably thawed and granted the permission. This time I had not the slightest difficulty, because Pauline gave me a letter of introduction to the Mother Superior and a private letter to Léonie and told the Mother Superior that it was her wish that I deliver in person that letter to Léonie.

I spent almost an entire day with Léonie, and she was as good and patient and gracious this time as before. We talked chiefly about her mother. Léonie spoke, I think, with more enthusiasm about Mrs. Martin than did her three Carmelite daughters. Perhaps the others spoke with equal ardor but I could not see their faces as they spoke and I could see Léonie's, and therefore Léonie's enthusiasm was more evident.

Léonie wrote for me that day the foreword to my book "The Little Flower's Mother." She says in the foreword, "My opinion is that my mother was truly a saint." Many of the anecdotes of the booklet ("The Little Flower's Mother") came first from the lips of Léonie.

I asked Léonie too for a message, and Léonie's message this time was as follows: "I ask of my little sainted sister to obtain for all the Americans who become members of her Society, the grace of a holy life and of a happy death."

During our conversation, the only departure from the subject of the Little Flower's mother happened this way: I said to Léonie, "Sister, you remember that you told me during my last visit that St. Thérèse gives you many favors."

"Yes," she said, "but I never ask her for anything for myself."

"Why not, Sister?"

"Because she is my sister," she said, not proudly, but so simply that I think it was at that striking remark more than at any other made by her or any of her sisters that I realized fully the close relationship between these nuns of Normandy and their sister in heaven. That simple sentence, "Because she is my sister" I remember more clearly than any other of Léonie's remarks.

Then she added "And I trust her to obtain for me, her sister, without being asked, all the graces that I need.

"One of her greatest favors to me," she continued, "was the privilege of spending three weeks at the convent of Carmel in Lisieux with Pauline, Marie, and Céline. You know, when I had entered the Visitation cloister and they the Carmelite convent, I naturally never thought to see them again on earth. But during the process of Beatification, when the Apostolic Commission was sitting in Lisieux taking depositions from all who knew Thérèse in life, they called me there for questioning. I was the only one here to be examined; so instead of coming here, they summoned me there and during the questioning I stayed in the convent with my sisters for three weeks."

Her face simply glowed as she spoke.

"I suppose you were very happy there, Sister," I said.

"It was heaven," she replied.

"Did you find your sisters changed?"

"No," she said, "they are older of course and the years of mortification and prayer have matured their souls, but they are just the same to me as they were at Buissonnets."*

"Do you not think, Sister, that Pauline is very saintly?" I asked.

"She is a saint," she declared. "I do not believe that there is a superior so esteemed. Pauline told me herself one day with her ravishing simplicity, 'Léonie, I do not know why my sisters love me so much. Since I have been superior I have never had to say the same thing twice.'

Then Léonie proceeded to tell me that Pauline had been made superior for life by a special decree of the Pope brought to Lisieux by Cardinal Vico. Pauline had had no intimation of the act of the Holy Father until Cardinal Vico read the brief in the convent chapel in the presence of all the sisters.

Pauline was at first stunned and then broke and exclaimed, "Oh, I can't, I am not worthy!"

But when Cardinal Vico said to her kindly, "Mother, it is the wish of the Holy Father, and what of your vow of obedience?" Pauline braced herself and said in a firm voice, "Be it done as the Holy Father wishes. I am a Carmelite and I obey."

"Do you think, Sister," I said "that Pauline is as much of a saint* as was the Little Flower?"

"No," said Léonie slowly. "Hers is not the same sanctity. God made Thérèse a great saint although she was so little. Pauline follows the same little way of humility and simplicity, but perhaps God does not wish to exalt her as He did Thérèse."

While I was with Léonie she showed me a letter written to her by the Little Flower. It was the last letter written to her by St. Thérèse and was written four days before the Little Flower's

---

* Buissonnets is the name given to the girlhood home of the Little Flower and her sisters. (Editor's Note.)

* Wherever in this book the word "saint" is employed, it is used without any intention of anticipating the judgment of the Church. (Author's Note.)

death. It has never been published, but I believe it is one of the most beautiful letters which St. Thérèse ever wrote. I will take it as a basis of the rest of our talk this evening.

The letter reads:

"My dear little sister: I am indeed happy to be able still to communicate with you. Several days ago I did not think I would have that consolation again on earth, but the good God has seen fit to prolong a little my exile. I am not afflicted by His plan, for I would not wish to enter heaven one minute sooner by my own will. The only happiness on earth is to try always to be pleased and delighted with the state in which Jesus places us. Your state is indeed beautiful, my dear little sister. If you wish to be a saint, that will be easy for you, because after all at the bottom of your heart the world means nothing to you. You can therefore, like us, occupy yourself with the one thing necessary, that is to say, to give yourself with devotion to exterior occupations, having for your one aim to give pleasure to Jesus and to unite yourself more intimately to Him. You say you wish that in heaven I would pray for you to the Sacred Heart of Our Lord. Be sure that I will not forget to give Him your messages and to ask from Him all that will be necessary for you to become a saint. Farewell, my little sister, so dear to me, I would wish that the thought of my entry into heaven would fill you with joy, since I could then love you even more than I do now."

It is with this ravishing simplicity that the Little Flower says farewell to her sister. But is it really a farewell? Is it not rather an invitation to an early meeting in heaven where there are no farewells?

Let us select from the letter one passage and attempt to glean from it for ourselves spiritual profit.

The passage to which I would call your special attention, my dear friends, is this: "You say that you wish that in heaven I would pray for you to the Sacred Heart of Our Lord. Be sure that I will not forget to give Him your messages." What familiarity with God, what intimacy with Our Lord do not these words imply! "I will give Him your messages." We would imagine that she were speaking of one in the next room; or that she were speaking of a close relative or intimate friend. She is speaking of Almighty God!

"I will give Him your messages." We can in our imagination picture our little saint delivering those messages of her sister to Our Lord. Let us construct in imagination that scene of her delivery of those messages in heaven. We may be sure that she did not deliver the messages through a third person, unless indeed sitting at the feet of Our Lady she whispered her request to Mary bending low to listen, to deliver those messages for her. We may be sure that Our Lord did not oblige her to deliver them kneeling before His throne, but that He permitted her to deliver them in as intimate a manner and with as close an approach as it is possible for souls to communicate with Our Lord.

"I will give Him your messages." Who but a saint and a saint as closely united to God as the Little Flower could use so intimately familiar an expression in speaking of God. To all the saints, to all men and women who lead spiritual lives, nourishing themselves spiritually by frequent prayer and frequent Holy Communion, to all such, God becomes what He was to the Little Flower, a familiar friend. To such spiritual people He is not a far distant being, away off in some corner of heaven sitting in cold and distant majesty on His throne. No, to really spiritual people He is a loving Father, a familiar friend, a companion. The companionship with Our Lord is one of the most consoling rewards that Our Lord bestows upon those who love Him with a whole-hearted personal love. That familiarity, that friendship, Our Lord bestows upon those who give Him that generous service that one would give to an absent and distant, but none the less, real friend.

Those who have never experienced this friendship of Christ, this sense of His nearness, approachableness and loveableness, cannot understand how such friendship with God is possible and are inclined to think it a delusion, but theirs is the blindness of ignorance and of fleshy materialism; they lack the keen sight of highly developed and sane spirituality. Those who have experienced this friendship of Christ and then lost it by falling back to lower planes of living, taste then bitterness far more bitter than the bitterness caused by the loss of any earthly friend. No one can depict their utter loneliness nor describe the ever-aching void in their hearts. But those who are experiencing this friendship of Christ are enjoying that peace which surpasses understanding and which the world cannot give nor take away. Their morning Communion, their morning visit with Our Lord they would never think of missing. They go to visit Him in the Blessed Sacrament for a moment every evening just as one would not fail to mount the stairs of one's home to say goodnight to a beloved father or mother. As they go about their daily duties they are conscious of being not only friends but intimate personal friends of Our Lord. That consciousness breeds in them no pride nor vanity; it produces just peace, the peace of knowing that they enjoy the close friendship of that Friend of friends, the Perfect Friend.

Such friendship with Our Lord is not only possible, my dear friends, but certain for all who will practice frequent Communion, daily visits to Our Lord in the Blessed Sacrament and frequent ejaculations to Him during the day, and that is a grace for which we should ask during this novena.

After our Blessed Mother and St. Joseph no one can better help us to win that friendship with Christ than that little saint of ours who loved Him so ardently and was so well beloved by Him in return; that little saint of ours who spoke of Him so familiarly in her letter to her sister, saying: "Be sure that I will not forget to give Him your messages."

Let us ask her tonight to obtain for us, gathered about her Shrine, the grace of close and personal friendship with Our Lord. And in all the requests we make of her, in all our petitions to her we cannot do better than to adopt her own expression and say to her in her own words: "St. Thérèse, we too have messages for you to deliver; tonight, Little Flower, give Him our messages; give Him the messages we send to Him through you."

Chapter Six

The World's Youngest Saint

For seven days, my dear friends, you have been listening to these little talks about the Little Flower-, these little stories of her told by her sisters who knew her in life. You have been listening so intently that there has been no doubt of the keenness of your interest in the Little Flower. But my dear friends, this Novena would utterly fail in its purpose if it created merely interest—if it did not create also resolution, reformation, and imitation of the Little Flower in our daily lives. Those resolutions we confidently expect as a result of the Novena and we hope and pray and know that the Little Flower will work an improvement in the lives of us all.

Permit me therefore in conclusion to ask you some pertinent questions.

Is there a father or a mother here tonight who through the sermons at these devotions has come to be intimately acquainted with the Little Flower's home life and yet has not altered their own home life accordingly? Have the fathers and mothers learned from the Little Flower's story the value of home influence? See what home training did for the daughters of Mr. and Mrs. Martin, the mother and father of the Little Flower. All their living daughters today are objects of universal admiration. One of their daughters has become a saint with the world at her feet, and this daughter who became a saint was the ninth and last child of her parents. Have the fathers and mothers here made their resolutions accordingly;

resolutions suggested by the thought that the Little Flower was the ninth and last child; resolutions not to discourage, but to foster vocations in their children; resolutions to correct whatever may be faulty in the home training they are giving their little ones.

Is there a young man here who during these novena devotions has come to admire the supreme beauty of the Little Flower's life and who is nevertheless conscious of the moral ugliness of his own life? If there is such a young man here, I say to him, "What effect has this novena had on you; what greater respect for womanhood in general ought not the story of St. Thérèse produce in you? For your benefit I repeat the message of the Little Flower's sister, 'Tell them that if they love my little sainted sister they will hold themselves aloof from all that is low and base and ignoble and go to Holy Communion frequently.'"

Is there a young lady here who perhaps congratulates herself because she has been thrilled by the beautiful story of the Little Flower, forgetting that admiration of St. Thérèse does not necessarily connote genuine devotion to her. Imitation is the only tribute that the pure and modest Little Flower will value. Is there a young lady here then who imagines that she is devoted to the Little Flower and yet who permits in her company keeping liberties which her own mother did not permit and which cause her heavenly Mother to turn away from her in pity and perhaps in disgust. If there is such a young lady here, I say to her, "What have been your thoughts during this novena to the Queen of Virgins and to the Little Model Virgin of Lisieux. What have you in common with the Little Flower?" You expect me to say that you have nothing in common with her, but instead I say that you have everything in common with her in this sense: that our little saint who spends her heaven doing good upon earth wants especially to help you. She understands your temptations. She understood the allurements of the world; she had wealth, beauty, charm, and everything that would incline her naturally to be worldly. She says in her Autobiography, "What would have become of me if the world had smiled on me?" She wants to help you. Surrender therefore to her sweet influence and after a sincere confession go out under her protection more perfectly to fulfill the law of God.

It is our prayer tonight that the Little Flower will bestow upon you all, fathers, mothers, young men and young women, all, the rose of the grace that you most need.

We say to St. Thérèse tonight, "Oh Little Flower, once when you were asked 'Will you look down on us from the heights of heaven, sister,' you answered, 'No, I will come down.' Come down then today amongst us who are gathered here about your Shrine. Some of us are suffering and need consolation and relief; some of us are sinners and need conversion. All of us are in need of greater love of Our Lord and of His Blessed Mother. Come then little Virgin of Carmel, descend into our midst and place in each of our hearts the grace of greater love of Our Lord and Our Lady."

That the Little Flower will enable you, my dear friends, always to heed the messages of her sisters, that she may always keep you, each one of you, under her sweet protection, that her promise "I will let fall from heaven a shower of roses" will be fulfilled in each one of you, that is our prayer tonight, and do you in return say a like prayer for me.

Saint Thérèse of the Child Jesus.
Design adopted at Rome for the great banner of her canonization, May 17, 1925.

Chapter Seven

"She's My Saint," Said the Holy Father

My private audience with the Holy Father in November was even more delightful than the April audience. The Holy Father asked many questions about the Society of the Little Flower and expressed surprise and pleasure at its growth. When I told him of the relics that I had obtained at Lisieux, he expressed his astonishment and said, "You have impoverished Europe in enriching America." I presented to him my books about the Little Flower, and he opened each one to the title page and read the title in English.

I showed him a colored picture of the National Shrine, and he made no attempt to conceal the impression its beauty made upon him. "It is magnificent," he declared, and he listened with patience and interest to my description of its rose symbolism.

I then asked him for a message for the members of the Society of the Little Flower in America, a message which I could deliver as his own personal message to them. (In April he had sent this message: "Tell the members of the Society that all should study carefully and imitate closely the humble life of St. Thérèse who was an exquisite model of perfect holiness."). This time, he paused, thought a moment and said, "Let us frame the message from Our Lord's own words, changed a little to suit this situation. Our Lord said, 'Unless you become as little children, you shall not enter the Kingdom of Heaven.' Let my message to the members of the Society of the Little Flower be then: Unless you become as this little child, Thérèse of our own time, you shall not enter the Kingdom of Heaven. That is to say," the Holy Father went on to explain, "that the proud and haughty do not enter heaven, that humility is the essence and foundation of holiness and that therefore it is no exaggeration to say that unless we become like this little child, Thérèse of our own time, we shall not enter the Kingdom of Heaven."

Then came the most memorable words of the Holy Father during our audience. During our conversation I had been referring to the Little Flower as "our saint," when the Holy Father suddenly interrupted me and said smilingly, "You say always 'our saint' and indeed it is true that she belongs particularly to you in America where she is so well loved. Continue to call her 'our saint', but in all humility I claim her in a special way as my saint. She's my saint; mine because she has been the guiding star of my pontificate and because she was the first I beatified and the first saint I canonized. She's my saint even though she is also yours in America."

Certainly nothing could be more touching and impressive than to hear the scholarly High Priest of Christendom speak so tenderly of the little girl-nun of Carmel whom he has chosen as his Patron. Those words of the Holy Father, uttered so gently and simply, "She's my saint," still ring in my ears.

I again asked him for his blessing on the members of the Society, which he gave, and then I asked him to grant certain indulgences to the members. He said, "Yes, we cannot do too much for those who follow St. Thérèse. But put your request in writing, and let it pass through the usual channels, and when it reaches me I will approve it."

He gave his blessing and left; and very shortly afterwards he approved this document issued by the Sacred Congregation and bearing the rich indulgences with which this volume terminates.

Indulgences

Granted by Our Holy Father Pope Pius XI on November 23, 1926 to the members of the Society of the Little Flower erected in The National Shrine of the Little Flower (Provincial Carmelite Church) Chicago, Illinois

1. A Plenary Indulgence under the usual conditions to all who enroll as members of the Society of the Little Flower. (This indulgence is given on the day of enrollment.)
2. A Plenary Indulgence to members of the Society of the Little Flower who visit the National Shrine, that being the Carmelite Church of St. Clara, or, this being impossible, any other church on the following Feast days: Nativity, December 25; Circumcision, January 1; Holy Name, January 2; Epiphany, January 6; Holy Family, January 9; Easter, Movable; Ascension, Movable; Corpus Christi, Movable; Sacred Heart, Movable; St. Joseph, March 19; Our Lady of Mt. Carmel, July 16; Assumption, August 15; St. Thérèse of Lisieux (The Little Flower), September 30; Holy Guardian Angels. October 2; St. Thérèse of Avila, October 15.
3. A Plenary Indulgence at the moment of death to be gained by members who have either confessed and communicated or who at least with a contrite heart pronounce, either vocally or mentally, the most Holy Name of Jesus, expecting death patiently as the penalty of sin.
4. (a) A Partial Indulgence of 300 days to be gained by members of the Society of the Little Flower as often as they attend any Little Flower devotion at the National Shrine.

(b) A Partial Indulgence of 100 days to members of the Society of the Little Flower as often as with a contrite heart they fulfill any work of piety or charity in accordance with the statutes of the Society.
5. An Indult by virtue of which all Masses said by any priest for the soul of a deceased member of the Society of the Little Flower benefit that soul as if the Masses were celebrated at a privileged altar. (Granted for seven years by the Apostolic Congregation of the Holy Poenitentiaria.)

Where the Little Flower Seems Nearest

Thérèse in the garden of Carmel.

Chapter One

To the Cloister Room

This booklet describes my third visit to the home of St. Thérèse.*

On my other two visits to Lisieux in 1925 and 1926 I had eagerly sought out every place associated with the Little Flower; exploring every nook and corner of the home of her girlhood; walked joyously down the streets sanctified by her footsteps; visited the school she had attended and talked with one of her teachers there. I had knelt reverently at the altar railing where she had received her first Holy Communion; talked with one of her cousins and playmates; visited the two venerable churches, St. James's and St. Peter's, where she had attended Mass and made her visits to the Blessed Sacrament with her father. I had gone to the cemetery to venerate the holy ground which for twenty-five years had held her holy remains. Then, awestricken, I had entered the public chapel of the convent and knelt before her beautiful tomb and said Mass there. I had enjoyed the singular privilege of speaking to her sisters in the convent parlor and then the grand privilege of saying Mass for them and giving them Holy Communion.

But in spite of all these privileges and experiences, in spite of all these, I was not satisfied; I left each time with regret.

---

* The chapters of this book were originally so many talks delivered by Father Dolan at the National Shrine of the Little Flower in Chicago and elsewhere, and the narratives have been preserved in their original form because it was thought that the narrative gains rather than loses interest and attractiveness in that vivid and animated form. (Editor's Note.)

Something was lacking. Something had been left undone. What was it? It was that I had not entered the cloister itself where she spent the last nine years of her life.

I said to myself "Oh, if I could only enter there. Because it was chiefly there in the cloister of the convent that our Rose bloomed; it was chiefly there that, hidden from all, she wove her robe of holiness. It was there in the cloister that she prayed, suffered, and died. There in the cloister was her little cell, sanctified by her constant presence. In there was the infirmary rendered ever blessed by her last sigh. Oh, if I could only enter there. What a happiness it would be to cross the threshold of the cloister and penetrate into its depths to find there the places where the Little Flower would seem nearest."

That was my regret. That was what had been lacking in my first two visits and I determined upon a third visit which, with the help of the Little Flower, I hoped would supply what the first two visits had lacked.

I first wrote to Rome to friends in the Vatican for permission to enter the cloister and I received the disappointing reply that Rome has no power to grant that permission, but the message added hopefully that Mother Agnes, the Superior of the convent, might possibly be able to grant my request.

I set out then for France and arriving again at the convent of the Little Flower I secured an audience with Mother Agnes and explained my desire. I was desolated upon receiving the answer that although she would gladly grant me the permission if she could, it was impossible for her or even the Bishop of the diocese to grant permission to enter.

"From whom, then, Mother," I said, "must the permission come?"

---

* Mother Agnes reported that daily, priests and bishops from all parts of the world are in Lisieux and that all want to visit the cloister. If a rigorous rule were not adopted, strangers would be in the cloister each morning and the solitude and silence

"No one can grant it," was her answer, "no one can enter this cloister except a Cardinal* or a priest who is accompanied by a Cardinal."

"Where, then, Mother," I asked, "will I find a Cardinal to accompany me?"

Naturally she did not know of a Cardinal who would be at my beck and call.

Then of a sudden I thought of Cardinal Dubois of Paris who had, in 1926, visited the National Shrine in Chicago, and venerated the relics there, and who, while there, had been my guest.

"If I secure Cardinal Dubois to come, Mother, may I enter with him and visit the cloister and say Mass perhaps in the infirmary or cell of the Little Flower?"

"Yes," she answered, "you can do all these things if you come with a Cardinal, but I think he will be too busy to come at this time of the year."

I waited just long enough to ask her to say a prayer that the Cardinal might come and then I was off to Paris to seek the presence of its distinguished Cardinal Archbishop.

I shall not stop to explain my difficulties in Paris. Suffice it to say that the Cardinal finally consented to come and fixed the day. On the day he appointed, a very happy day indeed, we set off together for Lisieux.

We were lodged that night in the Chaplain's apartment directly across the street from the convent, and as on a previous similar occasion I kept waking during the night fearing that something might happen while we slept to prevent the fulfillment of my long cherished desire. I wondered whether the Cardinal was well, and so on.

But nothing untoward happened; and in the morning, my heart beating fast, I accompanied the Cardinal across the street to the public chapel and entered. We went on up the center aisle, on past the tomb, on in through the gates into

---

demanded by the rule would consequently be impossible; hence the rule that no one may enter except a cardinal or a priest accompanied by a cardinal. (Author's Note.)

the sanctuary; then in through the inner sacristy until at length we stood before a great massive door—the door to the cloister itself—the door, the threshold of which I had so long desired to cross.

Let me pause here to explain an inscription on the door. There are written there in letters of gold these impressive words: "It was by this same door that St. Thérèse of the Child Jesus entered this convent the ninth of April, 1888."

What a touching scene that inscription recalled, the scene of the parting of the Little Flower from her father, a scene described by the Little Flower herself in these words: "On the day I was to enter the convent, after a last look at the dear home of my childhood, I set out for the public chapel of the convent, where together we all heard Mass. I did not shed a tear, but as I led the way to the cloister door, the beating of my heart became so violent that I wondered if I were going to die. I embraced all my loved ones; then I knelt for Papa's blessing, and he too knelt as he blessed me through his tears. To see this old man giving his child to God while she was still in the springtime of life was a sight to gladden the Angels.

"This is how my father announced my leaving home in a letter to one of his friends, 'Thérèse, my little Queen, entered Carmel yesterday. God alone could ask such a sacrifice, but He helps me so powerfully that my heart is overflowing with joy even in the midst of tears.'"

Indeed this magnificent Christian man, gladly giving all his children to the convent, presents a much needed example in this age when so many parents interpose refusals and delays and obstacles in the way of their children who are called by God to be priests or nuns. Had Mr. Martin refused to surrender Thérèse, there might never have been any Little Flower to bless the world with her fragrance and to shower her blessings on all the world.

Her father had a portion of his reward a few months later, January 10, 1889, on the day on which the Little Flower took the habit. On this day her father was reunited to Thérèse for a while at this same door of the cloister. On this day, the fathers of the postulants are permitted to come to the door of the cloister and escort their daughters to the public chapel where the fathers present to the presiding Bishop their daughters who are about to be clothed in the habit of Carmel. How happy must that venerable father have been when that cloister door opened and there appeared on the threshold his Thérèse, dressed in the gracious virginal habit of her clothing, a robe of white satin and lace of her father's own choosing! How happy he must have been to fold her once more to his paternal heart! His joy was expressed in his exclamation that morning when he saw her. "Oh," he exclaimed, as the Little Flower appeared in the doorway, "there is my little Queen."

The Little Flower says, writing of that morning, "Then Papa gave me his arm and we made our solemn entry into the public chapel. This was indeed his day of triumph. His sacrifice was now complete, for all his children belonged to God."

This is the kind of father from whom saints spring, and all fathers and mothers may learn from him the spirit of sacrifice they must possess when their children are called by God to the religious life.

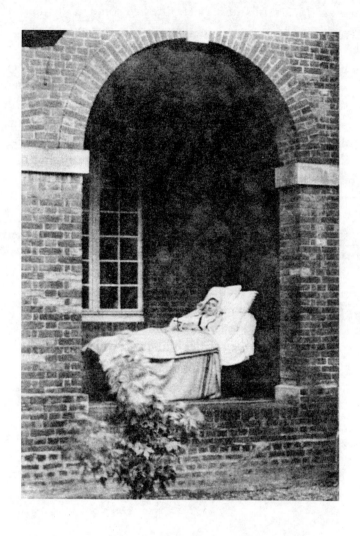

Thérèse enjoying her last few rays of earthly sunshine, as her time in exile draws to a close, 1897.

Chapter Two

The Infirmary

We stood before the door a few moments and then heard the bolts shoot back. The ancient door creaked on its hinges as it opened, and there before us were the sisters of the convent kneeling for the blessing of the Cardinal. After he had blessed them, the Cardinal presented us to Mother Agnes.

I had often talked with Mother Agnes through the grille in the convent parlor but I had never before conversed with her unveiled and face to face.* Four sisters were appointed to act as our guides and they conducted us out of the vestibule which leads directly to the cloister.

My eyes were everywhere, searching for places made familiar from the reading of the life of our saint.

First, through the pillars of the cloister, we glimpsed the garden which she often mentions in her Autobiography. The cloister pillars are not of twisted marble which are so admired in Italy, but of bricks which have long since lost their color, aged as they are, by the storms of time. It seems to me that there is a peculiar fitness that the cloister pillars should be that

---

* At this moment of our entrance there was not time for more than a word of greeting to Mother Agnes, but later this same morning when Mother Agnes came to the parlor to speak with me, she ordered the grilled opened, to my great astonishment, and I conversed with her unveiled and face to face. The topic of the conversation was confidential, and Mother Agnes does not wish to be described, but I can say that she is, in manner and speaking, all that you would expect the beloved sister and second mother of St. Thérèse to be. (Author's Note.)

humble in construction, since they were made famous by the humility and modesty and simplicity of St. Thérèse.

How abundant in memories were these disjointed flagstones of the cloister walk along which we passed! How many times had the Little Flower swept them with her broom! How many times had she passed over them on her way to the convent dining room, supporting the feeble and faltering steps of the invalid sister who had been committed to her care, supporting the sister with exquisite gentleness and with infinite patience.*

As we walked along I could not help but be impressed by the absolute silence that reigns in that isle of peace. How far we were from the busy, noisy world where men struggle for money and name and how strange that from that tiny room should go forth whispered words that were so soon to ring in the ears of all the world: "I will spend my heaven doing good upon earth"—words first whispered there, now known everywhere.

On another occasion as the Little Flower lay in that bed, a sister said, "Will you look down on us from heaven, sister?" She answered, "No, I will come down." She has come down since thousands upon thousands of times to give help to the tempted, relief to the suffering and to the needy, and consolation to the dying.

I thought as I stood there of that other saying of hers one day when she tossed about that bed in terrible agony, "If

---

* I cannot but quote here the Little Flower's own words describing one of her experiences as she led the aged sister along the cloister walk. The Little Flower writes: "One cold winter's evening when I was humbly leading Sister St. Peter along the cloister walks, there suddenly fell on my ears the harmonious strains of distant music. A picture rose before me of a richly furnished room, brilliantly lighted and decorated, and full of elegantly dressed young girls conversing together, as is the way of the world. Then I turned to the poor invalid; instead of sweet music, I heard her complaints; instead of rich gilding, I saw the bare brick walls of our cloister, scarcely visible in the dim flickering light. The contrast thrilled me, and Our Lord so illuminated my soul with the rays of His truth, in the light of which the pleasures of the world are but darkness, that not for a thousand years of such worldly delights would I have bartered the ten minutes spent in my act of charity." (Author's Note.)

people only knew how necessary it is to pray for the dying." These words she repeated constantly, "If people only knew how necessary it is to pray for the dying."

I remembered, too, that it was here in this bed that she had received her last Holy Communion, and I tried to imagine with what love she received Our Lord that last morning when, with the convent cloisters thickly strewn with rose petals, a young priest who had just been ordained and who was about to say his first Mass that morning in the convent, bore the Blessed Sacrament to the dying saint.

Then I remembered, also, what love of the Blessed Virgin had been expressed in that tiny bed. When they brought into that very room the miraculous statue of the Blessed Virgin which had smiled on the Little Flower and cured her in her girlhood, St. Thérèse fixed her gaze on that statue so lovingly that her sister, Marie, remembering the former miracle said, "Sister, what do you see?"

The Little Flower answered, in those well known words, "Never has the statue of Our Lady seemed so lovely, my sister, but today it is the statue whereas the other time, as you well know, it was not the statue but Our Lady herself who smiled on me."

Then St. Thérèse exclaimed, "How I love Our Blessed Lady; had I been a priest how I would have sung her praises. She should be thought of and spoken of more as Mother than as a Queen."

Then I glanced from her bed to the statue of the Blessed Virgin above the altar and tried to reconstruct the scene the night she died when, just as the convent bell rang the Angelus, the Little Flower raised herself and gazed with inexpressible tenderness upon that statue of Our Blessed Mother. It was then that the sisters kneeling about and following her gaze, repeated the beautiful prayer which the Little Flower herself had composed, "O, cherished Mother, Thou who didst smile upon me in the morning of my life, behold it is evening now, come and smile upon me once again."

Indeed where in the world should one find so many memories to touch the heart, as within those infirmary walls which saw and heard all that was said and all that took place during the last illness and last agony of our saint? So far I had occupied myself with an inspection of all that was to be seen in this hallowed sanctuary, but now it was time to kneel and to prepare for Mass. Imagine my feelings as I realized that I was about to say Mass there in that tiny room whose walls saw the last look of St. Thérèse, in that room whose walls still echo her last words, "My God, I love Thee."

I vested and offered the Mass for the members of the Little Flower Society in America, as the Cardinal had done before me, and then I turned to begin the prayers at the foot of the altar.

My feelings during the Mass would be impossible to describe because it is impossible to render into words that which only the heart can taste. But you can well imagine my emotions, particularly as I turned for the "Dominus vobiscum's" of the Mass, for then I saw, not the sisters kneeling about, but only the little white bed, so old, so poor and yet so rich, so rich in having been the place of repose of our saint during the agony which won so many souls to God, the place of repose of the saint when she uttered the words, "I will spend my heaven doing good upon earth," the little bed so rich in having heard, as it were, those last words, "My God, I love Thee."

So near was the altar of the tiny infirmary to the bed of our saint that as I turned for the "Orate Fratres" the vestments brushed the bed. I could imagine almost that she was there. Certainly there is no place in the world where one could feel nearer to her or where her presence could be more distinctly felt.

As the Mass went on, the seeming nearness of the Little Flower, the realization of the great privilege being accorded me caused me to feel how unworthy I was of that privilege, how unworthy to be called a soldier, much less a captain in her army. But no more of the Mass—I can't tell you more—there are no words.

As I left the infirmary to visit her cell about which I will speak in a later chapter, I turned to gaze once more upon the infirmary, and to impress upon my memory that hallowed sanctuary with its tiny bed. And so should you, dear readers, try to impress upon your memories the lessons this narrative should teach, lessons as revealed by the Little Flower on her infirmary deathbed; the lesson of constant prayer for the dying in accordance with her words, "Oh, if people only knew how necessary it is to pray for the dying"; the lesson of greater love of our Blessed Mother, as manifested by her words uttered there and by that last look of love at the sound of the Angelus bell; the lesson of greater devotion to the Blessed Sacrament as revealed in her last Holy Communion, and finally the lesson of greater love of God as expressed in her last words, "Oh, how I love Him: My God I love Thee."

The Little Flower fulfilling her duties as sacristan.

Chapter Three
The Chapter Hall

Upon leaving the infirmary, we were escorted by the four sisters with their noiseless step through the cloister again until we came to a corner in which, in a pretty little niche, is the statue of the Infant Jesus of which St. Thérèse, upon entering the convent, was given charge. This is the statue which the Little Flower used to dress so beautifully and surround with flowers and lights and say, "My little Jesus smiles at me now through my lights and flowers." The statue is a very beautiful one and has been left just as it was dressed by St. Thérèse for the Feast of the Nativity 1896.

Then we turned a corner and began to mount a staircase — the same that St. Thérèse used to mount to reach her cell. We, however, climbed with much lighter step than she, for you remember that she was so weak after her first hemorrhage that she used to mount these stairs one at a time, stopping at each step for breath, and then wearily dragging herself to the next.

The staircase terminates in a wide and long corridor from which there open the cells of the sisters. Each cell is dedicated to some Carmelite saint, and the name of the saint is written on the door of the cell.

On the walls of the corridor are written in large letters sentences taken, for the most part, from Holy Scripture— sentences that, in the cloistral silence, proclaim loudly the eternal truths. These two particularly caught my attention: "Today a little work, tomorrow eternal repose"; "When I hear the clock strike, I rejoice because I am nearer eternity. I have one hour less to pass in this land of exile."

These are specimens of the sentences that greet the eyes of the nuns whenever they walk along the corridor. How well the Superiors of these convents realize that statues, pictures and holy sentiments are spiritual helps, even for their cloistered sisters. How many of our Catholic parents have forgotten the value of such helps in their homes. In how many homes is there nothing on the walls or the mantelpiece to suggest a good thought, a prayer or an ejaculation? In your homes are there little family Shrines and Altars, and do pictures of Our Lord and His Blessed Mother occupy places of honor there? If not, let this description of the corridors of the Little Flower's Convent induce a resolution to supply what is wanting in your homes to suggest holy thoughts and aspirations.

As I walked along the corridor, I stopped at one of the windows and glanced again into the garden, and I recalled that it was there in that garden, that there occurred one day an incident that illustrates well the Little Flower's constant zeal for souls. One day, towards the end of her life, she and a little novice were walking in the garden. The Little Flower was so weak that she could scarcely drag one foot before another and every step was an agony. The little novice, seeing the torture that the walk was causing St. Thérèse said, with tears in her eyes, "Sister, please do not try to walk any farther." The Little Flower answered, "I walk for a missionary." She was enduring that torture because she hoped thereby to take upon herself some of the fatigue of a missionary priest whose labors for souls would be lightened by her vicarious mortification. "I walk for a missionary." She was walking for souls; in fact her every thought and her every act was directed to that end, to win souls for God. If we would imitate her, we too can offer up each day, little prayers and little sacrifices for priests, for missionaries and for the dying, and then we will feel, as she did, that by our prayers and sacrifices, we are in reality missionaries ourselves and are doing the work of priests.

We walked along past several cells with closed doors until we came to a large door which one of the sisters opened, saying, "This is the chapter room where our little saint made her vows."

There is an altar in the chapter room and before the altar at the Epistle side a candelabrum marks the exact spot where she stood when she gave herself to God under the vows of obedience, chastity and poverty.

Then the sisters directed our attention to a cabinet in the corner in which there are placed some very interesting souvenirs of St. Thérèse. There are her breviaries, or books for the recitation of the Divine Office; then there is the little book of the gospels, which she always carried over her heart, and the little book is opened to the page in which she wrote the entire Credo with her blood to manifest her faith at a time when her temptations against faith were at their height. The Credo is written in her regular, fine hand, which might be printing, and the letters are of course in red.'

The most interesting of all the articles in that cabinet, is the original Autobiography of the Little Flower, written on cheap blank-books such as are used by children in their early grammar school days.

"So there," I thought, "written on that common, cheap copy-book paper is the book that has been translated into every language, converted many a soul and aroused the admiration of the world. How strange that a little sister with no higher education should be able to sit in her cell, or in the convent garden, and pen a volume that for ten years at least has been the world's most widely read religious book."

Then there is, in her own handwriting, of course, her Act of Oblation, dated June 9, 1895; and also, the handkerchief which caught her tears of joy on the morning of her first Holy Communion.

After inspecting these things we were conducted again to the corridor.

"Now we will go to the cell of our saint," said one of the sisters.

Sister Geneviève outside of the Carmel of Lisieux.

Chapter Four
The Cell

We were nearing the Little Flower's cell, her room during the last years of her life; the cell in which the little girl of fifteen, who had once been so inclined to be proud and independent, had been transformed day by day into the great St. Thérèse.

A few steps further in the corridor and we were at the door of the tiny abode of our little saint. The cell is dedicated to St. Eliseus, who asked the double spirit of St. Elias; and we recalled that St. Thérèse, with sublime daring, had implored God to give her the double spirit of all the saints.

We reverently entered her cell, which is divided into two parts by a thin partition. The first part is a narrow oratory almost filled now by an altar, on which there is a facsimile of the statue of the Blessed Virgin of the Smile. It was in this oratory that St. Thérèse, the young novice mistress, received her novices and gave them the wonderfully wise counsels that are to be found in part in the supplement to her Autobiography. I recalled there, in the oratory of her cell, some of her sayings to her novices that had always particularly impressed me.

One day a novice entering her cell, paused, struck by the celestial expression on the countenance of St. Thérèse, who was sewing with alacrity, yet seemed lost in profound contemplation.

"Of what are you thinking?" asked the young sister.

"I am meditating on the Our Father," she replied. "It is so sweet to call the good God our Father." And tears shone in her eyes.

A novice once complained of being more tired than her sisters, for besides the common work, she had done another task, of which they knew nothing; and Thérèse answered: "I want to see you always like a valiant soldier who does not complain of his pains; who thinks very seriously of the wounds of his brother, and regards his own as mere scratches. Why do you feel this fatigue to such a degree? It is because no one knows about it. This feeling is natural to us; yet to wish that all should know when we suffer is a very commonplace manner of acting."

"I have asked God to send me a beautiful dream to console me when you are gone," a novice once said to St. Thérèse.

"Ah! that is a thing I should never do," said the Little Flower, "ask for consolation! It is so sweet to serve the good God in the dark night of trial; we have this life only in which to live by faith."

"When I receive a reproof," said a novice on another occasion, "I would rather have deserved it than be wrongfully accused."

"As for me," replied Thérèse, "I prefer being blamed unjustly, then I have no cause for self-reproach, and I offer this unmerited blame to the good God with joy; then I humble myself at the thought that I should be quite capable of doing that of which I was accused."

Then we passed from the oratory into that part of the room habitually occupied by St. Thérèse and which is properly her cell. We walked into it reverently indeed. It is a very small room, smaller than the infirmary, and in it there is a large window which lets in an abundance of light.

Along the wall is her little bed covered with a gray cloth. I touched the mattress of the bed. It was as of wood. It was on this hard bed of boards that the child accustomed to the comfort of her father's home had slept. Nevertheless at the sound of the bell in the morning, she shook off her fatigue, placed her crucifix on her pillow, and said with her characteristic cheerfulness and ingenuity, "My sweet Jesus, You worked and wept during Your thirty-three years on this poor earth; now it is my turn to struggle and to suffer."

There was of course no fireplace in the cell, and I could readily understand how cold it would be there during the winter months. How cold a room in which to sleep and in which to rise! Yet from the very moment in which Thérèse, as a girl of fifteen entered it, fresh from her own luxurious bedroom in her father's home, that cell was for her a paradise, and when she was obliged to leave it for the infirmary, she said, "I acquired a great deal of my happiness in this little cell and I have suffered so much in it that I would be glad to die in it."

Oh, the memories that cell evoked. If those walls could speak how many acts of virtue would they relate. It was there she received what she calls the first call of her Beloved. On Holy Thursday, 1897, she had obtained permission to remain in the chapel until midnight when she returned to her cell. She says, "Scarcely had I laid my head on the pillow when I felt a hot steam rise to my lips, and thinking I was going to die, my heart almost broke with joy. I had already put out our lamp, so I mortified my curiosity till morning and went peacefully to sleep.

"At five o'clock, the time for rising, I remembered immediately that I had some good news to learn, and going to the window I found, as I had expected, that our handkerchief was saturated with blood. What hope filled my heart! I was firmly convinced that on the anniversary of His death my Beloved had allowed me to hear His first call, like a sweet distant murmur, heralding His joyful approach."

The beauty of that passage, in which St. Thérèse joyfully welcomes the approach of death, would not be enhanced by comment, but we lesser souls cannot but envy her, whose life was such that death meant for her only a joyful meeting and union with her Lord.

I recalled as I stood there that it was here in this cell that the Little Flower made one day a very remarkable prophecy. The Little Flower's Autobiography was written under obedience and the Little Flower did not know as she wrote it that it would ever be published; but later in life, just before she died, she certainly seemed to foresee how widely it would be read, because one day Pauline brought the Little Flower the manuscript and asked her to reread a passage which seemed to Pauline incomplete. Pauline left her with the manuscript and returned soon to the infirmary and found Thérèse in tears.

"You are crying!" Pauline exclaimed.

Thérèse looked up with a strange expression and said, "Indeed, my sister, these pages will do a great deal of good, they will make better known the goodness of the good God," and then she added, in a tone evidently inspired, "Yes, sister, I feel all the world will love me. All the world will love me."

How to the very letter has been fulfilled her prophecy: "All the world shall love me." The Little Carmelite Sister who uttered these words in a little cell of that cloistered convent of Normandy is now loved and honored in every part of the world; daily her name is pronounced lovingly in the most remote villages of the globe and she is loved more tenderly and more generally with every passing day.

But I have enumerated only one or two of the incidents that we know took place in the cell in which we were standing. Besides what the Little Flower had told us, how much else took place in that cell? She says in her Autobiography, "many pages of my story will never be read upon earth." There were sufferings there, we may be sure, that have not been disclosed, and certainly there were consolations too. How many secrets did Our Lord reveal to her there? How many inspirations did He give? We cannot tell, but certainly in her cell we were standing on holy, holy ground and we were set on fire with the wonder of it, and we caught up there some of the fervor and devotion which made that cell so venerable and holy a place.

We left the cell reluctantly. I would have been happy to have spent hours there, As we left it, I recalled the Little Flower's words to her sister, Mother Agnes. Mother Agnes said to her one day, "When you are gone how sad I shall feel as I look at your little cell," and Thérèse replied, "My little mother, for consolation you must think how happy I am in heaven, and remember that a great deal of my happiness was acquired in this little cell."

Indeed, I thought, heaven is a kingdom which we might gladly purchase by passing a few years in so narrow a cell, and yet, to win heaven it is unnecessary for us to go to such extremes. We need only fulfill the duties of our state of life. We need only offer to God, as the Little Flower says, "the flowers of little sacrifices" and place God first in our lives always, and then some day, we shall see face to face and converse with the gracious, lovable occupant of this little cell, a visit to which terminated our sojourn in the cloister.

We left the convent slowly and reluctantly, and for many a day after, our souls were under the spell of the charm of the cloister and filled with all that we had seen and heard there. Our visit there made the Little Flower seem much closer to us, and if this description of it has made her seem nearer to you, it has attained its object, because the nearer she comes to us, the easier it will be to pray to her, and to imitate her.

The Little Flower's Mother

Madame Martin, age 35.

Chapter One

A Visit to the Little Flower's Mother's Home

I am going to open this book by repeating what is written in my "Living Sisters of the Little Flower", about my first visit to the home of the Little Flower's mother. I repeat the passage because it explains the genesis of this book and also because it is a fitting introduction to this biography. The passage to which I refer is: "Mrs. Grant, the custodian, took me first to the little chapel which has been built in the room in which the Little Flower was born. The room in which the Little Flower was born! What thoughts crowded into my mind as after our prayers we stood there in the little chapel room and read the inscription: 'In this room January 2nd, 1873, Thérèse Martin, now Saint Thérèse of the Child Jesus, was born.' How little did the Little Flower's mother guess that night of the future of her newborn girl. I thought, while I was standing there, of much that I had recently heard of the Little Flower's saintly mother who had never ruled the household at Lisieux, but who died in the same room in which I was standing, the room in which the Little Flower was born. In another chapter, I will tell you of the many anecdotes of the Little Flower's mother, that I heard from authentic sources while I was in France, and which, because they throw so much light on the saint's mother, will not only be interesting but extremely beneficial; especially to mothers of whom thousands in America are trying to fashion their households, as much as possible, after the Little Flower's family home as their model. After leaving the chapel, I stood at the head of the stairs with Mrs. Grant and said to her, 'Is this the staircase which the Little Flower used to mount calling out at each step, "Mama, mama," and refusing to mount until, she heard her mother's "Yes, darling," in answer?'

"'Yes, Father, it is the very same,' replied Mrs. Grant, 'I often think of that incident as I mount these stairs,' and then she added, 'The staircase has never been altered nor touched.'

"'What a patient and model mother Mrs. Martin must have been,' I said.

"'Oh, yes Father, I often think that someone should write a book about the Little Flower's mother. What a wonderful amount of good it would do if all mothers could know intimately the mother of the Little Flower.'

"'I had already half determined to write such a book,' I said, 'and now I have decided. If you will agree to pray that it will do the good that you have just prophesied, I will write the book and call it simply, The Little Flower's Mother."

"Mrs. Grant agreed, and the book will soon be forthcoming."

Now that I have explained the genesis of the present book, let me, without any further preliminary, begin the biography of the mother of our little saint.

Chapter Two
Her Parentage and Maidenhood

The Little Flower's mother was Zélie Guérin, a Normandy girl, born at Saint-Dénis-sur-Sarthon. She belonged to one of the most Christian and Catholic families of Normandy. During the revolution, her ancestors had given asylum to the persecuted clerics; and her own father, while still a boy, had not been a stranger to the ruses employed at that time by the Catholic gentry to hide the disguised priests. Her father's uncle was one of the priests who, in spite of the law which banished them, remained in the country to minister to the faithful, and was often hidden at intervals in the boyhood home of her father. Later her father participated, just as did the father of the Little Flower's father, in the campaigns of the Empire and of the Restoration. He served in the infantry and then retired to Alençon after forty years of military life.*

Mr. Guérin had three children, Marie-Louise, who became Sister Marie-Dosithée in the Visitation of Mans, Zélie, who was the mother of the Little Flower, and Isador, the youngest, who applied himself to the study of medicine.

Zélie Guérin was for a while a pupil of the Ladies of the Adoration at Alençon, and at school her successes and scholarly triumphs were numerous. After her graduation she determined

---

* The following is a resumé of the military service of Isador Guérin, the maternal grandfather of the Little Flower: Born on July 6, 1789, he entered the army June 6, 1809, and was under fire for the first time at the battle of Wagram. In another division he took part in the battle of Toulouse.

to serve Our Lord in the person of His poor. She confided her desire to the Superior of the Hôtel-Dieu, but after many intimate conversations, the Superior declared definitely and without any ambiguity, that such was not the will of God. One wonders how much of the basis of this decision was natural shrewdness, and how much the inspiration and revelation of God. The young lady was of course downcast and disappointed, but sustained by her strong faith she awaited, in the company of her parents and her younger sister and younger brother, the decision of Providence upon her life.

Her father had bought in 1843 at No. 42 Rue Saint Blaise in Alençon a comfortable home in which he lived with his children, but the classical studies of his son, and the cost of the education of his daughters, weighed heavily upon the budget of the aged soldier. Since Zélie was destined ultimately for matrimony, she felt the need of increasing her dowry and she stormed heaven for help. On the 8th of December, 1851, the Feast of the Immaculate Conception, she was suddenly interrupted in the middle of absorbing work, in which the play of the imagination could have had no place, by the interior voice which seemed to give her this order: "Make Alençon lace." It was the response of the Blessed Virgin to many petitions which Zélie had addressed to her.

Alençon lace is the finest in France and the only lace in the country which is made entirely by hand. Zélie Guérin studied the various steps in its manufacture and then she specialized in the assemblage of portions previously prepared, and finally she set herself to the enterprise of making the lightest and the most delicate tissue. Alençon lace is made with threads of costly linen, hand-spun to an exquisite fineness.

She had under her several employees who worked at their homes, but Zélie gave the orders, furnished the designs, and arranged and superintended the work. Very soon the Alençon lace of Zélie Guérin was classed among the most beautiful in the country, so that it was sold, not rarely, for five hundred francs a yard, the profits forming a considerable capital.

Chapter Three

Her Marriage and Early Married Life

Isador Guérin, the father of Zélie, lived not far from the church of Notre Dame. A certain Captain Martin had established himself with his son Louis on Rue Pont-Neuf in Saint Peter's parish.

At this time Louis Martin, active, industrious and endowed with a very delicate artistic sense, gave every promise of becoming an expert in the jeweler's profession.

The two families (Guérin and Martin) were not acquainted. In her daily prayers Zélie Guérin again and again demanded from God to find for her a husband, who would not only be a good Catholic, but a fervent Catholic, and she had already, with firm faith, asked from God the honor of having many children who would be all in some way consecrated to God.

One day she was passing over the bridge of Saint Leonard when she saw approaching a young man whose appearance was so noble and dignified and distinguished that no one could but bestow upon him a second glance. She did not know him, but an interior voice manifested to her, once again, the solicitude of God over her life. The voice said: "It is this young man that I have selected for you."

Not long afterward under circumstances that have not been revealed, Zélie Guérin and Louis Martin were introduced; and finally united in the bonds of matrimony in the church of Notre Dame in Alençon on the 13th of July, 1858. Their home was upon the Rue Pont-Neuf. The husband continued his chosen profession and Zélie her manufacture of Alençon lace, and the clientele of both became numerous and their material future was assured.

The newly married couple felt each day, increasingly, the benefit of their mutual labors. To her practical sense, and rare energy, and increasing activity; Mrs. Martin joined an admirable spirit of the deepest faith. One ambition dominated her life: she had appropriated for herself this maxim of St. Francis, "Labor, that in all things God may be better loved."

Mr. Martin's character was perhaps more calm and quiet. He had, by nature, a very marked taste for religious contemplation, and he was a model of patience and alert charity which gave to their common life a charm, which every day increased.

The intimacy of the union between the two spouses expressed itself most remarkably in the service of God and, specifically, in their love of Our Lord in the tabernacle; for every morning they assisted together at half-past-five Mass. They knelt together at the holy table, and although at that time frequent communion was not practiced in France, they received Holy Communion more than once a week. In spite of the absorbing work of the husband and the fatiguing labors of the wife, Mr. and Mrs. Martin observed rigorously the fasts and abstinences of the Church, although they lived at a time when the spirit of mortification had become enfeebled in the better French families.

This spirit of faith manifested itself even more touchingly in the intimacy of the home. Prayers were always said in common, the young couple always endeavoring to place into the "Our Father," the heavenly fervor of Captain Martin, (the soldier father of the Little Flower's father; observe the military ancestry of both the father and mother of the Little Flower) whose recitation of the "Our Father" it is said, no one could hear without tears. The Lives of the Saints were read every evening in their home, and in these lives the couple certainly must have recognized kindred spirits.

One day, as the young wife was reading the biography of Madame Acarie, who, after having given her children to Carmel, consecrated herself to God in religious life, Mrs. Martin exclaimed: "All her daughters Carmelites! Is it possible that a mother could have so much honor?"

Since this was the spirit of the wife, it is easy to understand why she approved so strongly the practice of her husband, the practice of giving one entire night each month to prayer before the Blessed Sacrament. Often she accompanied him on walks into the country, where they were wont to end every walk in some church, kneeling happily before a tabernacle too often deserted.

Mrs. Martin was always ready to relieve the miseries which came to her notice. One of her servants was taken ill with articular rheumatism. The servant's parents were poor and could not procure for her the necessary medicines and nursing care. Mrs. Martin devoted herself therefore, night and day for several weeks, to the care of the servant until she was entirely well.

Nothing was wanting in this family of true Christians except the power of transmitting their virtues to a numerous posterity. God answered the prayers of Mrs. Martin, and magnificently blessed his two faithful servants by giving to them within a few years nine children. They wished that each one of their little ones from their entrance into this world should be consecrated to the Queen of Heaven; so they gave to each of their children the name of Mary. Marie Louise,* Marie Pauline, Marie Léonie, and Marie Pauline, were the first four children to come to increase the joy of their home.

But the parents, in their desire to multiply here below the glory of God, demanded of Him through the intercession of St. Joseph, "a little missionary." They thought that their prayers had been answered when to the little girls, who already filled the home with laughter and song, was added a little brother,

---

* Marie Louise, the eldest, is the only one of the daughters who was not called familiarly in the family by her second name. Marie-Louise was always called simply "Marie."

who received the name of Marie Joseph Louis. Alas! he had hardly time to smile at his mother, for, five months after his birth, he took his place among the angels to intercede for his terrestrial family. Prayers and novenas were redoubled with great fervor. They must have, at any price, a priest, a child who would become a great saint. Again their prayers seemed to be answered in the person of Marie-Joseph-John-Baptist who also soon went to heaven to fulfill the mission that God had refused him here below.

After this, Mr. and Mrs. Martin believed that their prayers were not to be answered; they consoled themselves by recalling that the ways of God are not our ways and they did not ask any longer for a missionary, but who shall dare to affirm, considering the future history of one of their children that God had rejected their prayers?

When the two older sisters, Marie-Louise, who being the eldest was always called Marie, and Marie-Pauline, became old enough for school, they were sent to Mans under the care of the Visitation sister of Mrs. Martin, Sister Marie-Dosithée.

To defray the expenses of their education and at the same time to keep their home supplied with comforts, the courageous mother resolved to apply herself with new energies to the further development of her commerce in lace. She accepted large and numerous orders, gave long hours to the instruction of her employees, carried on a vast commercial correspondence, and filled the house with activity.

There was no room in her busy life at this time for recreation. She writes to her brother's wife, September 28th, 1872: "To tell the truth, the only pleasure I have is to sit by my window and assemble my Alençon lace."* Nevertheless she enjoyed keenly the charms of family life; they were almost her only earthly joys and she applied herself with simplicity, good grace and devotion to the fulfillment of all the duties of motherhood.

---

* One entire afternoon the author sat by the same window talking with the custodian of the home, Mrs. Grant, about the Little Flower's mother. (Author's Note.)

Mrs. Martin had, as we have said, a brother, Isador Guérin, who before becoming the grand Christian man, who was later the father of Marie and Jean Guérin, had been for a moment entranced, in the course of his medical studies, by the allurements of Parisian life. It was at this time of temptation that the Little Flower's mother wrote to her brother Isador the following letter:

"My dear brother:

"I am greatly disturbed about you. My husband every day makes many sad prophesies concerning you. He knows Paris, and he tells me that you will suffer temptations which you will not be able to resist because you have not enough piety. He tells me that he, himself, underwent those temptations and that he had need of great courage to emerge victorious from the battle. If you only knew, or if I could only tell you the temptations through which he passed! I beg of you, my dear brother, to do as he did. Pray, and you will not be swept away by the torrent. If you succumb once, you are lost. It is only the first step that counts on the way of evil just as in the way of good; after that one is swept along with the current. If you will only consent to do one thing that I am now going to ask of you, I will be more happy than if you were to send me all Paris. This is it— you live very near the church of Our Lady of Victory. Very well. Enter there just once a day and say just one 'Hail Mary' to our Blessed Mother. You will see that she will protect you in a very special way and that she will promote your success in this world and give you afterwards an eternity of happiness. That which I ask of you and promise you, my dear brother, is not due to any exaggerated piety of mine, nor is it without foundation, for I have reason to have confidence in the Blessed Virgin. I have received from her favors that I alone know. You know well, my dear brother, that life is not long. You and I will soon be at the end, and then we will indeed be happy to have lived in such a way that our last hour may not be bitter."

How much that letter reveals of Mrs. Martin's character, and is that letter not indeed a sermon in itself, a sermon on the brevity of life, and upon the efficacy of prayer, especially to the Blessed Virgin in times of temptation against holy purity?

Her brother so well profited by Mrs. Martin's advice, that soon, having established himself at Lisieux as a pharmacist, and having married the pious Mademoiselle Fournet, he became one of the most practical and militant Catholics of the region.

After his marriage, a very close intimacy existed between the Martins in Alençon and the Guérins in Lisieux. It was at Lisieux, at her brother's home, and accompanied by her children that Mrs. Martin spent those rare holidays that she permitted herself. It was to her brother's wife that she addressed most of the letters, as simple as they are distinguished, in which she traces so many charming tableaux of her family life and in which expressions of supernatural hope mingle with the tears of her troubles. These letters* preserved by Mrs. Guérin and afterwards recovered by Mrs. Martin's daughters are a precious mine of information concerning the Little Flower's mother, and some of these letters which so well reveal her character are reproduced on the following pages.

Mrs. Martin never permitted her brother to forget that she was his older sister, and that she therefore had a right to moralize in her letters to him. Of this trait we have this example. One day a rich lady of the village remarked to Mrs. Martin: "Oh how happy I am. I lack nothing. I have health; I have wealth; I can procure for myself and do procure for myself all that I desire. I have no children to trouble my ease and my repose. In fact, I do not know anyone who is more fortunate than I."

Mrs. Martin made these remarks the text of the following letter written to her brother on March 28th, 1864: "I must say to you, my dear brother, that thrice unhappy is he who

---

* These letters were obtained by Father Dolan through the Little Flower's sister, Pauline, and are here published in English for the first time. (Editor's Note.)

utters or cherishes such sentiments. My dear brother, I am so persuaded of the truth of what I say that at certain times in my life when I had reason to believe that I was happy, I could not think of it without trembling; for it is certain, and often proved by experience, that happiness is not found here on earth and that if by chance one enjoys happiness for a while, it is but a prelude to some catastrophe. I have experienced that often myself. No, my dear brother, happiness is not found here below and it is a bad sign when all prospers. God in his wisdom has thus arranged life so as to make us remember that earth is not our true home."

Her letters are not all filled with this high moralizing; many are about her children, who play around the table on which the lace is being made; others contain expressions of the great spirit of thanksgiving that overflows the soul of the young mother as she views the treasures that had been confided to her. For instance, she had placed her last born, Hélène, in charge of a nurse and she naively expresses her maternal joys in a letter to her brother on April 23rd, 1865: "I went to see Hélène yesterday. I do not remember ever to have experienced a throb of happiness like that which came at the moment that I took her in my arms. She smiled at me so graciously that I thought I was seeing a little angel. My little Hélène, when shall I have the happiness of possessing her permanently! I cannot realize that I have the honor to be the mother of so delicious a little creature."

Alas! the little one, five years later, was to flee forever the arms of its mother and leave in that heart, the love in which is so plainly revealed in the lines just quoted, an incurable wound.

A less remote sorrow came now as a prelude to many others which awaited Mrs. Martin. Captain Martin, her husband's father, died, on which occasion she wrote on June 26th, 1865, to her brother: "My husband's father died yesterday at one o'clock in the afternoon. He had received the last sacraments the day before. He died like a saint. As was his life, so was his death. As one lives, so shall he die. I would never have believed that his death could have so affected me. I am desolate."

Alas, she was soon to become all too familiar with the spectacle of death. In the years immediately following her father-in-law's death, her two sons died as we have already indicated. Then came the death of her own father, on which occasion she wrote to her sister-in-law on the 3rd of September, 1868: "If you only knew how holy a death he had. I hope, in fact I am certain, that my dear father has indeed been well received by the good God. I only wish that my death will be like his. I already have had masses said for him, and soon we shall have many more. His tomb will be near that of my two little Josephs."

On the following 1st of November she wrote to her brother: "If the good God has heard me, our dear father is today in paradise. Our poor dear father—he was not accustomed to suffer. As for me I am not at all frightened at going to purgatory; it is entirely natural for me to suffer. If the good God wishes, I shall, as I have told Him, suffer my father's purgatory as well as my own. I shall be content to know that he is happy."

To these sorrows was joined the anxiety caused her by the frail constitution of Léonie, her frequent illnesses, and certain difficulties that her education caused.

This mother, who in spite of her exquisite sensibility, had valiantly endured such trials, and who was strengthened rather than weakened by grief, was also able to bear without complaint the thousand and one difficulties and annoyances of the busy household.

But to her cares as mother, wife, and employer, there was now added her fears for the health of her sister, the Visitation nun, who now was threatened with tuberculosis.

She was the more afraid of losing her sister because Pauline and Marie had progressed marvelously under the direction of the Visitation Sister, Mrs. Martin's blood sister, and their budding virtue had been her chief consolation in the midst of her trials.

Marie was shy and reserved, and underneath her timidity was hidden a heart of gold.

Pauline was gracious and thoughtful, endowed with great talent, and was the joy of her teachers.

It was after the death of her father that Mrs. Martin began to value more highly the sweet and happy dispositions of Marie and Pauline and to realize the consolation that their amiable qualities could give to her in her trials.

She induced Marie to offer for the soul of her grandfather the pain of a certain dental operation. "This morning at eight o'clock," writes Mrs. Martin to her brother on January 5, 1869, "I took Marie to the dentist. She asked me if the operation would really help her grandfather. Upon my affirmative response, she did not cry at all in the chair and was so quiet that the dentist said he never saw so determined a child. This new examination of her tooth proved the operation to be unnecessary and the little tot then said to me, 'It is a pity; if it had been necessary, my poor grandfather would have been released from Purgatory.'"

In return for the pious education she gave her children, this Christian mother tasted even amidst severe trials the most comforting consolations of our faith. God planted some flowers in the rough path which she walked, but before she reached the end there were other trials in store for her.

On the 23rd of February, 1870, Mrs. Martin buried her fourth child, the little Marie-Hélène. The others who died were Marie-Mélanie and the two Josephs. After the death of Marie-Hélène the Little Flower's mother wrote on October 17th, 1870, to her sister-in-law, this letter:

"When I closed the eyes of my dear little children and prepared them for burial I was indeed grief-stricken, but thanks to God's graces I have always been resigned to His will. I do not regret the pains and the sacrifices which I underwent for them. People say to me, 'It would have been much better if you had not given birth to those whom you lost so soon after their coming.' I cannot endure such sentiments. I do not find that pains and sacrifices can at all outweigh or compare with the eternal happiness of my little ones, eternal happiness which, of course, would never have been theirs had they never been born. Moreover, I have not lost them for always. Life is short. Soon I shall find my little ones again in heaven."

Would that every mother and father could read that last letter. Surely its lessons are obvious: it needs no comment. Just let us recall that it comes from the pen of one whose last and ninth child became the great Saint Thérèse. If Mrs. Martin had been innoculated with certain current views, the world would never have been blessed with the fragrance of the Little Flower.

Towards the end of 1870, Mr. Martin gave up his jewelry business to one of his nephews in order to help more directly and more actively his wife's lace business which had taken on enormous proportions.

An era of great prosperity opened for the family, when suddenly there came an invasion of Alençon by the victorious Prussians. Mrs. Martin had to open her home to nine Germans who, though they avoided the more odious forms of violence, destroyed in a twinkling of an eye the good order established by the mistress of the home. She writes: "They put my furniture into a terrible state. The town is in desolation. Everyone except ourselves is in tears."

At this unhappy time Mrs. Martin's husband manifested the same courage as his valiant wife, as she herself is happy to testify in this letter: "Possibly, men from forty to fifty will be drafted. If my husband goes, I am prepared; I expect it, and he is not concerned; he says often that were he free he would like nothing better than to enlist."

At this time when a wife of the town had tried to hide her husband after he had been drafted by the order of mobilization, the heroic mistress of the Martin household wrote: "How is it possible that anyone could do such a thing?"

The war was ended before Mr. Martin was called to the colors. After the war, the family moved from their home on the Rue du Pont-Neuf to a house on the Rue Saint-Blaise. This property had become the heritage of Mrs. Martin upon the death of her father, and the home was destined to be the birthplace of the Little Flower. Céline had been born in the former home the year before, 1869. At this time the mother wrote: "Four of my children are already well placed (she refers to the four who had gone to heaven) and my other children will go also to that heavenly kingdom, laden with greater merit; for they will have fought a much longer time."

See how Christian hope always assuaged her sorrows and gave her that remarkable tranquillity and spirit of resignation so discernible in her letters.

The Little Flower and her mother.

Chapter Four

The Birth and Infancy of St. Thérèse

The two admirable Christians, Mr. and Mrs. Martin, now enjoyed in their new home several years of pure joy and intimate felicity. It was into this atmosphere of peace and piety and tenderness that there came, January 2nd, 1873, another baby, hailed as the others had been, with transports of joy. This time it was the little missionary, the object of so many vows and ardent prayers: Thérèse, the frail little missionary, who all unknown to her parents, was to win to God more souls than the most renowned apostles.*

This night, Pauline and Marie were home on vacation and were sleeping in a room on the second floor, when their father mounted the stairs with a light step announcing joyously, "My children, you have a little sister."

Then, kneeling, the daughters and the father gave fervent thanks to God.

Marie, the eldest sister, was chosen as the godmother of the Little Flower. The godfather, a son of a friend of Mr. Martin, lived at some distance, and his coming was so tardy that Mrs. Martin was greatly disturbed, and beseeched God not to let her little daughter die without baptism. Finally, January 4th, in the afternoon, all the family went to the

---

* Some may perhaps think that the details given concerning St. Thérèse are too minute and abundant. The canons of rhetoric might require abridgment; but the avidity of lovers of the Little Flower for all that concerns her has made me believe it would be well to penetrate, as far as possible, into the intimacy of that home which was so worthy of her. (Author's Note.)

church of Notre Dame for the baptism. In accordance with the vow of her parents, the little one received, like her other sisters, the name of Marie to which was joined Thérèse; the latter name prevailing in the usage of the family.

Thérèse, pure as a starry sky and white as snow, carried in the arms of Louise, the faithful domestic of the family, regained her home while the bells of Notre Dame sounded a joyful melody. Mrs. Martin was reassured now, and content.

The weeks rolled by illumined by radiant hopes. The mother resolved to nurse the child herself, for she thought that she discerned already a halo radiating divinely from the forehead of the little one. Once the mother, singing to the child, thought for a moment she heard the little one also feebly sing. Whether or not she did sing, the presage would be verified, for that soul, who just made its appearance into the Martin home, became indeed one of the world's greatest singers; singing God's mercy and goodness so sweetly that all the world has paused to listen. But soon the strength of the little one began to decline, and she seemed destined to follow to heaven the other four Martin children who had died in infancy. A new sorrow seemed about to come to the poor parents. The family physician did not conceal from them that the only possible remedy for the little one was to confine her to the care of a vigorous nurse.

Mrs. Martin had already employed, as a nurse for one of the other children, a strong peasant woman, Rose Taille; herself the mother of many children. Mrs. Martin resolved to try the remedy counseled by the doctor, and she writes to her brother's wife in 1873: "If it had not been so late I would have set out that night to find the nurse. How long the night was! Thérèse would not take the least nourishment, and during the night all the sad signs that preceded the death of my other little angels, manifested themselves; and I was sad at heart that my poor little last-born could not receive from me the least help in her weakened condition.

"At dawn I set out for the country to see the nurse. She lived on a farm three miles out of Alençon. I went myself, because my husband was away, and I was unwilling to trust my mission to any messenger. On the deserted country road I encountered two rough looking men who inspired in me a little dread, but I said to myself, 'If they kill me it makes no difference; I have the death of grief already in my heart.' Arriving at the home of the nurse I asked her to come to our house immediately. She replied that she could not leave her own children, but that she would come and bring Thérèse back with her to the farm and care for her there. Knowing that my little one would be safe and in good hands, I consented."

The two women returned together to Alençon before noon and at the sight of the dying infant the nurse shook her head discouragingly as if to say, "It is too late."

Mrs. Martin, utterly cast down by the livid color of the little Thérèse, went to her room, threw herself on her knees before a statue of Saint Joseph, and between her sobs, invoked that patron of desperate causes.

Then after her prayer, she descended the stairs and lo, the child at the breast of the nurse seemed to have taken new life and courage! It was but the happiness of an instant. Definitely overcome now by the malady, the little Thérèse fell back on the lap of her nurse and lay there immovable without breathing, without any sign of life whatsoever. Thinking the child was dead, the poor mother, amidst her tears, found in her faith and piety enough courage to thank God at that moment for the peaceful death of her innocent one. But lo, just then the little one reopened her eyes and smiled long and sweetly upon the thankful mother! This time Saint Joseph had done his work. Thérèse, in a few hours, was well enough to be carried to the country in the arms of her nurse.

There are extant some letters written by Mrs. Martin at this time, describing her visits to Thérèse at the farm home of the nurse. March 30, 1873, she writes to her brother's wife in Lisieux: "Up until last week Thérèse had been quite well and had even grown quite plump, but since last Friday she is suffering from an irritation of the intestines, and when the doctor came he found her in a high fever. Nevertheless, he tells me that he does not believe there is any danger. Today she is better, but I have serious fears. I cannot but think that she will not live. I have done everything possible to save my little one, and now if the good God disposes otherwise, I will try to endure, as patiently as possible, the sacrifice He asks of me."

Then at this time other trials came to Mrs. Martin. While Thérèse was still ill, Marie returned ill from school and was stricken with typhoid fever. For long weeks she languished at Alençon under the eyes of her mother. Mrs. Martin gave to her care most of the hours of the day, and often of the night. At the same time, she superintended the work of her lace workers. The poor woman bent under the burden, but her faith never wavered.

April 13, 1873, she wrote to her brother's wife, who had suffered a great material loss through fire: "Everyone has his cross to bear, but there are some who find the cross heavier than do others. You have just commenced to learn, my dear sister, that all in life is not roses. The good God sends suffering to us in order to detach us from earth and raise our minds to heaven.

"I do not ever leave my sick Marie and I sleep beside her nights. Under my present burden, I am sure that a special grace from God has been necessary, and has been given to save me from collapsing under it."

At this time, Mr. Martin undertook a pilgrimage of penance to win Marie's cure. On May 3rd, Mrs. Martin wrote to Pauline: "Your father left early this morning to make a pilgrimage for Marie. He left fasting and will return fasting in an effort to persuade the good God to hear his prayers. He will make the journey on foot, returning tonight about midnight."

God indeed heard the supplications of the parents for their two sick daughters. Slowly, and after frequent relapses, Marie became convalescent. Thérèse recovered from the intestinal malady and on May 5th, the mother wrote this reassuring news to Pauline: "Last Sunday, Rose, the nurse, without notifying us, brought Thérèse to our house. We were not expecting her, and at 11:30, just as we were seating ourselves at the table, Rose entered, accompanied by four of the children, and with Thérèse in her arms. Rose immediately gave the little one to me and then departed for Mass. But that departure did not please the little one at all. She cried until I thought she would suffocate. The whole house was in an uproar. It was necessary to dispatch one of the servants immediately to the nurse to tell her to return here with all speed after Mass. The nurse came in soon; she had rushed all the way from church. The baby was immediately consoled and became quiet. We were all surprised to find Thérèse so strong."

What consolation for Mrs. Martin after the fears and anxiety of the first months to be finally assured that Thérèse would live and wax strong.

Again, two weeks later, Mrs. Martin wrote to Pauline: "Thursday I saw the little Thérèse. Her nurse brought her, but Thérèse did not wish to stay with us, and sent forth piercing cries when she could no longer see her nurse. Louise, one of the servants, had to take her to Rose who was downtown selling her butter, and as soon as she saw her nurse, Thérèse began to smile and there was no more crying at all. She weighs fourteen pounds and she will be very gentle and later very pretty."

The acts of the infant Thérèse differ little from those that all mothers can observe, but in the two following letters, the mother declares that she seems to have observed the first unusual manifestations of the presence of the Holy Spirit in the little innocent soul. The first letter was written November 30th, 1873, when Thérèse was nine months old. Her mother, writing to Pauline, is describing the physical development of the Little Flower, and mentions the first reflection on the baby's countenance of the presence of divine grace in her soul. "I hope that little Thérèse will walk by herself in five or six weeks. Even now, if we place her upright near a chair, she will hold herself up well and never fall. She takes little precautions against falling, and seems very intelligent. I believe that her appearance will be better than the average. She smiles continually and has the expression of a predestined one. Never have I seen such an expression in your countenance or that of the older ones."

On the following January 11th, Mrs. Martin writes: "Since last Thursday my little Thérèse walked all alone. She is as sweet and delicate and pretty as a little angel. Her disposition is charming; I can see that already. How sweet her smile is! I long for the time when she can stay with me here at home."

Is it not remarkable to see this feeble child, hardly a year old, manifesting already by the sweetness and grace of her countenance, the presence of the hidden God who has taken his delights in her soul.

Rose, the nurse, brought Thérèse home permanently on April 2, 1874.

Now the calamities that threatened the Martin home seemed definitely averted. Marie had entirely recovered her health; Pauline continued to be the pride of her teachers and the consolation of her mother; the little Céline, vivacious and amiable, had not seriously suffered from certain illnesses that had inspired fear for a time; Léonie was making satisfactory progress at school. The two spouses forgot their recent agony in the midst of the caresses with which childish hands showered them. The Little Queen was the source of constant delight. Mrs. Martin wrote to her brother's wife January 1, 1874: "None of my children was so strong, except perhaps the first. She will be beautiful. She is already gracious and graceful. I admire her little mouth which, as the nurse says, is as small as an eye.'"

In the midst of these joys, Mr. Martin did not forget the duty of thanksgiving. In 1873, after the cure of his daughter, Marie, he went to make his thanksgiving at Notre Dame de Chartres. In October he went to Lourdes with a diocesan pilgrimage, and to these pilgrimages of thanksgiving the fervent Christian joined the most assiduous perseverance in his habit of monthly nocturnal adoration of the Blessed Sacrament.

On her part, Mrs. Martin, surrounded by pious children who gave early signs of religious vocations, stimulated in the way of piety and abnegation by her holy Visitation sister, applied herself more fervently than ever to become more intimately united with God. In the following letter, written November 1, 1873, (the eve of the Feast of All Saints) Mrs. Martin confides to Pauline and Marie, now reunited in the Visitation School at Mans, her determination to progress further in virtue: "I must now go to vespers to pray for my dear departed parents. There will come a day when you will render a like service for me, but I must so live that I will not have too great need of your prayers. I wish to become a saint. That will not be easy; there is indeed much to hew down and the wood is hard as stone. It would have been better to commence sooner when it would have been less difficult, but better late than never."

Of course, this is the language of humility, for as those who have followed her life so far and have read her letters know, she had long before this been far advanced in the struggle towards perfection.

God, who had designs on the little Thérèse, seemed to use to preserve her, means that sometimes seemed to defy the laws of nature. The following facts recounted by Mrs. Martin in her letter of June 25, 1874, presents an example of God's Providence over Thérèse: "Recently, I had a singular adventure with my little one. I go to Mass at half-past five. I did not dare at first to leave Thérèse alone, but seeing that she never awoke, I decided to push her crib so close to my bed that it would be impossible for her to tumble out. One morning, I forgot to move the crib. When I returned, and entered the bedroom, I did not see my little Thérèse.* At that moment, I heard a little cry and I saw her sitting on a chair near the bed, her head resting on a pillow. I cannot understand how she could have fallen from the crib into the chair. I have thanked the good God for preserving her from any harm. It was indeed providential, for ordinarily an infant would have fallen to the floor. Her angel guardian had watched over her, and the souls in purgatory to whom I had said prayers every day for her, protected her."

* Thérèse was then about one year old.

Thérèse manifested in a manner as charming as naive, a tender affection for her mother, and Mrs. Martin smiles deliciously at these manifestations of filial affection. She writes in 1874 to her two elder daughters, Marie and Pauline: "Picture the baby embracing me and passing her little hand over my face. I could see that she was greatly interested. The poor little one will not leave me; she is continually with me. She loves especially to go into the garden, but if I am not there, she will not stay there and cries until I return or until she is brought to me."

The pious mother was soon to experience through Thérèse joys more profound. Mrs. Martin had wished that the little one's first words should be words of prayer, and on the 18th of November, 1874, the little girl, hardly twenty-two months old, offered to "the good Jesus," the love of her child's soul and this in such terms and with such an accent that the mother was delighted. She writes to Pauline and Marie who were at school: "My little Thérèse becomes daily more and more sweet and gentle. She gurgles and hums from morning until evening. She sings us little songs, but it is necessary to be accustomed to her to understand them. She says her prayers like a little angel. It is ideal."

Soon Thérèse was taken to church, and it was wonderful to see the attraction that this child of two years manifested for the Mass, of which one would almost say she had already feebly divined the import. Let us listen to her mother describe her at this time; no one is better fitted than Mrs. Martin to be a witness to the action of divine grace on the little soul. The mother writes to her brother's wife, March 14, 1875: "Thérèse looks, and is, well. She carries on with us the most amusing conversations. She knows her prayers. Every Sunday she goes to vespers, and if by chance we cannot take her, she cries inconsolably. Some weeks ago, on a Sunday, it was raining. She started to cry, saying that she had not been to Mass! Unobserved for a moment by us, she opened the door and in the pouring rain started down the street in the direction of the church. I ran after her and brought her back, and her sobs continued for a good hour. She says to me very much aloud in church, 'Mama, I have prayed well to the good God.' When she doesn't see her father say his prayers in the evening, she asks, 'Why, Papa, do you not say your prayers? Have you been to church?' Since Lent began, I go to the six o'clock Mass, and she is often awake when I leave, and says to me 'Mama, I will be very good.' And she doesn't move until I return."

This little two-year-old girl, so inclined towards the things of God as to wish to go to church in the pouring rain, revealed to some extent by this unusual courage, the attraction for God which led the Holy Spirit to invite her to "refuse nothing to Jesus."

Mrs. Martin enjoyed to the full these first supernatural flashes upon the life of Saint Thérèse that we have so far related, but these joys of the Christian were not unmixed with the anxieties, though passing, of the mother. Thérèse struck her forehead against a table and the accident caused a wound which the mother at first feared would mark the little one for life. Then again, Thérèse scarcely recovered from one severe cold when she contracted another. But after these little troubles, the clouds lifted, and smiles came once more to the mother.

The picture of the Little Flower as a first communicant signed by all four of the living sisters of the Little Flower. The first signature is that of Pauline, the second of Marie, the third of Celine, and the fourth of Léonie.

Chapter Five

The Mother During the Girlhood of St. Thérèse

For some time now, the family enjoyed tranquil happiness. There exists a picture of the family, the children gathered about their parents in the sitting room of their home. The picture was taken one evening, probably in September, when Marie and Pauline were home on vacation. Under the brilliance of a lamp, each one is occupying or recreating himself according to his peculiar inclination. The father, whose grave countenance is already surmounted by white hair, has brought his paper, but he is more occupied with his children than with the news of the day, and is conversing with Léonie who is doing some scholastic work in preparation for the opening of school. Marie is leaning on the back of a large chair in which Mrs. Martin is seated. The mother is watching the little Thérèse who, kneeling against the mother's knee with hands joined and her eyes raised to heaven, is addressing "the little Jesus," Whom one would imagine she saw. Céline, also on her knees, mingles her prayers with those of her little sister who was always her playmate and companion. Pauline, always occupied seriously, interrupts her reading to smile at the angelic infant in conversation with God. What a delicious scene! How well it reveals the tastes and patriarchal customs of that most Christian family. Is it any wonder that God blessed that home with a saint?

The Martin family circle was not entirely closed to outsiders, but they mingled habitually with scarcely any but close relatives. Mrs. Martin's intimacy with her brother, the reader already knows. The better Mrs. Martin came to know her brother's wife, a woman of piety and character, the closer friendship between them became, and Mrs. Guérin became the confidant of the joys and sorrows of Mrs. Martin. The Martins went frequently to visit the Guérins in Lisieux, not because Mrs. Martin was really anxious for relaxation, but because she knew how Céline and Thérèse loved to play with their sweet little cousins, Marie and Jeanne Guérin.*

Once Mrs. Martin went to visit her sister, the Visitation nun, at Mans. The days of the sister, afflicted with tuberculosis, were numbered, and Mrs. Martin wished to present to her sister Thérèse who, having given such early signs of piety, might one day, who could tell, occupy a place in the choir of cloistered religious. Mrs. Martin writes to Mrs. Guérin of this visit in the following letter dated April 29, 1875. "My little Thérèse was very happy to take the train. Arriving at Mans she sat in the parlor of the convent as serious as a big girl. Then, I do not know what was the matter, she began to cry noiselessly, the big tears rolling down her cheeks. Maybe it was the grille that caused her fright. Soon she stopped crying and when my sister came she replied well to all questions as if she were taking an examination. The Mother Superior came to the grille, and I said to Thérèse 'Ask the good Mother to give you her blessing.' Thérèse replied 'My mother, do you want to come to my house?' And at this, of course, everybody laughed."

Thérèse, as the reader doubtless knows, was not entirely exempt from little outbursts that revealed her willful temperament, but Mrs. Martin watched over her carefully, insisted upon perfect obedience, and warned her husband when, during the first few months, she thought he showed a tendency to humor and spoil Thérèse, "his little queen." One evening Thérèse had given some resistance to her mother, and her mother had insisted on obedience and the

---

* See "The Living Sisters of the Little Flower" for an interview Father Dolan had with Jeanne Guérin, who was still living. (Editor's Note.)

little girl was not therefore in very good humor when Mrs. Martin was putting her to bed. Of the sequel, Mrs. Martin writes to Pauline, December 5th, 1875: "After she had gone to bed, she called to me that she had not said her prayers. I replied 'Go to sleep and you can say them tomorrow.' But she was not satisfied. To put an end to the trouble, her father went to her and heard her prayers. But she still was not satisfied; she wanted to say some other prayer that we couldn't understand. Finally, your father gathered something of what she meant, and said the prayer, and then we had peace until the next morning."

Vain and futile details, some one will say. Yes, if we were dealing with an ordinary infant. But what Christian will deny the interest of investigating the first traces of the divine influx on a soul which was to become such a furnace of supernatural love? And besides these letters picture the mother as well as Thérèse, and to picture the mother is the purpose of this book.

Thérèse is now nearly three years old and delights her mother by her progress in the little lessons she took with Céline. The mother writes to Pauline: "Thérèse has an intelligence such as I have never observed in any of you when you were so young."

Mrs. Martin now recalls her ambition as a young mother, "all her children consecrated to God"—what a joy! Marie, her first child, simple and modest and serious, now began to show indications of a vocation to the life of the cloister. Pauline had not become vain because of her constant scholarly successes, but was obedient and industrious and even more faithful to her exercises of piety than to her studies. This news from the Visitation school was a source of greatest joy to Mrs. Martin. She wrote to Pauline, December 5, 1875: "You are my true friend. You give me courage to endure life with patience. Be always the joy to others that you have been to me. The good God will bless you not only in the next world, but in this, because he is always happiest even in this life, who always bravely does his duty."

Mrs. Martin had, too, her own happy dreams. She gave over her rare hours of leisure to spiritual reading, reading that revealed the joys of religious life, joys that she had ambitioned as a girl, and which attracted her still, and to which she wished to lead her daughters. She wrote to Pauline, September 5, 1875: "I am reading the life of the holy Chantal. I am ravished with admiration. It is the more interesting to me because I love the Visitation. How happy are they who are called! I dream sometimes of the cloister and solitude. I do not know really, considering the ideas I have, why it was not my vocation to remain either an old maid or to enter a convent. I would now like to live to be very old so that when my children are all grown up, I could retire to the solitude of the convent."

Alas, these hopes of a long life and of an old age spent in the cloister were not to be attained. God had other designs on this wonderful woman who had already prepared for Him, from afar, five religious. By the merit of her sufferings heroically borne, she had formed the character of Marie and Pauline and by her intercession she was to obtain for the little Thérèse the graces which would make her one day a great saint, "the most pure victim of merciful love."

Chapter Six

The Mother's Influence upon St. Thérèse

"All my life," writes the Little Flower, "it has pleased Our Lord to surround me with affection. My earliest recollections are of loving smiles and of tender caresses; but if He made others love me so much, He made me love them too, for I was of an affectionate nature."

The influence of these holy affections and of those domestic virtues, of which the Little Flower has testified in the passage just quoted, Thérèse gives as the reason for her early attraction to all that is good and holy.

Let us note now some other acts which were performed by her parents daily before the eyes of Thérèse, acts which could not but develop in her, little by little, a high sense of duty.

The patience of the father, his charity to the servants and employees, his high sense of justice, all this we may be sure did not escape the little Thérèse, keen little observer as she always was. Then, too, the parents always observed strictly the Sunday rest, and kept rigorously the fasts of the Church, and the mother went much farther than the Church requires in penance and mortification. For instance, when Mrs. Martin, eight months before her death, was to undergo an operation of which we will speak later, she refused to take supper on the eve of the operation, saying that it was an Ember Day and she wished to keep the fast.

We might expect that, to such a devout mother, manifestations of the supernatural world would not be lacking, and indeed when I was at Mrs. Martin's home, talking with the custodian, Mrs. Grant, the latter, in answer to my remark that it must be a great consolation to live always in the Little Flower's home, replied, "Oh yes, there were miracles in this house." And then she related this story: "You remember, she said, "with what tenderness Mrs. Martin loved the little Hélène, who died at the age of five years. Well, one day shortly after Hélène's death, Mrs. Martin remembered a little fib that Hélène once told in the course of a childish conversation, and Mrs. Martin immediately went to the statue of the Blessed Virgin in her home and begged that if the little Hélène were being kept in purgatory because of that little fib that the Blessed Virgin would release her. Immediately, in answer to her prayer, a voice issued from the statue,* saying, 'Hélène is here at my side.'"

Such then were the exemplary lives constantly before Thérèse as models. Thérèse observed them closely and admired them greatly and loved them ardently. She tells us in her Autobiography: "You can hardly imagine how much I loved my father and mother, and, being very demonstrative, I showed my love in a thousand little ways, though the means I employed make me smile now when I think of them."

Aided and stimulated by this ardent affection, the piety of Thérèse increased day by day. She wished always to please her parents; she knew they were so perfect because they loved God so much; and so she comprehended very early in life that one must love greatly the good God, do all that He commands, avoid all that He forbids and she brought to this work of loving God, all the ardor of her intense nature. When her reason began to function, it occupied itself with eternal problems. The little child, for instance, was beginning to comprehend that eternal happiness is a recompense and that therefore one must earn it, merit it. Of this, Mrs. Martin writes: "Thérèse tells me this morning that she wishes to go to heaven, and that therefore she would always be as good as a little angel."

---

* This statue had been given to Mr. Martin before his marriage by a pious person of Alençon who had a reputation for sanctity. It is the same statue that later smiled upon and cured the Little Flower. (Author's Note.)

Thérèse had such a high notion of God's goodness that she thought, in her ingenuity, that He, even when offended, would not separate a child from its mother; hence, this naive dialogue reported by Mrs. Martin, October 29, 1876, in a letter to Pauline: "Thérèse (then three years old) said to me, 'Mama, will I go to heaven?' 'Yes, if you are good,' I told her. 'Oh Mama,' she answered, 'then if I am not good shall I go to Hell? Then, I know what I shall do: I shall fly to you in heaven, and you will hold me tight in your arms and how could God take me away then.' I saw that she was convinced that God could do nothing to her if she hid herself in my arms."

Another letter of Mrs. Martin's to Pauline showed how Thérèse served to alleviate her heavy burden: "My little Thérèse is my happiness. She will be good; I can see that already. She speaks only of God. She wouldn't for all the world miss her prayers. I wish you could hear her. Never have I seen anything so charming."

This family so intimately united, this atmosphere so amiable and sanely joyous and yet so holy and religious, with faith animating all their relations and penetrating all their acts, could not but react strongly on the character of Thérèse. Thérèse expresses this negatively in her Autobiography when she says, "I am sure that had I been brought up by careless parents, I should have become very wicked and perhaps have lost my soul."

Conversely, the facts are that she was brought up by superbly Christian parents, and therefore became very holy and saved not only her own soul, but countless others. That is the theme and purpose of this book, the raison d'être of every anecdote given herein, namely, to show that the holiness of the Little Flower is due in no small degree to her parents, to the training they, and especially her saintly* mother, gave her. One day in Normandy I told the Little Flower's sister, Léonie, that I was going to write this book about her mother, and that the theme of the book would be that the mother was a saint and that her

---

* Wherever in this book the word "saint" is employed, it is used without any intention of anticipating the judgment of the Church. (Author's Note.)

holiness, influence, training and prayers explained in no small degree the holiness of the Little Flower. Léonie declared that I was right in both propositions and gladly wrote that declaration so that it might be used in this book as a foreword.

Certainly, after God, it was to the living faith and example and devotion of her mother that Thérèse owed first her gentleness, and then her detachment from pleasure, and finally her determination always to give pleasure, cost what it might, to the good Jesus, Whom she saw her dear mother loved so ardently.*

We have passed in review some examples of piety, faith, devotion, courage, and resignation in trial that the mother gave to the Little Thérèse. These examples would doubtless not have affected Thérèse so profoundly if the mother had not been as affectionate as she was solicitous. It was by love that, little by little, the mother formed Thérèse to love also, to love even to the giving of her whole self to God, to love even to greater sacrifice and to death.

The tenderness of Mrs. Martin was not sentimental and soft, but virile. She was a strong character, who for all the world would not attempt to flatter or pamper her children or to overlook in them a dangerous inclination — but at the same time, she knew how to bestow on them signs of the most tender and most moving affection. She, herself, relates with what affection and condescension she responded to the loving, childish desires of Thérèse. She writes Pauline: "Thérèse will not even go upstairs alone without calling me at each step, 'Mama, Mama,' and if I forget to answer 'Yes, darling,' she waits where she is and will not move."

Such was the education of love without softness that Thérèse received from her mother, and how much of the Little Flower's love of God and desire to please Him is due to that admirable training?

---

* The influence of the Little Flower's sisters, especially Pauline, upon the character of St. Thérèse has been described in the author's book, "The Living Sisters of the Little Flower." (Editor's Note.)

Chapter Seven
Twilight and Dawn

February 24, 1877, Mrs. Martin received this letter from the Visitation Convent at Mans: "This morning your well-beloved sister, Sister Mary Dosithée, ended her edifying life by a death worthy of envy. Her presence of mind, her serenity, her devotion were admirable to the end."

"Now," wrote Mrs. Martin to her brother, "we have one more protector in heaven, for it would be difficult to close more holily so virtuous a life as our sister's."

This hope sustained Mrs. Martin in the sorrow the sad news caused her. She asked her children, especially Thérèse, to beg daily the heavenly protection of their aunt. Mrs. Martin herself prayed that the intercession of her pious sister, joined to that of the Blessed Virgin, would bring about a miracle of which she herself had need, as we shall now see.

When Mrs. Martin was a young girl, she had an accident; she fell violently and struck her breast against the corner of a table. The result was a lump, at first not very painful, but ultimately the lump became a decaying fibrous tumor, which, I suppose, we would call cancer. Without ever complaining, without interrupting her fatiguing labors, without omitting any religious or family duties, Mrs. Martin had borne valiantly for more than sixteen years the pain of this tumor, which was slowly doing its work of destruction. When the pain so increased that she could no longer hide her state from her dear ones, they called a doctor of Alençon, Doctor Prévost, who, seeing the hopelessness of the case, gave her, for form's sake, a prescription. "What is this for?" asked Mrs. Martin. And the doctor said sadly, "It is to console the sick."

Mrs. Martin's brother advised an operation and for this purpose brought his sister to a celebrated surgeon in Lisieux who declared, "It is too late."

Condemned by the doctors, and having the prospect of dying in the midst of the greatest suffering, the courageous Christian returned to Alençon, took up again her ordinary life, and had no other thought than to perform, to the end, without weakness or ostentation, her daily duties.

She wrote to her brother's wife, January 28, 1877: "You are too much concerned about me, my dear sister. I am not worried. I do not deserve that you should be so concerned about me; my life is not so precious."

Soon she gave up her lace business, and wrote, "I love the work and regret to give it up, but I can easily live on our income."

The image of death had become familiar to her; she could face it without trembling, but she thought that, since her Visitation sister was dead, her daughters needed her to superintend their education, so she begged her sister in heaven and the Blessed Virgin to give her back her health, and to this end she made in June, 1877, a pilgrimage to Lourdes. Marie, Pauline and Léonie accompanied her because she hoped that the urgent prayers of her pious children, joined to her own, would obtain from Mary Immaculate her cure.

The journey* was more fatiguing than had been foreseen. Insufficient warmth, poor food, and the difficulty of finding suitable lodging in Lourdes, all contributed to make her condition worse. She plunged four times into the water of the sacred pool of Lourdes, but alas her pains were not alleviated.

---

* Many of the facts concerning Mrs. Martin, reported in these pages, were told to me by Léonie, the Little Flower's sister; others were found in a French book recommended to me by Pauline. The book is entitled La Vie de Sainte Thérèse, by Laveille, to whom I am greatly indebted. (Author's Note.)

Once home she wrote to her brother's wife, June 24, 1877: "I would have been doubly happy to have been cured, because of the happiness it would have caused you, but alas the Blessed Mother has said to us as she did to Bernadette: 'I will make you happy, not in this world, but in the next.'"

On the return journey from Lourdes to Alençon, Mrs. Martin joined the other pilgrims in chanting with full voice the customary hymns—this in the presence of her daughters, silent, sad and despondent.

Her husband, with Céline and Thérèse, met the train. They had passed a difficult week, always expecting a happy message that never arrived. The husband was, of course, saddened, and Céline and Thérèse were astounded that the Blessed Virgin had not heeded their innocent prayers. Mr. Martin was surprised to see his wife return as gaily as if she had obtained the grace that she desired.

"That attitude of mine," wrote Mrs. Martin to her sister-in-law, "gave him new courage, and my resignation brought good cheer to the household."

The cheerful attitude of Mrs. Martin was assumed out of pure charity towards her loved ones. To her daughter Pauline, whose piety the mother knew and whom she wished to habituate to facing trouble, Mrs. Martin wrote her true sentiments. Her letter to Pauline read: "Are you still angry with our Blessed Mother because she did not make you dance with joy? . . . Do not look for much joy on earth, for if you do you will be disappointed. As for me, I know by experience to what extent to rely on the joys of earth, and if I did not live only for the joys of heaven, I would indeed now be miserable."

Nevertheless, to console her dear ones, and to maintain her own courage, the poor mother continued to pray for a miracle. She wished once more to visit at Lisieux her brother's family, which had always been so dear and helpful to her. She planned on bringing Céline and Thérèse with her, and writing to her sister in-law about their keen desire of accompanying her, Mrs. Martin said in her letter of July 8, 1877: "The youngest

(Thérèse) will be the most impressed by the journey. She will remember all her life that when she was two years old, we left her home when we went to visit you, and when she speaks of it now, the tears always come. She is a charming little creature, my little Thérèse. I assure you that she will amount to something."

The little child who wished to be taken along on a visit to Lisieux, could not of course foresee the cruel event that would prevent the journey.

Relentlessly, the disease progressed. The months of July and August were marked by intolerable pain; no sleep, no peace, no rest for the invalid on her bed of suffering where she passed most of her twenty-four hours.

She saw clearly the gravity of her own condition, and with that faith which had been the light and consolation of her life, she prepared herself for the inevitable. She wrote on July 15, 1877, to her sister-in-law: "I have resigned myself to my fate. It is absolutely necessary that I lose nothing of the little time that remains for me to live. These are the days of salvation that will never return; I wish to profit by them."

And to assure herself of the grace of final perseverance, and to give to the end to her family an example of fidelity to religious duties, she dragged herself for the last time, the first Friday in August, to the morning Mass in the parish church. At each step, her breast and neck were pierced as with a dagger. Acute pains in the entire right side obliged her frequently to stop and rest. Nevertheless, she went on and in this condition heard the entire Mass, and drew from the Sacrifice of Calvary renewed on the Altar, courage to meet the last struggle.

The following weeks saw the progressive dissolution of the poor body which collapsed under the action of the implacable disease.

Thoughtful of her daughters to the end, she determined to spare Céline and Thérèse the sight of her pain, and arranged to send them during the day to the home of friends. Thérèse, in the following passage from her Autobiography, gives us her memories of these days:

"All the details of my mother's illness are still fresh in my mind. I remember especially her last weeks on earth, when Céline and I felt like little exiles. Every morning, a friend came to fetch us and we spent the day with her. Once we had not the time to say our prayers before starting and on the way my little sister whispered, 'Must we tell her that we have not said our prayers?' 'Yes,' I answered. So very timidly Céline confided our secret to her and she exclaimed, 'Well, children, you shall say them.' Then she took us to a large room and left us there. Céline looked at me in amazement. I was equally astonished and exclaimed, 'This is not like Mama, she always said our prayers with us.' During the day, in spite of all efforts to amuse us, the thought of our dear mother was constantly in our minds, and I remember that my sister once had an apricot given to her and she leaned towards me and said, 'We will not eat it, I will give it to Mama.' Alas, our beloved mother was much too ill to eat any earthly fruit; she would never more be satisfied but by the glory of heaven. There she would drink the mysterious wine with Jesus at His Last Supper, to share with us in the Kingdom of His Father."

One more day of earthly joy was reserved for the mother. Marie, who had been the tutor of Céline and Thérèse that year, decided that since vacation had come they would have closing exercises at home, just as in the public and private schools. To encourage her sisters, and to distract the mother, a distribution of prizes was arranged. Marie writes to her aunt, "I assure you that it was all very beautiful. The room was ornamented with garlands of roses. The presidents of the august ceremony were Mr. and Mrs. Martin. Yes, my dear aunt, Mama also wished to assist. Céline and Thérèse were dressed in white, and would that you could have seen with what triumphant manner they received the prizes which Papa and Mama distributed."

It was the last smile the family gave to her who was about to leave them. Eight days later she wrote to her brother,

August 16: "My strength is gone. If the Blessed Virgin does not cure me, it is because my time is come, and the good God wishes me to rest with Him in heaven."

On the 26th of the same month, Mrs. Martin was given Holy Viaticum, and Mr. Martin himself, walking before the priest with the Blessed Sacrament, bore the candle from the church to the home into which Our Lord entered to fortify his dying servant for the last journey. Thérèse was present and guessed the coming solemn separation, but believed that her heroic mother, even though she was returning to God, would not entirely abandon her dear little daughter.

Thérèse writes in her Autobiography: "The touching ceremony of Extreme Unction made a deep impression on me. I can still see the place where I knelt, and hear my poor father's sobs."

Mrs. Martin, so well prepared, broke the ties that bound her to earth on August 28, 1877, at midnight. She was 46 years old. Twilight had given place to the dawn! Who can doubt that she went straight to heaven?

Thérèse writes: "The day after her death, my father took me in his arms, and said, 'Come and kiss your dear mother for the last time.' Without saying a word, I put my lips to her icy forehead. I do not remember having cried much, but I did not talk to anyone of all that filled my heart. I looked and listened in silence and I saw many things which they would have hidden from me. Once I found myself close to the coffin in the passage. I stood looking at it for a long time. I had never seen one before, but I knew what it was. I was so small that I had to lift my head to see its full length and it seemed to be very big, and very sad."

After the funeral, the family returned to their home and Thérèse writes: "We were all five together, looking at one another sadly, when our nurse, overcome with emotion, said, turning to Céline and me, 'Poor little dears; you no longer have a mother.' Then Céline threw herself into Marie's arms crying, 'Well, you will be my mother now.' I was so accustomed to imitating Céline that I should have undoubtedly followed her example, but I feared Pauline would be sad, and feel herself left out that she too had not a little daughter, so, with a loving look, I hid my face on her breast, saying in my turn, 'And Pauline will be my mother'."*

The days following the funeral were indeed lonely and sad. The family left the house only once, and then to go to the cemetery. Mr. Martin sold his business and property and determined to move to Lisieux, where Mrs. Martin's brother and sister-in-law, to whom Mrs. Martin had been so attached, might give him and Pauline the benefit of their advice, counsel and help in bringing up the little motherless children. On the following 5th of September, the Martin family moved into the famous Buissonnets at Lisieux, where Thérèse was to find her vocation to the Carmel of Lisieux and there reach the summit of heroic sanctity.

Mrs. Martin's body was later brought to the Lisieux cemetery and she and her husband were buried together there. When I knelt before her tomb, I could not bring myself to pray for her, but rather to her. So, dear reader, do you say a prayer to this holy woman whose life, mirrored in these pages, has, I hope, taught you lessons which it would be superfluous for me to formulate. We may be sure that not only Thérèse, but, her mother are in heaven now and that they are ready and anxious to help all those who wish to imitate them. That they will help all my readers to follow in their footsteps is the author's constant prayer.

---

* The Little Flower's mother had by gesture, as she was dying, indicated her wish that Pauline was to assume the maternal mission from which God was taking her. (Author's Note.)

An Hour with the Little Flower

(Little Flower Series—Number One)

Thérèse as a novice embracing
Our Lord's cross in the Carmel garden.

Chapter One

The Little Flower's Secret of Happiness

"Our hearts were made for Thee, O Lord, and they shall be restless, 'till they rest in Thee."

(St. Augustine)

People are sometimes puzzled by the popularity of the Little Flower and inquire, "Why should this little girl saint attract to herself from all over the world such great multitudes?" Various explanations are given: The charm and sweetness of her life which, like the perfume of roses, cannot be resisted; her unique and attractive promises, "I will spend my heaven doing good upon earth; I will let fall from heaven a shower of roses;" her favors showered so abundantly upon her lovers.

One other explanation of her popularity, I think, is this: Acquaintance with the Little Flower teaches every soul the secret of happiness, and having learned that secret from the words and example of the Little Flower, thousands are full of gratitude to her; they come to love her and loving her, they strive to win for her the love of others, who in turn come to love her and repeat the process, and thus her popularity is, partially at least, explained. Perhaps there are some who have not yet learned from the Little Flower her secret of happiness. Let us, therefore, glance at her life and try to learn that secret.

The Little Flower, as a girl, was no more indifferent to this world's pleasures, no less subject to worldliness and pride and vanity than we are. As a little girl she liked to hear herself praised and to hear her beauty remarked. As a girl she was vain of her pretty dresses, eager for earthly friendships and so proud that once, when her mother offered her a penny if she would humbly kiss the ground, the Little Flower refused to bend.

Yet the Little Flower was not many years old before she learned the emptiness of dress and praise, and of all those things that gave pleasure to her as a mere child. We find her when only ten years of age spending her holidays "thinking," as she said. "Of what do you think?" she was asked, and she answered, "Oh, about God, about the shortness of life and about the length of eternity." She grasped thus early in life this tremendous truth, this secret of happiness, that life is so short and eternity so long that it does not pay to live for the fleeting pleasures of life, but only for the enduring happiness of eternity.

What happened, once she had grasped this truth? This girl so bright, so charming, so beautiful, so talented, so blessed with riches that she could have had the best the world could offer, turned her back upon the world and entered the Carmelite convent; henceforth to live under a rule which is the most severe and austere and rigorous of all the rules of religious orders. She took this step, not because she did not know or appreciate what the world had to offer her and what pleasures were open to her outside the convent, but because she had learned what many of us will never learn until we are on our deathbeds; that mere pleasure in any form will never satisfy the heart of man. She said to herself, "Since this world passes and with it all its cares and anxieties, all its joys and sorrows, all its hopes and wishes; since it passes, and with it all those who dwell therein, whether they have met with its frowns or its smiles, whether they have experienced its evil or its good; since all that concerns me thus passes, what is worth my solicitude here except to love God and labor for eternity." She entered the convent because she was convinced that this world's pleasures cannot give full happiness to any creature and because she was convinced that to be in the close friendship of God is the greatest happiness possible in this world.

Let us briefly demonstrate that the Little Flower was right in her decisions. That worldly pleasures, even though not sinful, cannot satisfy the longings of the human heart is a matter of so common experience that we need not demonstrate it here. Pleasures of every kind pass quickly, and leave a void. Men and women of great wealth and capacity for pleasure are not distinguished for happiness, as you know. Ask any man, who has been a pleasure seeker and a luxury lover and has then turned more completely to God's service in mortification and self-denial; ask such a man when he was happier, in indulging his passion for pleasure or in practicing mortification for the love of God, and he will tell you that there was no solidity, no permanence, no depth to his former pleasures; whereas now he is experiencing the greatest happiness earth can give, namely the consciousness of following closely in the footsteps of Him Who said, "If any man would come after Me, let him take up his cross and follow."

What is true of legitimate pleasure is much more true of sinful pleasure. How many of us are there, who have had to learn by experience, that sinful pleasures bring bitterness, disheartening bitterness, instead of the happiness they promise. Who does not know that an accusing conscience takes all the joy out of the pleasures that stolen money will buy? Who does not know that sins of the flesh, instead of bringing happines, give way very quickly to remorse, and wretchedness, and shame. Such sinful pleasures mean dead innocence, and memories full of bitterness. Oh, we all know from sad experience the bitterness of the consciousness of sin, and never is this bitterness more disheartening than in the case of one who has been serving God well, basking in the sunshine of God's smile, when suddenly, through pride or carelessness, or neglect of prayer, the storm of sin breaks and leaves destruction in its wake. Then the poor soul awakes, and viewing the wreck of its happiness, knows then what it should have known before; that there is no happiness in this world except the consciousness of being in the friendship of God. Oh no, sinful pleasure never yet satisfied the sinner's heart. So we might go down through the list of worldly pleasures and find, not one, nor any combination of them that will satisfy the heart of man. As St. Augustine says, "Our hearts were made for Thee, Oh Lord, and they shall be restless until they rest in Thee."

My dear friends, let us imitate the Little Flower in her correct estimate of the worth, or rather the worthlessness of earthly pleasures. We need not imitate her in leaving the world and entering the convent, but, living in the world, we can imitate her by acting upon the principle that, although worldly pleasures should have a place in our lives, this place is second, not first. God must come first. In our pursuit of worldly pleasure, God must not be neglected.

We can imitate the Little Flower in other ways also. For instance, let us not envy those who are better able to provide themselves with earthly pleasures than we are. They are no happier than we, and in more danger. There is comfort in these thoughts for those who have lost fortune or health; for they have lost but worldly goods. Their misfortune or illness is short, and heaven is before them. Instead of envying the healthy, the wealthy, the pleasure-mad, the successful men and women of the world, the true followers of the Little Flower in imitation of Thérèse are content with what God sends, are not too eager for worldly pleasure because they have learned from her, to use the words of the Novena Prayers, "the difference between the passing things of time and the joys that never end." They have learned "to be dissatisfied with all that ends with time" and to fix their eyes upon heaven in imitation of the Little Flower.

The Little Flower went through life as in her girlhood she passed through the fields, under the stars, in walks which she describes in these words: "I would ask my father to lead me on through the fields under the stars and lifting up my head that I might see nothing of this unlovely world, I would walk on gazing at the starry sky." So she went through life, her eyes fixed upon heaven. So must we go through life, our eyes fixed not upon the passing things of earth, but upon the eternal joys of heaven.

This, thousands have learned from the Little Flower. Thousands seeing the happiness of the Little Flower have learned to seek and find happiness, as she sought and found it, not in pursuing fruitlessly the will-o'-the-wisp of pleasure, but in giving an adequate amount of time and energy to God.

Young men, surrounded by the allurements of a pleasure-mad age have looked at the white, unruffled and lovely brow of the Little Flower and have learned from her to find their happiness in peace and in purity. Young ladies, formerly completely absorbed in the pursuit of passing popularity and of good times, have been caught by the spell of the charm of the Little Flower, and have learned from her to give God more of their time and energy; and they have thus added to their own charm and beauty of character, and increased their own happiness. The afflicted, the sick, the poor, and the unfortunate have learned from her to gaze into eternity and, foreseeing their happiness there, to be content with their earthly lot.

This then is one explanation of the popularity of the Little Flower: She teaches to all who come near her the secret of happiness, namely, to give God first place in our lives, and to subordinate all pleasure seeking to Him. That all of us may learn this secret; learn to give God always, and under all circumstances, first place, is our prayer to the Little Flower this evening. "Continue to send upon the world a shower of roses, the sweetness of whose perfume will draw all souls from the passing things of time to joys that never end.

Compassion and love for our sorrowful Savior radiate from the recollected face of the Little Flower.

Chapter Two

St. Thérèse, Our Guide in Sorrow

"Blessed are they that mourn: for they shall be comforted."
(Matt. 5, 5)

My dear friends, you who are assembled here tonight are lovers of the Little Flower. You are here because you love her, and are devoted to her and wish to honor her, and also because you wish to obtain more favors from her. You have heard that she prophesied and promised that she would spend her heaven doing good upon earth; that she would obtain from Our Lord, and let fall upon earth, a shower of roses, and one or many of these roses you hope to obtain during this Novena. There is one rose in particular which you can all be sure of obtaining from her for the mere asking, a rose which we all need, but a rose which, if not warned, many may forget to ask from her. I intend to advocate tonight the cause of that particular rose which I say we need and ought to ask from the Little Flower, and which I know she will be particularly happy to let fall upon those who ask it of her. The rose of which I speak is a certain virtue for which the Little Flower herself was remarkable. Let us glance at her life and see what this rose of virtue is, to which I refer.

But by way of a preliminary to an examination of her life, permit me to ask a question or two. Have you ever been puzzled by the problem of suffering in the world? Have you ever heard anyone say, or have you said yourself under some trial or sorrow, "Why, why does a good God so afflict His people? What have I done that I should be so afflicted? I have never been a sinner. From my youth I have always kept God's law. Why, then, is God so cruel as to send me illness or poverty or bring disgrace upon my children, or take away my loved ones, my friend, or my wife, my husband or my child, as the case may be? Why does God inflict so cruel a fate upon me? I can understand why He sends these evils to sinners. To sinners these misfortunes come as punishment and as a means of awakening them to conversion. But why does God send physical and mental anguish and heart-break to me who have always been a good Catholic?"

For answer, my dear friends, to these questions, which have perhaps occurred at one time or another to all of you, let us turn to the life of the Little Flower. You know her life; you know her goodness; she never offended God by a single serious sin. We say we are good Catholics, but surely no one of us would presume to claim the virtue of the Little Flower. As good and holy as any one of us may be, she was far more holy and therefore she deserved the most tender treatment from God whom she loved so tenderly and served so faithfully. She deserved well of Him; let us see how He treated her.

From her earliest childhood until the moment of her death He made her life one long, almost uninterrupted pain. Her brief, young life was crowded, simply filled with suffering. Never was a family as intimately and closely bound together by ties of tender affection as were the members of the family of the Little Flower, and yet one by one they were torn apart. One by one, the Little Flower had to part from her loved ones and each parting was like death, each parting almost intolerable to a soul so deeply affectionate as the Little Flower's.

Her first great sorrow, which came when she was but a child of four, was the death of her mother. To appreciate what supreme anguish her mother's death caused the Little Flower it is necessary to read in her life the accounts she herself gives of the close and intimate union that existed between them. She tells us that her mother's death and her father's sobs at the deathbed were ever after as vividly graven upon her memory as if it all had just happened. "After my mother's death," she says, "I was utterly desolate, lonely, and always in tears."

She took her sister Pauline as her second mother, and yet soon this second mother, Pauline, her most intimate friend, was lost also. Pauline left the Little Flower behind and entered Carmel. The Little Flower says of this parting, "O how great was my anguish. I saw that life is made up of sorrows and separations and I wept bitterly, for I did not yet understand the joy of self-sacrifice."

There was also in her childhood much physical pain, and, besides, her every earthly friendship, she says, ended in bitterness. Early in life, after one of her very first Holy Communions, she offered this prayer, "O my Lord, make me look upon all comfort as bitter."

And she tells us that God granted her prayer. How strange it is to us, who are impressed with the beauty and the sweetness of the Little Flower's life, to reflect that there was in that life no comfort, only sorrow.

Before the wounds I have described had time to heal, there came another fresh sorrow, the parting with another sister, Marie, who, since Pauline's departure had been the inseparable companion and confidant of Little Thérèse. Then came to the Little Flower periods of spiritual desolation; then the thwarting of her whole-souled desire to enter Carmel; long, tedious delays and seemingly insurmountable obstacles.

After that came the sad fate that befell her beloved father. Never was a father more dearly loved by a daughter than was Mr. Martin by the Little Flower. And this dearly loved father now met a fate far worse than death. He was stricken with paralysis and not only his body gave way, but also his mind. The anguish of the Little Flower at this sad fate may well be imagined. She tells us that she learned during this trial how Our Lord's sufferings pierced Mary's heart, for even so was she, the Little Flower, pierced by the pains and abasement of him she cherished above all on earth.

Then there came spiritual trials, long stretches of spiritual dryness, a long and cruel dark night of the soul, which was like total abandonment by God. Then there came, towards the end, the physical pains of her last illness, accompanied by a fierce onslaught of temptations against faith. The evil one whispered to her, "Ha, heaven, which has been your one thought and goal all your life, heaven does not exist." A voice kept whispering to her, "God, whom you love so tenderly, does not love you." She tells us that she would not have imagined such torments possible as she suffered from those temptations during her prolonged last illness. Until the end God flooded her soul with pain.

Last night I turned over, rapidly, the pages of her Autobiography to see upon how many pages I would find the words cross, suffering, sorrow, pain, and equivalent words, and I found very few, practically no pages, from which these words were missing. Her life is a record of sorrow. It was sorrow bravely, cheerfully, lovingly borne; it was sorrow which she even sought, but it was sorrow nevertheless.

So that is how God treated His Little Flower, who loved Him so tenderly. He gave her a cross to bear from the cradle to the grave. He repaid her love with pain. He did the same with His Own Blessed Mother, the Mother of Sorrows. He treats all His saints and loved ones similarly, sends them sorrow, pain, separations poverty, sickness, disappointments, misunderstandings, and trials of every description all their lives. Let us not wonder then that we have trials in spite of the fact that we do not sin. Let us not say, "Why does God send such fierce and continued trials to us who have always been good?" It is God's way to send more sorrow to good people than to sinners, and more sorrow to saints than to ordinarily good people.

"But that doesn't explain it," you will object, "to say 'that's God's way.' What I want to know is WHY is that God's way?"

Well, my dear friends, I will give a partial explanation. A complete explanation would keep us too long, and besides, there is, this side of heaven, no really complete explanation of God's dealings with men. Some day in heaven we'll understand.

> "Not now but in the coming years
> We'll read the meaning of our tears.
> We'll know why clouds instead of sun
> Hovered o'er what we had planned
> Why smiles had ceased when just begun
> Some day in heaven we'll understand."

Yes, until we reach heaven we will not completely understand God's plan of sending so much sorrow to good people, but even now we can give this partial explanation: sorrow is necessary in God's plan to keep our thoughts upon heaven and to make us live for the next world. Surely no one here will deny that it is a law of his own life and of the lives of others he has observed, that a man forgets God in prosperity and turns to God in adversity. Sorrows, trials, crosses, make us turn to God and make us lean more heavily upon Him and depend upon Him more absolutely. Sorrow makes us think. It shows us that here we have no lasting city. It gives the lie to those who say that we have our destiny here. It raises our minds to the life above and beyond where there will be no sorrow. We think sometimes in our ignorance and pride that we do not need trials, but God sees in His wisdom that only for the suffering we endure, we would become bewitched by the vain and fleeting pleasures of this life and cast all care of our eternal salvation to the winds. Pain has opened heaven to thousands who otherwise would have been lost. The Little Flower herself realized how much of her holiness she owed to sorrow and trial, for she often exclaims in her Autobiography, "What would have become of me if the world had smiled on me?" Yes, God takes the things of earth from us, takes material goods from us, takes friends and relatives from us, in order that we may find happiness in Him. The great Catholic poet, Francis Thompson, expresses his thought in these lines:

> "All that I took from thee I did but take,
> Not for thy harms,
> But just that thou mightest seek it in My Arms."

That is one reason then for God's way of sending sorrow to those He loves. By sorrow He prevents those He loves from leaving Him, from forgetting Him. By sorrow He keeps those He loves.

There are other reasons that might be given in explanation. We might explain the happy effect of suffering, how it ennobles the sufferer and forms a strong and spiritual character. We might explain in detail the words of St. Ignatius, "God's way in dealing with those whom He intends to admit soonest after death into heaven is to purify them in this world by the greatest afflictions." We might enter into these explanations, but to explain why God sends sorrow to good people is not my purpose tonight. I do not wish to explain but merely to state the fact that God does send sorrow to His friends and this not in punishment but in love, for some good purpose, sometimes discoverable by us and sometimes hidden from us.

Why do I emphasize tonight that fact that God does send sorrow to those who love and serve Him? Because, my dear friends, you who make up this assembly tonight in honor of the Little Flower are not sinners, but good people; you are God's friends and sorrow is therefore going to come to you in greater measure than it comes to many other people. It comes to all, as you know, good or bad, and it comes to so many and in such measure that three-fourths of the world is asking, "Is life worth living?" Suffering in one form or another makes up no small portion of everyone's life, but it will come to you, as God's friends, more abundantly than to others. To know that it is coming, and to make up your minds to it, to face the prospect of sustaining a large measure of pain and trouble in your passage through life, to face that prospect will tend to make you resigned to it. It will not surprise you then when it comes, for you will have faced the prospect all along and so it will neither appall nor overwhelm you. We shall have our cross whether we will or no. The more we resist it the heavier it becomes. No man has such a heavy cross as the one who expects and tries to go through life without a cross. Resignation, patience and the expectation of a cross will make it almost lose its weight. Expect sorrow and you will be better able to bear it, and that is why I have called your attention to its coming.

I have called your attention to it in connection with the sufferings of the Little Flower and of the Blessed Virgin, and of all the saints and friends of God, because you will thus connect your sorrow with theirs, and in this association there is consolation. It is most consoling when trouble comes to remember that God is not punishing you, but treating you as He treated the Little Flower, as He treated His Own Blessed Mother, not punishing but, in His love and wisdom, sending what He knows is best for you. That trial which falls upon you as a cloud is not a cloud but only the shadow of His Hand outstretched caressingly. No sorrow can embitter you; no trial can overwhelm you or make you lose patience and resignation, if you will only have the faith to see that the sorrow, whatever it is, that envelops you like a dark cloud is not in reality a cloud but only the shadow of God's loving Hand outstretched caressingly.

Try to summon the faith that is necessary to look at every sorrow in that way. Faith it is that is necessary to bear sorrow patiently; faith, I mean, in God's providence and goodness, in His wisdom and love, faith that whatever He sends is best. Try to bear ever in mind that nothing happens except by God's permission, that the most apparently cruel sorrows are in reality sent by God in love for the best and eternal interests of all concerned. Father Tabb expresses this truth in the lines:

> "This life is but a weaving between my God and me.
> I do but choose the colors; He weaveth steadily.

Full oft He weaveth sorrow, and I in my foolish pride
Forget He sees the upper, I, the under side."

That is the rose of which I spoke in the beginning, the rose which we should all ask of the Little Flower this evening, the rose of the virtue of expecting and bearing sorrow resignedly and patiently, believing that whatever is, is best.

The Little Flower, who knew so well how to suffer, who had such deep faith in God and God's goodness, who suffered so much and so bravely and cheerfully, that Little Flower is surely the one to get that rose for us from Our Lord. He will not refuse that rose to her. And she who learned so well the value of suffering will not refuse to ask Him for that rose for us.

Let each one not fail then to ask during this Novena for that rose which we all need or may need soon, the rose of bearing sorrow patiently and resignedly. If we ask that much, the Little Flower may of her own accord let fall another rose, the rose of bearing sorrow not only with patience and resignation, but also with love and good cheer. With good cheer, for, after all, what matters a rough road since it leads to the palace of the King? On earth the King's Blessed Mother was the Mother of Sorrows. Now, She is the Queen of Heaven. The Little Flower, whose earthly sufferings we have described, is now basking in the sunshine of the love of all the court of heaven, reunited to her dear ones, experiencing now, in the eternal embrace of Him she loved so well, the delayed reward of her service, a happiness more glorious than she ever dreamed. For Our Lord left us not only the bitter legacy of sorrow but also a magnificent promise: "Blessed are they that mourn for they shall be comforted!" "You shall indeed lament and weep and be made sorrowful, but your sorrow shall be turned into joy and your joy no man shall take from you. For eye hath not seen, nor ear heard nor hath it entered into the heart of man to understand the things that God hath prepared for them that love Him, in that City that is to come."

Chapter Three

The Mighty Promises of the Little Flower

"I shall spend my heaven in doing good upon earth. I shall let fall from heaven a shower of roses."

(Words of the Little Flower.)

We have learned that there are many making this novena who never made a novena to the Little Flower before, and it has also been brought to our attention that at every novena service there are many non-Catholics in attendance. It will not be inappropriate then this evening to sketch the life of the Little Flower and the history of devotion to her. Even those who are very familiar with her life will not find this repetition irksome, for the Little Flower's story is to adults what fairy tales are to children—perennially interesting and fascinating, no matter how often repeated. Indeed, there is something of the fairy tale about the history of the Little Flower. There is so much that is unusual and marvelous about it; it is so full of wonder, as we shall see.

The Little Flower's name in the world was Marie Thérèse François Martin. When she entered Carmel, she took the name of Sister Thérèse of the Child Jesus and of the Holy Face, but she is known everywhere as the Little Flower, the name which in humility she gave to herself, for she looked upon herself not as a great captain in God's army, not as a stalwart oak in God's kingdom, but as a simple, humble, little flower in God's garden.

Although it is certainly true that the Little Flower is the best known woman of modern times, her life may be told in a single sentence. The lives of the great men and women of this world may not be told in a sentence but the life of the Little Flower may be told just that briefly and here is the sentence: She was born in 1873 in Alençon in France, and at the age of fifteen she entered a Carmelite convent, where she died at the age of 24, in 1897. How apparently insignificant and unimportant is that life which may be so briefly sketched. She worked no miracles; she never was in the public eye; there was nothing remarkable about her life except her mighty prophecies, "I will spend my heaven doing good upon earth. I will let fall a shower of roses." These prophecies she repeated constantly and confidently. She was certain of their fulfillment.

Suppose that some free thinker heard of these promises during the Little Flower's lifetime; suppose that someone had said to some skeptic of France, "There is a nun in Normandy, in a cloistered convent, who maintains that her work will begin after her death; that after her death she will become known everywhere—draw thousands of souls to God by spending her heaven doing good upon earth?" What would this unbeliever have said? He would have maintained that she was suffering from delusions. He would have predicted, "She will never be known five miles from her convent."

Yet how wonderfully her promises have already been fulfilled. She has been dead but twenty-eight years and yet she is the most widely known and best beloved woman of modern times. She would be scarcely fifty years old if she were alive today and yet she is a saint, canonized, as we now understand canonization, sooner after death than any other saint in the history of the Church. She is dead only a few years and yet she has already become the best beloved of the saints and devotion to her is more widespread than devotion to any other saint excepting the members of the Holy Family. Thérèse Martin, who was born so obscurely and lived so hidden a life, who died at the age of twenty-four, when most people are beginning their life work, nevertheless foreknew and prophesied that after her death her work would begin; that after her death she would draw thousands of souls to God. And lo, already the whole world is running after her; her pictures look down from the walls of millions of homes; thousands of hearts are raised to her every day in prayer. The Holy Father himself deigns to honor her with the very first canonization of the Holy Year. The great Cathedral of St. Peter was illuminated for the first time since 1870 with sixty thousand torches, in her honor, on the day of her canonization. Her roses are let fall everywhere; roses of grace and healing. She numbers among her lovers the Holy Father himself, bishops, priests, nuns, young men and young women; people of all ages and conditions of life-children. She lived and died in obscurity, yet she has in a few short years captured the hearts and captivated the affections of the entire world.

What would the Little Flower have said if it had been prophesied to her, while she was alive, that only twenty-eight years after her death the Holy Father, moving amid scenes of surpassing splendor, would solemnly enroll her name on the registers of the saints? Would she have been surprised? I think not. She would have smiled in her simple way and have said, "Yes, God will make me known just that soon in order that my work may better be accomplished, my work of bringing thousands of little souls to Him." She would not have been surprised if it were prophesied to her that she, who in life was not known five miles from her convent, should in death be honored thousands of miles from her birthplace; honored by so many thousands, who every Tuesday crowd the Chicago Carmelite Church in which her American National Shrine is situated, that the attention of the whole city is attracted and even non-Catholics frequently stop us on the streets near the church and ask: "Father, may non-Catholics go in to see Little Thérèse?"

Yes, the popularity of the Little Flower is one of the wonders of modern times. It is a standing marvel that the girl who never lifted her finger to become known should in so few years have won over the world, and this according to her own promise made with miraculous foresight.

What explains her popularity? First, God's will. God saw that the modern world was buried in pride, prayerlessness and immorality. Accordingly, He sent to that world a messenger, the Little Flower, and her message was the necessity of prayer; the worth of humility; the beauty of purity. Since the Little Flower was the embodiment of these virtues, God provided, in His providence, that she, His messenger, should become known so soon. The spread of her devotion is God's will. That is one explanation of her popularity.

Her popularity is explained also by the fulfillment of her promises. Everyone who practices habitual devotion to the Little Flower has experienced the marvelous power of her intercession. She has indeed kept her promise of "doing good upon earth," of "letting fall from heaven a shower of roses"; roses of every kind of material and spiritual favors. Five volumes have already been written called "The Shower of Roses," each one containing account after account of marvelous favors attributed to the intercession of the Little Flower. A constant stream of acknowledgments of favors received by the members of the Society of the Little Flower pours into the central offices of the Society in Chicago daily.*

How may we win the favor of this "wonder-worker of our own time"? First, by laboring to make her better known. She has revealed that the surest way to her favor, the chief means of securing her roses, is to labor to make her better known, in order that she may deliver her message to souls who do not

---

* Those who wish information concerning conditions for membership in the Society of the Little Flower, united with the Confraternity of the Scapular, should write the National Headquarters, Carmelite Monastery, 6401-6413 Dante Ave., Chicago, Ill. 60637

now know her. We may win her favor secondly by imitating her virtues. It is inconceivable that the Little Flower would bestow her favors indiscriminately upon all who come to her, independently of their state of soul. It is absurd to think that she would grant her favors as readily to those who come to her in a state of unrepented sin as to those who are in the friendship of God. No doubt God has given her the gift of miracles, not for her own sake, but for His. His purpose is to attract attention to her, His messenger, in order that she may deliver His message, the message of the possibility of happiness in goodness; the message of the necessity of prayer and humility, the message of the beauty of purity and of the possibility of intimate friendship with God.

The conclusion from all this, my dear friends, is that those who accept this message of the Little Flower and try to become, like her, pure, humble, prayerful and little in God's sight, are the ones most likely to receive favors from her. Let us look upon the Little Flower then as God's messenger and let us accept her message. Let us make the resolutions that are suggested by the thoughts presented this evening and we will thereby become worthy to receive the roses that she lets fall from heaven with the lavishness of a queen.

The coat of arms of Jesus and Thérèse.

Chapter Four

Comfort for Sinners from the Life of St. Thérèse

"Fear makes me shrink and benumbs me; my way is not the way of fear. The Lord is good and His Mercy endureth forever and ever, and it is my special mission to glorify His infinite Mercy."

(Words of the Little Flower)

The subject which has been chosen for tonight's sermon is: "Comfort for Sinners from the Life of the Little Flower." This subject seems very strange; it would appear at first thought that there is no comfort for sinners in the sinless life of the sinless Little Flower. And yet there is a very great abundance of comfort for sinners in the Life of the Little Flower, as we shall see.

One of the difficulties felt frequently by those who wish to serve God well is the memory of their past sins. This consciousness of their past unfaithfulness is an obstacle to their spiritual growth and advancement; it acts as a barrier between them and God; it prevents them from coming close to God. Such souls lack confidence in God.

Time and again, both in and out of the confessional, we meet sinners who cannot be convinced that God will or can forgive them their sins. These souls also lack confidence in God.

Now it is precisely for her confidence in God that the Little Flower was most remarkable. There are some saints who were struck by the justice of God, who were almost overwhelmed by the thought of God's justice, by the thought of the rigorous judgment to which they would be subjected by God. Their way was the way of fear. Not so with the Little Flower. She tells us repeatedly that her way is not the way of fear, but the way of love, the way of confidence. "Fear makes me shrink and benumbs me," she says; "my way is not the way of fear—only with love can I go—and not only go, but fly forward on my way." In her Autobiography the Little Flower expressly undertakes to teach others—yes, to teach sinners—to have as much confidence in God as she had.

Hence, since it is confidence in God that sinners lack when the memory of their past or present sin keeps them from God, and since it was confidence in God that the Little Flower practiced and preached all her life, we make the claim that there is an abundance of comfort for sinners in the life of the Little Flower. If we can only catch a little of her confidence, if we can learn tonight from the Little Flower the secret of her confidence in God, then never again will the memory of our sins act as a barrier between us and God.

Let us then examine the words of our little saint and learn from her that, no matter how numerous or serious our sins have been, we can and should have confidence in God.

In the account of the Little Flower's virtues as presented to the Holy Father in petition for her beatification, the virtue of confidence in God is the very first of her virtues mentioned. There are few pages in her Autobiography in which there is not some reference to the mercy of God, some very beautiful and poetic thought about God's mercy, some very striking way of impressing us with the mercy of God. But before we quote any of these passages let us remove a possible objection that might be in the minds of some. Some might say, "What is the use of emphasizing, for the comfort of sinners, the Little Flower's confidence in God; I too could approach God with confidence if I were sinless; her sinlessness is the secret of her confidence."

But no, my dear friends, the Little Flower expressly tells us that her sinlessness was not the secret nor the foundation of her confidence. These are her words, "If I draw nigh to God with love and trust, it is not because I have kept from mortal sin. Were my conscience laden with every imaginable crime, I would not have one whit less confidence; heart-broken and repentant, I would throw myself into my Saviour's Arms. He loves the prodigal son; I know His words addressed to Magdalen, to the adulterous woman, and to her of Samaria. Who could make me afraid? I know His mercy and His love; I know that once I had thrown myself in His arms all my numberless sins would disappear in an instant like drops of water cast into a furnace."

What great consolation is there in this passage for us poor sinners! The Little Flower would have not one whit less confidence, she says, if she were guilty of every imaginable sin; she would not be afraid. Do not hesitate, she tells us, on account of your sins, to come close to God; just be sorry and throw yourselves in His arms; trust in His mercy and at that moment all your sins will disappear like a drop of water cast into a furnace.

Oh, now that the Little Flower has told us that it is not because she was free from sin that she trusted in God so confidently; now that she has told us that she would have had equal trust in Him if she were like us, sinful; now we are more ready to listen to her beautiful thoughts, which all of us may make our own, about the mercy of God.

In a very remarkable passage freighted with consolation for sinners the Little Flower discusses the justice of God. She tells us, "I know that God is just and that His justice affrights many souls, but, instead of frightening me, His justice gives me joy and confidence." Then she explains: "Because to be just means not only to show severity towards the guilty, but also to recognize our good intentions and our weakness. It gives me joy to think that God is just, because that means that He knows all our weaknesses and all the frailty of our nature and takes them into account."

What could be more comforting to sinners than to remember these words of the Little Flower just quoted, to remember that God's justice will not be exercised exclusively in meting out punishment for our sins, but also in making allowances for our weakness and frailty and good intentions? What could be better calculated to cure despair and to bring to the sinner hope and comfort than this wonderful thought of the Little Flower's that even God's Justice, to say nothing of His Mercy, will lead Him to make allowance for our frailty?

In another passage the Little Flower says that she found by experience the futility of trying to hurry matters in dealing with some souls; "For I have learned," she says, "that there are some souls for whom God waits with patient mercy, giving them light and strength by degrees." Maybe there is a soul here tonight who has almost surrendered to despair on account of repeated failure to progress, but who will be comforted and inspired to hope by this thought that perhaps "God is waiting for him with patient mercy, giving His light and strength by degrees."

Another passage full of consolation for sinners is one in which she tells the story of being given a task which she judged was beyond her strength. What was her course? She says, "I took refuge in God like a frightened child that hides its head on its father's shoulder and I begged Him to do the work while I remained in His arms." The task was easily accomplished, she said, "But had I done otherwise, had I confided in my own strength, I should have lost the battle." Again what a lesson is here for us when we are frightened by the strength of our passions and by the weakness of our resolution; we need only fly to Our Lord, make ourselves little, beg Him to fight for us and all will be well.

Then the Little Flower goes on to elaborate the sureness of this expedient of making oneself little and flying to the arms of Jesus like a frightened child to a good father. "Oh, Jesus," she says, "if only I could make known Thy wonderful condescension to all little souls. If Thou shouldst find a soul however poorer and weaker than mine who was willing to surrender itself to You as I have described, Thou wouldst load that soul with more stupendous favors than Thou hast given me." The Little Flower had all of us, yes, even the worst of us, in mind when she penned these words. If we will but surrender without reserve to God, if we will make ourselves little and fly to Him and beg Him to work for us, God will load even the weakest of us with favors as great or greater, says the Little Flower, than those He conferred upon her.

The Little Flower, in her Autobiography, asks, "What good earthly friend would refuse to forgive you, no matter what had been your offense, if you could whisper to him your heart-broken sorrow?" Would you have it in your heart to refuse to forgive one who had offended you, if he came to you humbly begging forgiveness and confidently relying on your merciful goodness? What mother would reject her son coming to her sobbing his repentance? And do you think, she says, that you, or any earthly father or mother is more kind, more tender, more merciful than Almighty God? Will God be outdone in mercy by any of His creatures? Do you not know that God is infinitely more good and merciful and kind than you, or any earthly friend or mother or father?"

Again the Little Flower, in one of the most beautiful passages of her Autobiography, compares the sinner to a baby trying to climb a stairs, and she compares God to the baby's father watching his baby's efforts from the head of the stairs. The baby tries and falls back, tries again and slips back again, and the father watches pityingly, but the moment the baby realizes its helplessness and reaches out its arms for the father's help, the father descends with all speed and takes the babe in his arms and they mount together the impossible stairs. So, too, we sinners need only hold out our arms to God, making ourselves little and humbly acknowledging our helplessness and God will come down to us, take us in His arms and we will mount together any stairs, no matter how impossible. An earthly mother never loves her child more, says the Little Flower, than when after some fault the child flies in tears to the mother's arms for forgiveness. So God never loves us better than when we, like helpless little children, go to His arms confidently relying on His goodness and mercy.

We could go on indefinitely giving from the Autobiography of the Little Flower one passage after another in which she expresses in poetic language and beautiful comparisons the mercy and goodness of God, mercy so boundless that no sinner need fear to approach Him confidently; goodness so stupendous that no sinner need despair of becoming a great saint.

But enough has been said to send home our point that there is an abundance of consolation for sinners in the sinless life of the sinless Little Flower. We have seen tonight in quick succession a series of pictures presented to us by the Little Flower; a picture of Mary Magdalen and of the prodigal son; a picture of a child in its mother's arms sobbing for forgiveness knowing full well that she is already forgiven; a picture of a frightened child hiding its head on its father's shoulder and whispering its fear; a picture of a baby being taken from the stairs into its father's arms—pictures all of them, of the sinner, humble and little and repentant, and on the other hand of Almighty God, kind and gentle and good and merciful. God is represented to us thus by the Little Flower to teach us that we must not fear to go to Him; to teach us where our place is, namely, in His arms, not sulking in the distance, afraid of Him, denying, by our fear, His goodness and mercy, but confessing, by our confidence, His love. That is our place—in God's arms—and there we must remain, conscious ever of our weakness. As long as we remain there whispering our helplessness, acknowledging our weakness, so long will we be safe and secure from any onslaught of temptation. But if we "grow up," that is, if we become, not little, but big, independent, relying on our own strength, forgetting to tell Him in prayer of our need of Him, if we thus "grow up," we will become too proudly heavy even for God's arms and He will let us try our proud strength and we will fall.

But please God, we will not forget our weakness. Remembering our frailty we will, for that very reason, rely on the strength of God our Father, and going into His arms we will remain there always.

Let us ask the Little Flower tonight for that rose, the rose of unfailing and unforgetting confidence in and reliance upon God. Let us ask her to let fall from heaven this rose, this little rose, of becoming and remaining little enough to go to and stay in the arms of Our Lord. Thus, just as the Little Flower, little enough on earth to remain in God's arms, is now the playmate of the angels; so we, likewise, little enough to remain ever in God's arms, will one day be found with the Little Flower in the "nurseries of heaven."

The assembled sisters of Lisieux.

Chapter Five

The Little Flower's Love of Our Lady of Mt. Carmel

"Were I Queen of Heaven and Thou Thérèse, I would still wish to be Thérèse that I might see thee Queen of Heaven."
                        (Words of the Little Flower)

As you all know, today, the feast of Our Lady of Mount Carmel, is one of the greatest feasts in the Carmelite calendar.[*] It was therefore one of the greatest feasts in the convent life of the Little Flower. It is called the "Scapular Feast" because on this day the Church celebrates Mary's bestowal upon the world of the brown scapular, which forms part of the holy habit of all Carmelite priests and nuns. The story of that scapular which the Little Flower as a girl, before she was permitted to enter Carmel, so ardently longed to wear, which she so often kissed, in which she lived and in which she died; the story of that scapular has been told so often during this novena that we need but sketch it today.

In the thirteenth century, the Carmelite Order, the oldest of all the orders and the first to be dedicated to the Blessed Virgin, was being persecuted in Europe. St. Simon Stock, the General of the Order, had long prayed to the Blessed Virgin for some sign of her approval of the Order dedicated to her. Finally the Blessed Virgin appeared at St. Simon, and holding

---

[*] This sermon was preached on the Feast of Our Lady of Mt. Carmel, the closing day of the third of the five Solemn Novenas held in Chicago at the American National Shrine each year in honor of the Little Flower.

out the brown scapular, said to him: "This is the privilege I give to you and to all Carmelites: Whosoever shall die wearing this scapular shall never suffer the pains of Hell." Catholics ever since, in spite of scoffers, trust confidently that the Blessed Virgin will keep her promise. Catholics know that there is no power in the cloth itself, but they do know that it is Mary's badge, Mary's uniform given by herself to men, and that Mary, according to her promise, would never allow any one to lose his soul who has sufficient trust in her, sufficient faith in her, sufficient love for her to wear her uniform day and night at all times and under all circumstances until death calls.

That scapular has been worn, ever since it was given, by all devout clients of the Blessed Virgin. It was worn by the Little Flower and she loved it well, loved it as Mary's badge, as Mary's uniform. O, we haven't time today, with such crowds waiting outside, to speak adequately of the Little Flower's devotion to Mary and of Mary's love for the Little Flower. Just let us recall again that Mary smiled on her at the very dawn of her life; that of all the orders, the Little Flower chose to enter the Carmelite Order, the Order of Our Lady of Mount Carmel. Just let us recall those beautiful and poetic words of the Little Flower which so nicely express her burning love of the Queen of Heaven: "Were I Queen of Heaven and Thou Thérèse, I would still wish to be Thérèse that I might see thee Queen of Heaven."

A portion of the love of the Little Flower for our Blessed Mother may be experienced, and is experienced, I think, by every devout Catholic. There comes a time in every devout Catholic's life when his devotion to the Blessed Virgin suddenly develops into a very real, very personal, very close intimacy with the Blessed Virgin never before experienced. Up to this point he has said daily prayers to the Blessed Virgin, has had frequent recourse to her, especially in emergencies, but those prayers had about them a certain formality and coldness. They were motivated more by duty than by love. But suddenly and unaccountably, the Queen of Heaven seems to come very close to him. He realizes, with a depth of conviction never before experienced, that she is in very truth his Mother; that she has for him all a mother's care and solicitude and love. He finds himself thinking of her not as one far removed from him, away off on her throne in heaven, but as one near to him, as a companion; he begins to speak to her more often, as one would to a companion. His faith in her develops to such an extent that he knows, although he has been given no new evidence, that he is indeed a child of Mary and she his Mother, and that he is being guarded in a very special way by her. He begins to depend more absolutely upon her. He relies less and less upon his own strength and more and more upon hers. He can almost feel the protecting mantle of Mary about him and thus a new feeling of strength and security takes possession of him; he does not dread the future so much now, because somehow his strength feels the strength of two. It is as if the veil of the other world had been lifted, as if he could see his Blessed Mother walking with him on the road of life clasping his hand in hers, and he knows now that there never will be any danger that he will stray to the left or to the right with her as his guide and protector. With this new conviction there comes a great gratitude and a great love for the Blessed Virgin; his devotion to her becomes an intense and loving personal attachment of a son for a mother, and every morning he greets her and recommends himself to her almost as soon as he has opened his eyes. Throughout the day there are many loving ejaculations to her, and in the evening there is always a deeply affectionate prayer of thanksgiving to her that another day has been spent for God and in God's friendship. Thus his devotion to her brings both a new beauty and a new security into his life and he wonders why his devotion to Mary was not as personal and intimate before.

That is a description of what devotion to Mary may become in the average Catholic. What then must have been the Little Flower's devotion to Mary? How much more intimate and beautiful and loving and trustful must have been her devotion to Mary! The answer to these questions must be left to your imagination.

Today let us rather ask what happiness devotion to Mary has brought the Little Flower in heaven. We know that the Little Flower's greatest joy in heaven is union with God, the Beatific Vision, the love of Our Lord; but just second to that happiness, union with Mary is her greatest joy. Oh, what must it mean to the Little Flower to see and be with Mary to whose order she belonged, whose habit she wore, whose features she so often tried to picture! What a joy it must be to that ardent soul of the Little Flower to enjoy the perpetual companionship of the Queen of Heaven! What love our Blessed Mother must be bestowing upon the Little Flower! No fond earthly mother ever hung over her firstborn with the tenderness like unto that with which Mary bends in heaven to Thérèse. The smile Mary gave to the Little Flower when Thérèse was a girl is only a faint representation of the smile which our Blessed Lady continually bestows upon the Little Flower now in heaven. The Little Flower is continually basking, I am sure, in the smile of Our Lady of Mount Carmel; she is ever near the throne of the Queen persuading the Queen to go with her whenever, in her childlikeness, she goes to visit the nurseries of heaven, where the Little Flower in her littleness and our Blessed Mother in her Queenly graciousness are ever at home among the little ones of heaven.

I wonder what the Little Flower is doing in heaven today, the first Feast of Our Lady of Mount Carmel since her canonization? We can imagine Our Lady sitting upon her throne in heaven at the right hand of Our Lord of His throne, and we can imagine the Little Flower sitting beside them, sitting at their feet, kissing ever and anon Our Lady's brown scapular which Mary has let fall lovingly over the Little Flower's shoulder. All three of these heavenly personages are gazing down today upon the ceremonies taking place in every Carmelite convent and every Carmelite monastery and church the world over. I can see the Little Flower in an ecstasy of happiness clapping her hands in joy, like the child she always was and is, as she sees the thousands celebrating the scapular Feast, the feast of Our Lady of Mount Carmel; as she sees the thousands gathered here and there and everywhere, all wearing Mary's badge, the scapular, all expressing their love today for Mary and Mary's livery. I can imagine her particularly happy to see the thousands here in this American National Shrine in a Carmelite church so far from her convent home. Then I can see Our Lord stooping to say to the Little Flower, "Since this is the first feast of Our Lady since your canonization, ask Me what you will and I will grant it to you," and I can see the Little Flower hesitating and then reaching up to whisper to Mary, who stoops to listen. Our Lady nods her head in approval at the words of the Little Flower who then turns to Our Lord to say, "O my dear Lord, this is not my feast, but the feast of Our Lady and so this is the boon I'll ask; a boon which the Queen approves; a boon not for me but for her: Let all those thousands who visit my shrines today in all countries learn this day to love Mary more and to value her scapular more highly."

That is exactly the boon which the Little Flower has already conferred upon us, upon all who made this novena; she has brought us closer to Mary. See how here, in this Carmelite sanctuary, she has kept her promise of letting fall her roses, roses of greater devotion to Mary, roses of greater knowledge of and greater love of the Blessed Virgin. Thousands during these nine days have learned what they did not know before, the close connection between the Little Flower and the scapular and Our Lady of Mount Carmel, and having gained this knowledge, thousands have resolved to imitate the Little Flower more closely in her love of Mary and in her devotion to the brown scapular of Mary. All this is the Little Flower's work. Every resolution, every confession and Holy Communion of this novena, is her work. What a marvelous fulfillment of her promise, "My work begins after my death; I will spend my heaven doing good upon earth."

The Little Flower is very near to Mary today, and therefore let us ask her for many of her roses, but for this rose especially, greater care never to be without the scapular and greater devotion to Mary; a devotion constant and ardent enough to lead us one day to heaven where the Little Flower today is enjoying the loving smile of heaven's Queen, Our Lady of Mount Carmel.

Chapter Six

Lovers of Thérèse Love Mary

"O Cherished Mother, I think that I am more fortunate than you, for I have you for Mother and you have not, like me, Mary to love."

(Words of the Little Flower)

In the midst of the world-wide chorus of approbation of devotion to the Little Flower there are discernible a few feeble but jarring notes of discord. Some of the members of our Society have come to us lately and requested that we solve, from the pulpit, this objection which had been proposed to them: "Devotion to the Little Flower involves neglect of the Blessed Virgin." At first we were disinclined to think that there was any need of considering this objection as serious. But there is danger that good people might be confused by this objection and therefore we shall answer it publicly today.

It is difficult to answer with moderation this charge, because it touches the honor of the little saint whom we all love so well, and because it is hard to understand how devotion to her could be so misunderstood. Certainly those who made this objection never attended these devotions; certainly they know little of the Little Flower and less of Catholic teaching; for it is not Catholic doctrine, as you all know, that devotion to the Mother of God requires that we pray only to her and not to the saints. We shall try, however, to be temperate in our condemnation of the authors of this objection and shall try to turn the objection to good account by making it serve to enforce our knowledge of the Little Flower and of her devotion to the Blessed Virgin.

It is said that devotion to the Little Flower involves neglect of the Mother of God. For answer, let us turn to the novena prayers just recited. There we find in the prayer that precedes the Litany of the Little Flower these words: "O Little Thérèse of the Child Jesus, make our troubles thine own and intercede for us to Our Lady Immaculate, whose flower of special love thou wert, to that Queen of Heaven who smiled on thee at the dawn of life. Beg her as Queen of the Heart of Jesus to obtain for us the grace we yearn for so ardently." So, instead of neglecting our Blessed Mother, we, who participate in these Little Flower novena exercises, turn, at the very climax of the novena prayers, to the Blessed Mother and ask her to sponsor the petitions of the Little Flower.

Two of the five annual solemn novenas of nine consecutive days in honor of the Little Flower have a relation to Mary, the one in May, Mary's month, and the one in July preceding the feast of Our Lady of Mt. Carmel. During this latter novena, one part of each service is held at the shrine of the Little Flower, the other at the altar of our Blessed Mother.

Again, what of the sermons here every Tuesday? How few of them contain no reference to the Blessed Virgin! How few of them contain no illustration of the Little Flower's love of the Mother of God! Who of you has not heard that the Little Flower's chief devotion, after devotion to Our Lord, was devotion to His Blessed Mother? Who of you, who attend these devotions regularly, is not familiar with Mary's smile upon the Little Flower during the latter's childhood? Who of you does not know that it was on account of her love of Mary that the Little Flower entered the Carmelite Order which was the first order to be dedicated to the Blessed Virgin? Who of the members of our Society is not familiar with these words of which the Little Flower was the author; words amongst the most beautiful ever penned concerning the Blessed Virgin: "Were I Queen of Heaven and Thou, Thérèse, I would still wish to be Thérèse that I might see thee Queen of Heaven." Could there be love of Mary more tender than that which prompted the beautiful words just quoted, or these other words which she wrote in a letter to Céline, "Sometimes I find myself saying to the Blessed Virgin, 'O Cherished Mother, I think that I am more fortunate than you, for I have you for Mother and you have not, like me, Mary to love.' "

All these points, the time of the solemn novenas, the character of our devotions, the place given to Mary in the novena prayers and in sermons—all these points make it self-evident that devotion to the Little Flower does not involve neglect of Mary. Charity does not forbid us to wish that the authors of this objection might attend these devotions before they utter criticisms of something of which they seem to know little. Charity does not forbid us to wish that they might familiarize themselves with the life of the Little Flower before they misinterpret our little saint by accusing her of diverting souls from the Blessed Virgin. The Little Flower leads souls to God, leads them to God through His Blessed Mother. No one who really loves the Little Flower can help but love Mary also, and the more we know of the Little Flower and the more we love her, the greater shall be our love for the Blessed Virgin.

May our Blessed Mother enlighten all who do not understand this fact. May she show them that she could not be displeased, could not be other than greatly pleased, at the honor paid to Thérèse, who is her latest daughter of Carmel to be sainted; Thérèse, who loved her so tenderly, Thérèse, who, we may well imagine, has not ceased since she entered heaven to gaze lovingly into the countenance of heaven's Queen, Our Lady of Mount Carmel.

Some of you may have heard other objections similar to the one just answered. It is sometimes hinted that devotion to the Little Flower has not complete ecclesiastical approbation. It is claimed that it is a novelty which will soon wear out. It is asserted that devotion to the older saints is just as good. Let us answer these objections also.

"Devotion to the older saints is just as good." Of course devotion to the other saints is good. No one of us should, no one of us does, cease to be devout to the other saints because of devotion to the Little Flower. No one of us is advised to give up devotion to the older saints. But that the older saints of the sixteenth, seventeenth, eighteenth, and earlier centuries are offended at or jealous of devotion to the little saint raised up by God in the twentieth century is utterly ridiculous. We must remember that no matter who it is that seeks to discredit devotion to the Little Flower, his words have no shadow of authority, for the Little Flower devotion has for it the highest authority on earth the approbation of the Holy Father. And if that be not sufficient, it has for it also the approval of Almighty God, for God has given to the Little Flower the gift of miracles, and miracles are letters of recommendation which God gives to His messengers to men.

The Holy Father not only raised the Little Flower to sainthood, but he went out of his way to give her the very first canonization of the Holy Year. He not only approves devotion to her, not only recommends it, but positively calls upon the faithful to be devout to the Little Flower and to imitate her. These are the words of the present Holy Father: "There is a call to the faithful of every nation, age, sex, and condition of life to follow the little way which led St. Thérèse of the Child Jesus to the very summit of heroic virtue." Once the Holy Father has spoken, the words of no one else count. Those who are more solicitous than the Holy Father for the honor of the older saints could easily find in papal utterances what would induce them to become lovers of the Little Flower.

It remains to be seen whether devotion to the Little Flower is a novelty which will soon wear out. The Little Flower says no; she says that she will continue to do good upon earth until time shall be no more. She says, "I shall not rest until the Angel shall have announced, 'Time is no more.' Then only shall I rest and rejoice when the number of the elect shall have been complete."

Let us say a prayer this evening to the Little Flower for those few who do not yet understand her little way, for those few who seem to be actuated by a strange hostility toward our beloved little saint. The Little Flower deserves no enemies. She would have no enemies if all were intimately acquainted with her. She will have no enemies; her enemies will become her friends, if we by prayer and counsel can persuade them to read with open minds the irresistible life of the most irresistible and lovable of all our lately-canonized saints, the Little Flower.

Saint Thérèse prayer card.

Chapter Seven

The Veneration of the Little Flower

"If I shall touch only His garment, I shall be healed."
(Matt. 9, 21.)

Since we so often venerate the relics of the Little Flower as a part of our devotions, a word about relics and their veneration will not, I think, be inappropriate this evening.

Let us try to imagine some scoffer witnessing the close of the Little Flower devotions here, crowds of people pressing to the front of the church to kiss the relic of the Little Flower. What would that scoffer say or think? "What nonsense," he would say, "what absolute superstition, to think that there is any virtue or power in that small piece of bone of a dead nun! What idolatry! Who can deny, after witnessing this scene, that Catholics are what they are so often called, unthinking, over-credulous, superstitious idolators, hopelessly behind the times?"

I wonder how many could answer this scoffer's objections. I hope that everyone present is sufficiently well instructed in his faith to be able to answer, if he were asked, "Why do you kiss that relic; what is the teaching of the Church concerning relics; why is the veneration of relics not a superstitious, but a reasonable, intelligent practice of which no modern thinking Catholic need be ashamed, but of which he may rather be proud?"

Lest there be some who are not thoroughly intelligent in their practice of venerating the relic, let us explain briefly the Catholic doctrine concerning relics and their veneration.

The word "relic" means something which remains, that which is left, and therefore some part of the body or clothes remaining as a memorial of a departed saint. Our relic is a piece of the rib of the Little Flower.

Now, in the first place, the Church emphatically does not teach, nor does any intelligent Catholic believe that there is any magic power or physical curative efficacy residing in the relic itself. There is no power intrinsic to any relic. There is no virtue whatsoever inherent in any bone or part of the bone of any saint. So much for that erroneous interpretation of our practice of venerating relics.

Secondly, notice, my dear friends, that we use the expression "venerate relics." We do not adore them, we do not worship them; that would be idolatry. We venerate them, that is, we honor them; we honor relics with a veneration which, though it is bestowed on material objects such as bones, ashes or garments, does not rest in these material objects, but goes beyond them to the saints they commemorate. When we honor a relic we are in addition, and chiefly, honoring the saint whose relic is concerned.

What practice could be more reasonable and intelligent than to honor the relics of the saints? It is an impulse that is common to all men to hold in honor everything that is intimately connected with the person whom they love or esteem. If Catholics are to be condemned for honoring the relics of the saints, then must he also be condemned as superstitious and unintelligent who preserves a lock of the hair of his beloved mother long since dead. So must they be condemned as superstitious who look with awe upon the sword of Washington or upon the pen with which Lincoln signed the act which freed the slaves. So must they be condemned who preserve and honor the actual handwriting of General Grant in his monument on Riverside Drive in New York City, or who preserve the home of Shakespeare and the letters of Longfellow. If there is nothing superstitious in preserving and honoring the homes and handwriting and the weapons of great men, how much less superstitious is it to honor, not so much the home or the handwriting, but part of the very body of one who is especially dear to God; part of the body that was once the temple of the Holy Ghost and which will one day be raised up unto the likeness of Jesus into heaven where the spirit that once inhabited that body now dwells.

Ashamed of such a practice? On the contrary, we are proud and happy that we have such a memento of the Little Flower to honor. We all love her and there are those of us who love her much and who in venerating the relic give expression to their ardent love of her who has let fall upon them a shower of roses. As we present the relic at each service to the people, we say to ourselves, as every once in a while some lover of the Little Flower kisses the relic with more than usual fervor, "There is a soul who has been touched by the beauty and sweetness of the life of the Little Flower; whose heart has been moved to great gratitude by the favors of the Little Flower. There is a soul to whom the Little Flower is a friend and a companion." No superstition there; no, only love, love for the dear little saint of our own times who has done so much for us all.

In conclusion let me say that although we do not believe that relics have any inherent or indwelling magical power or curative efficacy, yet we do know that God, in response to prayerful veneration of relics, has often chosen to make those relics the instruments of miracles of grace and healing. The Gospel of Saint Matthew relates an instance of Our Lord's use of a material thing, His garment, to work a miracle of healing: "And behold a woman who was troubled with an issue of blood twelve years, came behind Him, and touched the hem of His garment. For she said within herself: 'If I shall touch only His garment I shall be healed.' But Jesus turning and seeing her, said: 'Be of good heart, daughter, thy faith hath made thee whole.' And the woman was made whole from that hour." (Matt. 9; 20-22.) We hope for such graces when we kiss the relic and our hope is not a superstitious, but an intelligent one, because what wonder if God who answers prayer should choose, as His instrument of answer to prayer, the revered memorial of the body of her who on earth lived only for Him and gave Him naught but love. In the new Little Flower Bulletin all will read of many instances in which God chose the relic of the Little Flower, our relic, to work not miracles perhaps, but marvelous favors.

Our scoffer, I think, is answered. Let me add that the most unintelligent and illiterate and uneducated person who kneels at this altar railing and kisses in love the relic of the Little Flower and hopes to obtain thereby some favor from God, knows more than the most highly educated, but unbelieving, university professor. For the illiterate person knows what the proud professor does not know: that God exists, that God listens to prayer, that when we honor His saints and their memorials, we honor Him, and that He is often pleased to grant to the humble veneration of a relic of a saint a miracle of grace. Therefore, my dear friends, let us venerate the relic of the little Ssint reverently and lovingly, not believing that there is any magic power in it, but hoping that God will use this portion of the body of the Little Flower as the instrument of His answer to our prayers.

Chapter Eight

The Little Flower Still Lives*

"St. Thérèse, made glorious by thy Spouse after death, pray for us."

(Invocation from the Litany of the Little Flower)

Twenty-eight years ago today, at seven o'clock in the evening, St. Thérèse, the Little Flower of Jesus, died. During her last illness she had said, "The death I desire is the death of Jesus on the Cross." Her prayer was heard to the full; her agony was intense. Toward the end she asked the Mother Superior, "Mother, is not this the agony?" and the Mother replied, "Yes, my child, it is the agony." The Little Flower once more made an act of perfect resignation and with a loving glance at her crucifix, she added "Oh—I love Him—my God—I love Thee."

These were her last words. Scarcely had she uttered them when her pure soul fluttered from her body and flew to the throne of God in heaven.

The Little Flower was dead—and yet on this anniversary of her death we do not grieve, but we rejoice.

Why? Because she is not dead. Only after her death did she begin to live. On that day of her death twenty-eight years ago she did indeed leave her convent cloister but only to walk in two worlds—the peaceful realm of heaven and the troubled

---

* This sermon was preached in 1925 on the first feast of the Little Flower, September 30, the anniversary of the Little Flower's death.

The Little Flower in the Carmel garden.

realm of earth, and she has been vitally active in both worlds ever since. When the Little Flower died, no one outside the convent heeded the passing of her soul; even in France, to say nothing of America and other distant countries, there was no one aware of her life or of her death. And yet almost overnight, the whole Catholic world knew of her and raised suppliant hands to her. And immediately, in answer, and in fulfillment of her promise, "I will spend my heaven doing good upon earth," her smile fell like a benediction upon all mankind. Twisted limbs were straightened; hardened sinners looked into her pure eyes and sought the confessional; faith came back like the rushing tide into souls that had denied their God. She passed the boundary of the Catholic world and sought out the homes of unbelief; she brought Protestant ministers to the feet of Peter and pagans to the foot of the Cross. She was with the missionaries in Africa and China, and the foreign missions were soon put into her hands, put under her protection. She became the friend not of women only, but she sought also and won the hearts of mature men. Soldiers of France in the Great War placed themselves in her keeping as they went over the top. French aces carried her picture in their machines and dedicated their planes to her. Oh, no, the Little Flower is not dead. She continues today to teach our age lessons of modesty and innocence more powerful than all the preaching from Cathedral pulpits. In heaven she is vitally active. It is reported that lately she appeared to a Carmelite of France and said, "In the kingdom of heaven I am like a queen; I distribute graces according to my pleasure."

And here at her American National Shrine she lives. She moves among us, a vital, beneficial presence. She filled this church ten times today, and for the last nine days, and she fills it that often every Tuesday the year round in any and all weather. She is alive to the crowds who come. She smiles into their eyes; she catches and holds their hearts with the spell of her charm. They open their arms to receive her roses, roses of healing, roses of greater love of God, roses of strength against temptation, roses of relief from trial and trouble, roses of resignation, roses of the gift of prayer, roses of the virtues — humility, patience, purity. The roses drop and are caught by the members of her Society here, and it would be impossible to convince them that their Little Flower is not alive. Day after day her roses fall and day after day the Little Flower becomes dearer to our hearts as we fall deeper into her debt. Surely today we who love her will resolve to become more like her, to make her known to others, to help her to live in the hearts of others and to do in others' hearts the work she has done in ours.

May the roses which you now hold in your hands, my dear friends, be the symbols and the promise of the heavenly roses which the Little Flower shall let fall upon each of you today; today which is not so much the day of her death as her birthday, the birthday of God's favorite child to whom, because she never refused God anything upon earth, God refuses nothing in heaven; the birthday of God's favorite child "made glorious by her Spouse after death."

An Hour with the Little Flower

(Little Flower Series—Number Three)

The Little Flower in the Carmel of Lisieux.

Chapter One

The Special Vocation of the Little Flower to Love God

To realize that the Little Flower's special vocation was love of God, it is only necessary to read carefully the following passages from her writings* in which the Little Flower plainly expresses and joyously proclaims love as her special vocation.

Before we quote the words in which the Little Flower expresses her vocation, let us see how great her ambitions were, how ardent and all-embracing were the desires that led to her choice of the vocation which would fulfill all those desires.

The Vastness of Her Ambitions

She was not content to be merely a nun, not content to be merely a daughter of Our Lady of Mt. Carmel, not content merely to be a spouse of Christ. She would be all that and more. Although she had a marked contemplative vocation, her strong, active mind, consumed with the love of God, at times impelled her to be out and doing wherever the conflict was fiercest instead of being caged within the convent walls. She tells us of these desires in the following passage written in words of fire; a passage which reveals satisfactorily the ardor of her love:

"To be Thy Spouse, O my Jesus, to be a daughter of Carmel and by my union with Thee to be the mother of souls, should

---

* Generous quotations from her writings are given because it is the writer's effort to give the Little Flower's own words the widest possible distribution. Notably important passages are printed in italic type in order that the hasty reader may not miss the significance and beauty of such passages.

not all this content me? Yet, other vocations make themselves felt, and I would wield the sword. I would be a priest, an apostle, a martyr, a doctor of the Church; I would fain accomplish the most heroic deeds; the spirit of the crusader burns within me and I would gladly die on the battlefields in defense of the Church. A vocation to the priesthood! With what love my Jesus would I bear Thee in my hands when my words brought Thee down from heaven! With what love, too, would I give Thee to the faithful. Like the prophets and doctors I would be a light unto souls. I would travel the world over to preach Thy name, O my Beloved, and raise on heathen soil the glorious standard of the cross. One mission alone would not satisfy my longings. I would spread the gospel in all parts of the earth even to the farthest isles. I would be a missionary but not for a few years only; were it possible I would wish to have been one from the world's creation and to remain one until the end of time. But the greatest of all my desires is to win the martyr's palm. Martyrdom was the dream of my youth and the dream has only grown more vivid in Carmel's narrow cell. Like Thee, O my adorable Spouse, I would be scourged, I would be crucified; I would be flayed like St. Bartholomew; plunged into boiling oil like St. John, or, like St. Ignatius of Antioch, ground by the teeth of wild beasts into a bread worthy of God. Like St. Agnes and St. Cecelia, I would offer my neck to the sword of the executioner and like Joan of Arc murmur the name of Jesus at the burning stake. Open, O Jesus, the book of life in which are written the deeds of all Thy saints. Each one of these deeds I long to accomplish for Thee."

Such then were her desires, vehement, ardent, burning, all-embracing. There was no height to which she would not ascend, this little girl within whose breast there beat a heart so big that there is no word in any language with which adequately to describe it. Who can cite another saint in whose heart there burned more ardent desires, more dizzily high ambitions than burned in the heart of the Little Flower? It is not exaggeration but literal truth to say that Our Lord selected as His messenger to the twentieth century a girl with a heart more ardent even than the burning heart of St. Paul, His messenger to the first century.* Accustomed as we are to be thrilled by the vehemence of St. Paul's cries of love, we are more thrilled, we are carried away by the vehemence of the Little Flower's outburst in her canticle of love. In that song of love, quoted in the preceding paragraph, in that fiery outburst of holy enthusiasm, in that bounding vehement expression of what she would like to do for Our Lord, she appears to us as a St. Paul, a St. John, a St. Joan of Arc, as a St. Agnes, a St. Cecilia, all in one, and our love of God is at once dwarfed and enkindled in comparison with the overwhelming conflagration of love that burned in the heart of her whom, we find it difficult to realize, was only a girl. Here we have but another instance of the power of God - His power to choose the weak to confound the strong. He has illustrated His power by giving this little Carmelite a heart which in its capacity for love is simply astounding to the students of the human heart. She would not be satisfied to be a St. Paul, a priest, an apostle, a missionary, a martyr. No, a mission to one century would not satisfy her. She would be a missionary from the world's creation until the end of time. How could such all-comprehensive desires be realized?

Difficulty of Realizing Her Desires

She herself appreciated the difficulty of realizing such vast ambitions. "To such desires, to such folly, what answer, O Jesus, wilt Thou make?" How could such a child realize such ambitions? "Is there on earth a soul more feeble than mine?" Yet He deigned to supply in her a realization of those desires which He Himself had planted. He had work for her which would satisfy her longings, as wide as the universe and as extensive as time. "Yet precisely because of my feebleness Thou hast been pleased to grant my least, my most childish desire and now Thou dost will to grant those other desires more vast than the universe."

---

* The Little Flower herself tells us: "I can conceive here on earth of no love comparable to that with which Thou hast favored me without any merit of my own."

Her Own Description of the Realization of Her Ambitions

Now let us listen to her description of the manner in which her desires were realized. At first her failure to find work big enough for her ambition was a torture. "These aspirations," she said, "became a real martyrdom. I one day sought relief in the Epistles of St. Paul and my eyes lighted on the the twelfth and thirteenth chapters of the First Epistle to the Corinthians. There I read that all cannot become apostles, prophets, and doctors: that the Church is composed of different members; that the eye cannot also be the hand."

"The answer was clear, but it neither satisfied my longing nor brought me the peace I sought. 'Then descending into the depths of my nothingness, I was so lifted up that I reached my aim.'* Without being discouraged I read on and found comfort in this counsel: ". . . Be zealous for the better gifts. And I show unto you yet a more excellent way.'*

"The Apostle then explains how all the better gifts are nothing without love, and that charity is the most excellent way of going in safety to God. At last I had found rest.

"As I meditated on the Mystical Body of the Holy Church, I could not recognize myself among any of its members described by St. Paul, or was it not rather that I wished to recognize myself in all? Charity gave me the key to my vocation. I understood that since the Church is a body composed of different members, she could not lack the most necessary and most nobly endowed of all the bodily organs. I understood, therefore, that the Church has a heart—and a heart on fire with love. I saw, too, that love alone imparts life to all the members, so that should love ever fail, apostles would no longer preach the Gospel and martyrs would refuse to shed their blood. Finally, I realized that love includes every vocation, that love is all things, that love is eternal, reaching down through the ages and stretching to the uttermost limits of earth.

* St. John of the Cross.
* I Cor. 12:31.

"Beside myself with joy, I cried out: 'O Jesus, my Love, my vocation is found at last—MY VOCATION IS LOVE! I have found my place in the bosom of the Church, and this place, O my God, Thou hast Thyself given to me: in the heart of the Church, my Mother, I will be Love! Thus shall I be all things and my dream will be fulfilled.'"

Commentary on Her Description of Her Special Vocation

Reduced to its simplest form, the Little Flower in the passage just quoted sees the Church as a body with many members, some of which are priests, others missionaries, others martyrs, others apostles. But the body of the Church possesses not only members, but also a heart, a heart on fire with love, a heart that imparts life to all the members, so that should this heart of love fail, the members (apostles, missionaries) would cease to function. Consequently, whosoever has a place in the heart of the Church, which is love, is doing the work of all the members, doing the work of priests, bishops, missionaries, and martyrs. Whosoever does the work of love in the heart of the Church not only supplies energy to all the members of the Church but is herself a priest and an apostle, a missionary and a martyr. No single one of these vocations would satisfy the ardor and ambition of Thérèse. She wanted to have all these vocations. Consequently she chose the vocation of love; chose a place in the heart of the Church, a place that includes every vocation, a place which made her a priest, a missionary, an apostle, a martyr, as she desired. Hence her outburst, "Beside myself with joy I cried out: 'O Jesus, my Love. My vocation is found at last. My vocation is love. I have found my place in the bosom of the Church and this place, O my God, Thou hast Thyself given to me. In the heart of the Church, my Mother, I will be love. Thus shall I be all things and my dream will be fulfilled.'"

Her Vocation to Love to Last until End of Time

Let us note here that her vocation, her work, was in her own mind not to last merely to the end of her earthly existence. No, it was not even to begin, so to speak, until her death, and was to last until the end of time. Let us listen to her words uttered just before her death: "Mother," the Little Flower exclaimed one evening when Mother Agnes of Jesus went to the infirmary, "some notes from a distant concert have just reached my ears and there has come to me the thought that soon I shall be listening to the sweet melodies of Paradise. This thought, however, gave me only a moment's joy. ONE HOPE ALONE MAKES MY HEART BEAT FAST, THE LOVE I SHALL RECEIVE AND THE LOVE I SHALL BE ABLE TO GIVE. I feel that my mission is soon to begin, to make others love God as I love Him, to teach souls my little way. I will spend my heaven in doing good upon earth. No, there cannot be any rest for me until the end of the world, till the angel shall have said 'Time is no more.' Then only shall I take my rest." Again in one of her last letters the Little Flower wrote: "My real reason in welcoming death is that I shall then be of far more help to souls that are dear to me than I am now while on earth." Once when a sister was speaking to her of the happiness of heaven, Thérèse interrupted, saying: "It is not that which attracts me." "What is it then?" "Oh! it is love! To love, to be beloved, and to come back to earth to make love loved."

In view of these words of the Little Flower, then, we must, if we believe anything supernatural about the Little Flower, believe that as she said, her work, her vocation is to give "love of God," inspire love of God to little souls as much in 1926 as in 1897, and as much in 2026 as in 1926 if the world lasts that long. Here is something unique in God's dealings with men, but the promise of the Little Flower is plain—her vocation begins after her death, and it is to teach souls to love God. She had desired a mission not for a few years only, nor confined to one place, but a mission worldwide and limitless in point of time, and God granted that desire, she says, of teaching love to all men at all times. She is about to teach you, dear reader, now; follow on, then, with the explicit intention of being taught by this divinely appointed teacher of our own time.

Other Passages Concerning Love as Her Special Vocation

Now let us assemble other passages from her writings in which she refers to her work of love, her special vocation.

After the Little Flower tells us in her Autobiography that she has found her vocation, realized her desire of being all things and of embracing every vocation, she continues her song of love: "I do not ask for riches or glory, not even for the glory of heaven. That belongs by right to my brothers, the angels and saints. But I ask for love. One thought is mine henceforth, dear Jesus, it is to love Thee. Great deeds are forbidden me. I can neither preach the gospel nor shed my blood. But what does it matter? My brothers labor in my stead, while I, a little child, stay close to the throne and love Thee for all those who are in the strife. My brothers are all who labor for souls, priests, confessors, missionaries and all the officials of the Church." For these, her brothers, she offers her acts of love and her works of love; "I, a little child, stay close to the throne and love Thee for all who are in the strife."

In a letter to her sister, Pauline, she says: "Jesus! I would so love Him! Love Him as never yet He has been loved."

In her Autobiography she exclaims: "The science of love! Sweet is the echo of that word to the ear of my soul. I desire no other science."

In another letter to Pauline, she says: "I do not will that creatures should possess a single atom of my love; I wish to give all to Jesus, since He makes me understand that He alone is perfect happiness. All shall be for Him, all! And even when I have nothing to offer Him I will give Him that nothing."

In a letter to her cousin, Marie Guérin, she says: "I know of one means only by which to attain to perfection: LOVE.

Let us love, since our heart is made for nothing else. Sometimes I seek another word to express love, but in this land of exile the word which begins and ends is quite incapable of rendering the vibrations of the soul; we must then adhere to this simple and only word: TO LOVE.

"But on whom shall our poor heart lavish its love? Who shall be found that is great enough to be the recipient of its treasures? Will a human being know how to comprehend them, and above all will he be able to repay them? There exists but one Being capable of comprehending love; it is Jesus; He alone can give us back infinitely more than we shall ever give to Him."

In her Autobiography we find these passages: "O Jesus, I ask of Thee only peace, peace and above all, love, love without bound or limit. Jesus, let me for Thy sake die a martyr; give me martyrdom of soul or body: Ah! rather give me both, the one and the other." "I have no longer any desire unless it be to love Jesus even to folly. Yes, love it is, that draws me."

In a letter to Pauline, she says: "At any cost I will cull the palm of St. Agnes, if not by shedding my blood, then it must be by love."

In one of her letters to her "missionary brothers," the Little Flower says: "I ask you to say for me each day this little prayer which includes all my desires: 'Merciful Father, in the name of Thy sweet Jesus, of the Blessed Virgin and of the saints, I pray Thee that my sister be fired with Thy spirit of love and that Thou wilt grant her the grace to make Thee greatly loved.'

"If God should take me soon to Himself, I ask you to continue each day this same prayer for in heaven my desire will be the same as on earth, to love Jesus and to make Him loved."

Again she exclaims: "Oh! my well Beloved! I understand to what combats Thou hast destined me; it is not on the battlefield that I shall fight; I am a prisoner of Thy love. Freely have I riveted the chain which unites me to Thee and separates me forever from the world. My thought is love. With it I shall chase the stranger from the kingdom. I shall make Thee to be proclaimed King in the souls of men."

The Little Flower wrote to her sister, Céline: "Céline, during the fleeting moments that remain to us, let us save souls! I feel that our Spouse asks us for souls. Above all for the souls of priests. It is He who bids me tell you this. There is but one thing to be done here below: To love Jesus and to save souls for Him that He may be more loved. We must not let slip the smallest opportunity of giving Him joy. We must refuse Him nothing. He is in such need of love." This quotation sums up briefly the philosophy of her life.

One of the most remarkable passages in her Autobiography follows: "At times I experienced thrills of love for God, in fact undoubted raptures. One evening feeling at a loss to tell Jesus how much I loved Him and how keenly I desired He should be everywhere served and glorified, I was heartbroken at the thought that never a single act of love could reach Him from the deep pit of Hell. At this I cried out that with all my heart I would readily consent to be cast down forever into that place of torment and revolt if by doing so I could turn the hatred of the lost into love. Of course, that would not have glorified Him, for His only wish is for us to be happy, but love often makes one feel inclined to say foolish things without number. Speaking in this way did not mean that I desired heaven any less but in those days heaven for me was nothing but love and I felt that nothing could tear me apart from His love."

Just before her profession in Carmel in September, 1890, she wrote to her sister Pauline, "Before starting, my Beloved asked me in what land I wished to travel and what route I wished to follow. I told Him I had only one desire, that of reaching the summit of the mountain of love. Thereupon roads innumerable spread before my gaze, but so many of these were perfect that I felt incapable of choosing any of my own free will. Then I said to my Divine Guide, 'Thou knowest the spot I desire to reach and for Whose sake I would climb the mountain. Thou knowest Him Whom I love and whom alone I wish to please. For Him only I set out on this journey. Lead me therefore by the paths of His choice. My joy shall be full if only He be pleased. And Our Lord took me by the hand and led me." In the same letter, we find these words: "I am happy, nay, most happy, to be without all consolation. I would be ashamed were my love like that of those earthly brides who are forever glancing toward their bridegroom's hand to see if some present has not been brought them; or else at the face to catch the loving smile which fills them with delight." Thérèse, the little spouse of Jesus, loves Him for Himself. She only looks at the face of her Beloved to catch a glimpse of the tears that delight her with their hidden charm. She longs to wipe away those tears. "Jesus, Jesus, Oh! I would so love Him. Love Him as He has never yet been loved!"

"It is for the love of His creatures that the Creator of the universe pleads. He is all athirst for love. Oh, my God! Love is repaid by love alone. I have found how to ease my heart, by rendering Thee love for love."

All the aspirations of her ardent soul are crystallized in these ardent words: "Jesus! I would so love Him! Love Him as never yet He has been loved." And her last words were but the echo of her whole life. "Oh, I love Him! My God—I—love—Thee." Thus did she realize her dream, to live of love, to die of love. "I desire no sensible consolation in loving. Provided Jesus feel my love, that is enough for me. Oh! to love Him and to make Him loved . . . how sweet it is! I have but one wish, one desire: to love Jesus above everything else, to love Him to excess, even unto folly. Yes, it is love that draws me."

The foregoing variety and multiplicity of quotations will leave no doubt about the legitimacy of our thesis that the special vocation of the Little Flower was love. What follows under the heading, "Her Oblation of Herself as a Victim of Love," will show the climax to which her vocation of love led her.

Chapter Two

The Little Flower's Oblation of Herself as a Victim of Love

The Little Flower not only wished to live of love but also to die of love. There burned within her heart a consuming desire to die at last a victim of love for God. It is this phase of her love that we shall consider here. It is the dominant note of her life. She pleads and argues with her Divine Spouse, in the following poem, to grant her this greatly coveted favor of dying for love of Him.

> Remember, Jesus sweetest Word of life,
> That Thou didst die for love of me;
> Oh, let me be with holy folly rife,
> That I may live and die for Thee.
> Thou knowest, Lord, my heart's supreme desire:
> To make Thee loved and straight in martyrdom
>   expire.
> Oh, hear my ardent cry,
> I long of love to die!

In this poem the Little Flower implies that Our Lord would take an unfair advantage if, having died for her, He did not permit her in turn to die for Him. Just how she planned to die for Him—to die of love of Him—and just what relation her act of oblation as a victim of God's love has to her desire to die for Him, the following pages will explain. This

Thérèse at the age of fifteen, shortly before her entrance into the Carmel of Lisieux.

explanation necessitates first a preliminary explanation of her theory of the divine lift or elevator.

The Divine Lift

The heart of a saint is never satisfied. Never does it say, "Enough." In spite of growth, it aspires to grow greater and greater until its ambitions in some ways extend even to infinity. It seeks to go forth and lose itself in the shoreless and fathomless abyss of eternal love. For the realization of such ambition, created love does not suffice. God's love must be borrowed if the saint's boundless desires are to be realized. In other words, if the highest summit of Divine Love, the goal of a saint, is to be reached, a very special intervention of God is necessary. The way up the mountain is too rugged, too steep to be climbed by any creature; to reach the summit of God's Love, the soul must be carried by God.

Now to apply all this to the Little Flower. She desires to become a great saint. She saw herself however at the foot of the high mountain of holiness which she was too weak to climb. But she was not discouraged. She counted on God. She knew that the good God does not inspire desires which He does not intend to grant. She set about to search, in her emergency, for a way up the mountain which she was too weak to climb. What she needed, she decided, was an elevator such as is found in the houses of the wealthy, a heavenly elevator by which she, too weak to climb, would be carried to the summit of the mountain of love – of perfect love. To find such a lift, she searched the Holy Scriptures and found there that God would carry the little ones who came to Him. "Ah, then," she said, "here is the solution of my problem. I need only become little, become a child, abandon myself in childlike confidence and childlike love into the arms of God and He will carry me

---

* This quotation is taken from the ninth chapter of the Autobiography and is addressed to Mother Mary of Gonzaga, the Prioress of Carmel at the time Chapter Nine was written.

to the highest summit of love." Now let the Little Flower herself tell all this in her own inimitable way.

"You know, Mother,* that I have always desired to become a saint, but in comparing myself with the saints I have ever felt that I am as far removed from them as a grain of sand trampled underfoot by the passerby is from the mountain whose summit is lost in the clouds.

"Instead of feeling discouraged by such reflections, I concluded that God would not inspire a wish which could not be realized, and that in spite of my littleness I might aim at being a saint. 'It is impossible,' I said, 'for me to become great, so I must bear with myself and my many imperfections, but I will seek out a means of reaching heaven by a little way—very short, very straight and entirely new. We live in an age of inventions: there are now lifts which save us the trouble of climbing stairs. I will try to find a lift by which I may be raised unto God, for I am too small to climb the steep stairway of perfection.'

"I sought to find in Holy Scripture some suggestion of what this desired lift might be, and I came across those words, uttered by the Eternal Wisdom Itself: 'Whosoever is a little one, let him come to Me.'* I therefore drew near to God, feeling sure I had discovered what I sought. But wishing further to know what He would do to the 'little one,' I continued my search and this is what I found: '. . . You shall be carried at the breasts, and upon the knees . . . As one whom the mother caresseth, so will I comfort you.'*

"Never have I been consoled by words more tender and more sweet. O Jesus! Thy arms, then, are the lift which must raise me even unto heaven. To reach heaven I need not become great; on the contrary I must remain little, I must become even smaller than I am."

Practical Reflections

* Prov. 9:4.
* Isa. 66:12-13.

As a practical reflection let us answer here this question: What must he do who wishes, like the Little Flower, to become a great saint, to reach the summit of love and yet who realizes his own powerlessness?

He too must follow the Little Flower's "Little Way"; he must make use of the Divine Lift. But how may one avail himself of this lift? Let him place himself in God's arms in childlike love and confidence and absolute self-surrender and God will do the rest. We must note however that one does not remain idle after thus placing himself in God's arms. He must still exert himself to give God joy while God is carrying him. In what are our efforts to consist? In corresponding with His graces, in repeating and continuing to repeat the acts of self-surrender, child-like love and confidence by which we so place ourselves in His arms, in practicing all the acts noted in Part Two of this pamphlet. Let us not imagine that it suffices to surrender oneself once for all to God's arms; while there we must continually repeat our acts of surrender to Him, telling Him continually, as did the Little Flower, that we love Him, depending upon His strength entirely, asking Him in love and confidence to carry us safely.

A further step in this complete surrender to God is the offering of oneself as a victim of God's love, which forms the object of our next inquiry.

What Led the Little Flower to Offer Herself as a Victim of Love?

Just as the desire for greater love led the Little Flower to place herself in God's arms to be carried up the mountain of love, so a desire for still greater love, while being carried, led her to offer herself as a victim of love. The history of her act of oblation is as follows: Two great loves, the love which she felt for God, and the love which she felt God had for her, enkindled in her an ardent desire of being wholly transformed into love so as to be able to render to Jesus love for love. In other words she wished to love Him if possible as much as she saw herself loved by Him, but the

---

* I John 4:16.

best means of being transformed into love is to draw to oneself, in order to be consumed, the love which is in God or rather which is God Himself, for "God is charity."* Inasmuch as God is love He is a fire, a consuming fire. When wood is exposed to fire it burns. In the same way if a soul were to expose herself to the flames of the love pent-up in the heart of God, would not she too be consumed? And just as the wood becomes fire in contact with fire, would not she become love by contact with love? She would. Therefore she offered herself as a holocaust to the merciful love of the good God. In that way she enabled herself to render to her Father in heaven, love for love, and to love Him as she is loved by Him. Hence, she will thus have found the means of appropriating to herself the flames of love of which the Blessed Trinity is the eternal source. To love the good God she will have at her disposal the very love and, if I may say so, the very heart of God. At the same time she will satisfy one of the most earnest desires of His adorable heart, which is to diffuse Its love. The need of loving and of being loved is infinite in God and this need is fully satisfied in the very bosom of the Blessed Trinity. But love has a tendency to communicate itself and in order to be able to diffuse His love God created men, and men, as we know, at least the majority of them, scornfully reject His loving advances. Thus act not only the disciples of the world, but even a very large number of Our Lord's own disciples. How rare are they indeed who surrender themselves unreservedly to the tenderness of His infinite love! Still the good God ceases not to urge them in the most touching manner. Continually repelled, He returns continually to the charge. He multiplies His kindnesses, His calls, His acts of forgiveness, but most often it is in vain. What then will become of that infinite love with which Jesus wishes to set the world ablaze but of which the world wants nothing? Shall it forever remain pent up powerless in the bosom of the adorable Trinity? Pondering this problem, the Little Flower said to herself that if souls were to offer themselves as victims of holocausts to His love, then the good God, glad not to restrict the flames of infinite tenderness pent up within Him, would not fail to consume them rapidly, and immediately she offers herself to receive into her heart all the love that sinners disdain. This it is that makes her cry out: "O, Jesus, let me be that happy victim! Consume Thy little holocaust in the fires of Divine Love."

It was on the 9th of June, 1895, the feast of the Holy Trinity, that St. Thérèse pronounced her act of oblation as a victim of holocaust to the merciful love of God. Assuredly this date deserves to be remembered because it consecrates a memorable day for the little souls called to walk in her footsteps and her Little Way of love; the day which saw made on earth and ratified in heaven the consecration of the first of the little victims of the merciful love of God. It shall be to the eternal glory of St. Thérèse of the Child Jesus to have, by very special design of Divine Providence, opened up and traced the way for them, rendering it accessible to even the humblest and weakest souls, provided they be generous and confident and content to surrender themselves unreservedly to the infinite, merciful love of the good God.

The Act of Oblation Itself

(The essential part of the act of oblation is printed in italic type. This act of oblation was found after the death of the Little Flower, in her book of holy Gospels which day and night she carried next to her heart.)

"O my God, Most Blessed Trinity, I desire to LOVE THEE and to MAKE THEE LOVED, to labor for the glory of Holy Church by saving souls still on earth and by delivering those who suffer in Purgatory. I desire to accomplish Thy will perfectly, and to attain to the degree of glory which Thou hast prepared for me in Thy kingdom; in one word, I desire to be a saint, but I know that I am powerless, and I implore Thee, O my God, to be Thyself my sanctity.

"Since Thou hast so loved me as to give me Thine only Son to be my Savior and my Spouse, the infinite treasures of His merits are mine: to Thee I offer them with joy, beseeching

Thee to see me only as in the Face of Jesus and in His Heart burning with love.

"Again, I offer Thee all the merits of the saints—in heaven and on earth, their acts of love and those of the holy angels; and finally I offer Thee, O Blessed Trinity, the love and the merits of the Holy Virgin, my most dear Mother; it is to her I entrust my oblation, begging her to present it to Thee.

"Her Divine Son, my well-beloved Spouse, during His life on earth told us: 'If you ask the Father anything in My Name He will give it to you.'

"I am certain then that Thou wilt hearken to my desires . . . My God, I know it, the more Thou willest to give, the more dost Thou make us desire. Immense are the desires that I feel within my heart, and it is with confidence that I call upon Thee to come and take possession of my soul. I cannot receive Thee in Holy Communion as often as I would; but, Lord, art Thou not Almighty? . . . Remain in me as in the tabernacle—never leave Thy little victim.

"I long to console Thee for the ingratitude of the wicked, and I pray Thee take from me the liberty to displease Thee. If through frailty I fall sometimes, may Thy divine glance purify my soul immediately, consuming every imperfection like to fire which transforms all things into itself.

"I thank Thee, O my God, for all the graces Thou hast bestowed on me, and particularly for making me pass through the crucible of suffering. It is with joy that I shall behold Thee on the Last Day bearing Thy scepter, the Cross; since Thou hast deigned to give me for my portion this most precious Cross, I have hope of resembling Thee in heaven, and seeing the sacred stigmata of Thy Passion shine in my glorified body.

"After exile on earth I hope to enjoy the possession of Thee in our eternal Fatherland, but I have no wish to amass merits for heaven. I will work for Thy love alone, my sole aim being to give Thee pleasure, to console Thy Sacred Heart, and to save souls who will love Thee forever.

"At the close of life's day, I shall appear before Thee with empty hands, for I ask not, Lord, that Thou wouldst count my works. . . . All our justice is tarnished in Thy sight. It is therefore my desire to be clothed with Thine own Justice and to receive from Thy Love the eternal possession of Thyself. I crave no other Throne, no other Crown but Thee, O my Beloved! . . .

"In Thy sight time is nothing, one day is as a thousand years.

"Thou canst in an instant prepare me to appear before Thee.

"In order that my life may be one act of perfect Love, I OFFER MYSELF AS A VICTIM OF HOLOCAUST TO THY MERCIFUL LOVE, imploring Thee to consume me without ceasing, and to let the flood of infinite tenderness pent up in Thee overflow into my soul, that so I may become a very martyr of Thy love, O my God!

"May this martyrdom, having first prepared me to appear before Thee, break life's thread at last, and may my soul take its flight, unretarded, into the eternal embrace of Thy merciful love.

"I desire, O well-Beloved, at every heartbeat to renew this Oblation an infinite number of times, till the shadows fade away, and I can tell Thee my love eternally face to face!

> (Signed) MARIE-FRANÇOISE-THERESE
> of the Child Jesus and of the Holy Face.
> Feast of the Most Holy Trinity,
> This ninth day of June,
> In the year of grace, 1895

300 days Indulgence, each time recited by the Faithful with contrite heart and with devotion.

A Plenary Indulgence, once a month, on the ordinary conditions, for those who shall have recited it each day during the month.

Notes Concerning the Oblation

1. The reader should reread and study carefully especially the last three paragraphs of this oblation.

2. Let us note that it is a question of an oblation of ourselves to the merciful love of the good God, and that in making it we offer ourselves to this infinite love in order to draw that love to us.

3. Its first effect then is to cause the love of the heart of the good God to overflow into the soul who has offered herself. Consequently the soul remains before Him like a little vase in front of the ocean; the act of oblation has opened the floodgates and hollowed out the channels through which the waters pass unretarded. Henceforth, this happy soul shall be inundated with love.

4. We may note, too, a second effect of the oblation. Notice that St. Thérèse uses yet another expression which she was careful to underline; she speaks of tenderness. She implores the good God "to let the flood of infinite tenderness pent up within Him overflow into her soul." This is because she does not forget that God is a father and that the love which descends from the heart of a father into the heart of his child presents itself under the most sweet form of tenderness. It is this infinite tenderness then that she calls into her soul and to which she surrenders herself.

5. Note the difference there is between an oblation to the justice of God and the oblation of His merciful love.

    To offer ourselves to justice is to call down upon ourselves the chastisements reserved for sinners, and thus to enable Divine Justice to satisfy itself whilst sparing the culprits. By virtue of that oblation, the victim soul appears in the Church like a lightning conductor raised upwards towards heaven to attract the thunderbolt and preserve the neighboring buildings from it. And, as Saint Thérèse remarks, that offering is noble and generous, since by it we ask to suffer that others may be spared. We cannot, in truth, serve as a lightning conductor except by agreeing to serve as a target for the anger of God exasperated against the crimes of the world.

Victims of love vow themselves not to the justice of God but to His infinite tenderness. They do not offer themselves directly to suffer, but to love and to be loved; nor as victims of expiation to repair, but as victims of holocaust to be wholly consumed. They are not the conductor which attracts the lightning, but the victims exposed to the fire of heaven in order to receive its flames.

6. Here a question arises: "Is this martyrdom of love exempt from suffering, or if there be suffering in it, what exactly is its function?" Answer: Let us say at once that there is no martyrdom without pain, not even the martyrdom of love, for if, according to the testimony of the Imitation, we cannot live in love without suffering, much less can we, without suffering, live on love and die of love. This is the place to recall the beautiful saying of St. Augustine, "To him who loveth, nothing is hard. Or, if something is hard, that becomes a suffering loved, and this suffering is sweet in the eyes of love." But here again we must remark that suffering is not the end or the direct effect of the act of oblation. It may become a consequence of it, but it is not to suffering or with a view to suffering, that we consecrate ourselves. We consecrate ourselves to love with a view to love. It is true, however, that love bears within itself a germ of suffering and this usually develops with it. It is impossible to love God ardently without suffering. The act of oblation may, (note the word may), involve the following five kinds of suffering: First, it is a suffering to see Him so little loved and so gravely

offended. Second, it is a suffering not to love Him ourselves as much as we desire. We suffer from the narrowness and powerlessness of a heart which can now no longer suffice to contain the flood of tenderness which comes to us from the heart of God, and by which it is, as it were, submerged. Third, the soul that loves Jesus suffers too, or rather aspires to suffer and of herself tends to suffering, because in her eyes suffering is no longer that repellent thing, so hard to nature, from which everyone shrinks; it is Jesus suffering, Who extends His arms to her. Love invites a resemblance and Jesus is a Spouse of blood. Fourth, love urges on to generosity and there are exchanges of love which can be made only on the cross. Love in time tends with all its force to union, and since the cross has been the deathbed of Jesus, it has become the sacred abode whither He, the Divine King of Love, invites souls, His chaste spouses, to come and consummate their union with Him in suffering and in death. Fifth, there is yet another reason why every soul that loves Jesus ardently loves suffering too and gladly accepts it. It is because she finds in each cross presented to her a most efficacious means of purchasing souls for Him. To love Jesus suffices not for her love; she wants at all costs to win over to Him other hearts that will love Him eternally. She wants to save sinners for Him, but sinners are saved only by the application of the infinite merits of Our Lord. Grace alone can convert them, and grace, the seat of the bloody sacrifice of Calvary often reaches their souls by a mysterious channel hollowed out and kept clear by the voluntary immolations of pure souls continuing in the Mystical Body of Christ the sacrifice of the cross. Those whom Jesus has purchased by His death we can save by suffering.

Conclusion

For all those reasons suffering is the inseparable companion of love. Still, great as its necessity and importance may be to victims of love it has no more than a secondary function. It goes only in the second place and ever under the guidance of love.

7. Here let us answer an objection: Will not the good God to Whom we surrender ourselves by the oblation to merciful love, at least avail Himself of it to send crosses and trials without measure? Without measure? Certainly not! The trials willed by the good God are never willed without measure, but are always proportioned to the supernatural energies which an ever-preventing grace has been careful to develop previously in the soul. There is always proportion between the trial and divine help. But will not God at least send exceptional sufferings which He would never have demanded but for this oblation to love? That is His own affair and His own secret and it depends upon the designs He has for each particular soul. Let us say merely that it is not a necessary consequence of the act of oblation. It is true that Saint Thérèse wrote that "To surrender oneself as a victim of love is to offer oneself to every anguish, to every bitterness, for love lives only on sacrifice, and the more a soul wills to be surrendered to Love, the more she must be surrendered to suffering." But those words, spoken in a particular case for the consolation of a person sorely tried, were not what St. Thérèse habitually taught to the souls whom she wished to induce to make this act of oblation. In fact, in dealing with them, she insisted on just the contrary, in order to convince them that they had naught to fear and all to gain, assuring them that the direct result of this donation is to draw down not crosses but abundant mercies.

Without doubt God is Master, and the Cross being one of His most precious treasures, He usually gives it abundantly to His beloved ones. But that is so, whatsoever be the spiritual way followed. And the great advantage here is that the cross, by becoming the fruit of love, becomes, like it, gentle and sweet. In that sense we may say that what results from the act of oblation is not always more suffering, but more strength and facility to bear joyfully the measure of suffering intended for us by the good God.

This is what happens in practice: once a soul has consecrated herself as a victim to merciful love, she ought to believe, for it is true, that everything Providence sends her in answer to her oblation is the work of love—that is to say, determined, willed, chosen by love. Consequently, the good pleasure of God should appear to her all impregnated and radiant with love and she must surrender herself to it, as she did to love itself — filially, lovingly, and also with confidence, her eyes closed, without seeking to penetrate the secrets that her Father in heaven wishes to keep hidden from her. Let her only consider it as certain that He in His infinite wisdom and goodness will never require of her sacrifices above her strength. Love will know how to be forbearing in its demands and will ever proportion them to the treasures of energy that its own grace shall have developed in her.

But still, if God has in regard to that soul more lofty designs of perfection, if especially He intends to associate her efficaciously with His work of redemption for the conversion of sinners and the sanctification of other souls, there is reason to believe that He will lead her on by slow degrees to greater sufferings. But He will know how to do so with a sweetness at once strong and gentle. He will make her experience the austere and profound joy of suffering for love's sake, and in that way He will inspire a longing for suffering. This longing can even become so ardent that only great and continual sufferings will be capable of satisfying it. We see this clearly in the case of Thérèse. In proportion as Jesus sent her crosses, her thirst for suffering increased. But then, in the end she had gone so far, she said, as to suffer no longer, so sweet was suffering to her. Then there was nothing like pain for giving her joy, and suffering united to love was the only thing that appeared to her desirable in this vale of tears.

How then could she regret the consequences of her donations to love, painful though they were? That explains why, at the height of an agony without consolation, when the chalice was full to the brim and the pains so great that the dying child acknowledged that never had she believed it possible to suffer so much; she said also, and repeated several times, that she did not repent of having surrendered herself to Love.

So shall it be for all souls whom God will lead through love to the Cross. Not one of them shall ever repent of having surrendered herself to Love, whatsoever trials may result from it.

8. The principal effect of the act of oblation: The designs of providence, however, are not the same for all the little victims of merciful love, and there are some amongst them who shall neither know those great trials nor those great desires of suffering. They shall be none the less true victims of holocaust, most pleasing to God, for, according to the judgment of St. Thérèse, it is not these desires which delight the Heart of Our Lord. What most pleases Him in a soul is to see her love her littleness; it is the blind trust she has in His goodness. Love of suffering is merely an accidental effect of the martyrdom of love.

Its essential and by far the most desirable result is to make the soul live in the constant exercise of love, or, as St. Thérèse says: "in one act of perfect love."

Now when love takes possession of a soul to this extent, it becomes master of all her powers and animates all her works. Consequently, every action she does, even the most indifferent, bears the divine imprint of love, and its value becomes immense in the sight of God.

That is not all. Divine love cannot tolerate the presence nor even the trace of sin in the soul that is wholly surrendered to It. Doubtless the offering to merciful love does not render one impeccable; it does not prevent every fall. A little victim may still be guilty of infidelities. But love which penetrates her and surrounds her, renews her, so to speak, each moment and ceases not to consume her, destroying in her all that could displease Jesus.

9. We can foresee then, what will be the death of a victim of merciful love who shall have been to the last faithful to her oblation: an enviable death, if ever there was one; and experience proves that such has always been the case. As for the judgment that is to follow this happy death, St. Thérèse in her trustful simplicity believed that it would be as if there were none, so eagerly would the good God hasten to recompense with eternal delights His own love, which He could see burn in this soul.

Still, it would be rash to think that it suffices to have pronounced the formula of the Act of Oblation in order to escape all condemnation and so to avoid purgatory. St. Thérèse has been careful to say that words alone are not sufficient. The soul must surrender herself really and entirely. For she is consumed by love only in so far as she surrenders herself to love.

The soul must have lived, too, in accordance with the holy exigencies of love and in the exercise of charity, uniting love of her neighbor to love of God. Thus we can once more admire with what wise discretion Sister Thérèse knew how to remain ever within the exact bounds of truth and keep herself free from all exaggeration, even at the very height of her confidence.

All the foregoing remarks enable us to judge of the excellence of the effects of the oblation to the merciful love of the good God.

10. Let us remember in conclusion that the act of oblation is not intended to be made merely by a few privileged souls. A very great number are called to make it. Such were the thoughts and desires of little Thérèse and the closing lines of the story of her life show us that such was also on earth what it still must be in heaven the object of her ardent prayer: "I entreat Thee, O Jesus, to let Thy Divine gaze rest upon a vast number of little souls. I entreat Thee to choose in this world a legion of little victims worthy of Thy love." Why should not each one who shall read these lines, if he feel interiorly the call of grace inviting him, repeat after her and with her: "Grant, O Jesus, that I might be that happy victim."

May the Little Flower inspire all who read this book to desires of love as great as those that led her to express in her canticle of love the burning desire to possess every vocation. May she lead all to the dispositions necessary to be carried up the mountain of love on the Divine Lift, to the purity of Love and the littleness of heart necessary to make the Act of Oblation, as a victim of God's merciful love.

Little Thérèse discovers the intial of her name in the sky.

Chapter Three

Practical Rules for the Practice of Love of God

In addition to and in conjunction with, or independently of the Act of Oblation of self as a victim of God's merciful love, how shall we in a practical way express our love of God? In other words, how, whether or not we have made the Act of Oblation, shall we practice the little way of love of the Little Flower. Let us, in answer, set down here five rules:

Rule 1: Let us seek always to give pleasure to the good God.*

"I have ever remained little," says the Little Flower, "having no other occupation except to gather flowers, the flowers of love and of sacrifice and to offer them to the good God for His pleasure." This watchful care to give pleasure to the good God animated her constantly even in the least actions, dominating the other supernatural motives, excluding all motive of personal interest. And she summed up in those words, "to give pleasure to the good God," the whole secret of holiness, not only for herself, but for others. If you wish to become a saint, she wrote to one of her sisters, that will be easy for you. Have but one end only: to give pleasure to Jesus. Our first rule then is to be ever on the alert to profit by every opportunity, by the least opportunity, even in the least actions, of giving pleasure to the good God. To be even more brief, our first rule is always to be watchful—to give pleasure to Jesus. But how shall we give pleasure to Jesus? Let the succeeding rules supply the answer.

---

* Throughout this section the reader will especially notice how often in the Little Flower's phrases there recur the words: "the good God"; she wished ever to emphasize thus the goodness of God. The reader should notice also how often reference is made to "trifles", to "little deed", to "the very least actions".

Rule 2: Let us strew before Jesus the flowers of little sacrifices.

Let St. Thérèse herself explain this rule: "How shall I show my love, since love is proved by deeds? Well, the little child will strew flowers . . . she will embalm the Divine Throne with their fragrance, she will sing with silvery voice the Canticle of Love.

"Yes, my Beloved, it is thus my life's brief day shall be spent before Thee. No other means have I of proving my love than to strew flowers; that is, to let no little sacrifice escape me, not a look, not a word; to make use of the very least actions and do them for love. I wish to suffer for love's sake, and for love's sake even to rejoice; thus shall I strew flowers. Not one shall I find without shedding its petals for Thee . . . and then I will sing, I will always sing, even if I must gather my roses in the very midst of thorns—and the longer and sharper the thorns, the sweeter shall be my song."

Nothing is easier than this rule of the practice of holy love. It is so simple that anybody can grasp it, even a child could understand it; and that is not surprising since it is love put within the reach of little ones. To love is, then, to act in all things through love; it is to do all, to accept all, to suffer all with a view to giving pleasure to the good God because we love.

Nothing is either easier, or more practical. Anyone, no matter who, can do it with a good will and the help of grace. And God never refuses this grace to those who ask it. And it is always and everywhere possible, in all conditions of life and states of the soul, as well in aridities and powerlessness as in the midst of consolations. Listen to St. Thérèse discovering to us the little ingenious ways of her ever watchful love: "In times of aridity, when I am incapable of praying, of practicing virtue, I seek little opportunities, mere trifles, to give pleasure to Jesus—for instance, a smile, a pleasant word when inclined to be silent and to show weariness. If I have no opportunities, I at least tell Him again and again that I love Him; that is not difficult, and it keeps alive the fire in my heart. Even though this fire of love might seem to me extinct, I would still throw little straws upon the embers, and I am certain it would rekindle."

To sum up then, we are to be ever on the alert to let no possible sacrifice, during our everyday routine, escape us; let us offer our very least actions to Him, a smile when we are inclined to be surly, a pleasant word even when we are most fatigued. By such trifles we shall please Him. And when no such opportunity offers, we can "tell Him again and again that we love Him." No one can compute the number of those who in the streets, offices, homes and shops of our cities, have the habit of whispering frequently to themselves, as they go about their work, the ejaculation, "Sweet Heart of Jesus be my Love." Such souls should be apt pupils of Little Thérèse, but they should bring more confidence and daring to their ejaculatory prayers and say, instead of "be my love," the "I love Thee" of St. Thérèse and not only "I love Thee" but her other more ardent expressions such as "Jesus, I would so love Thee, love Thee as never yet Thou hast been loved."

Souls who make such ejaculations will not be long in reaching the summit of the mountain of love. They will find their way very soon to the divine lift and there make their act of oblation to the merciful love of the good God.

Rule 3: Let us profit by the very least opportunities and never lose an opportunity.

By this rule our attention is called to the fact that big things are not expected of us, nor are big things often at hand. Ordinarily, in the course of the usual day, there are only very little things that we can offer to the good God. Little Thérèse herself said, "I am a very little soul who has never been able to do any but very little things." Precisely because there were only little things at hand, did she wish never to lose any of them. "All shall be for Him, all!" No opportunity of overcoming self must be lost. Every opportunity for little sacrifice must be taken. Not one flower did St. Thérèse find without shedding its petals before Jesus through love of Him. Not one! Oh, how far that goes! Only a great soul could conceive such a desire; only a great saint can realize the desire. Those little sacrifices, taken separately, are trifles, but let us try to realize what supreme generosity, what universal renunciation, what colossal strength of will, what continual self-forgetfulness is necessary never to miss even one such trifle. When we have pondered this and then remember that the Little Flower never missed one such trifle, never gave God aught but love, we wonder how anyone could say that her life was an ordinary life or that there was nothing miraculous in it. Is it not miraculous that she should have spent years of days without missing the least opportunity to give God pleasure? Such a life is not ordinary, but marvelous; it is the life of a great saint. We should not be led by the consideration that the Little Flower performed no great austerities to imagine that her little way is easy. Her little way is more wonderful and more difficult than the practice of severely penitential exercises. The Little Flower is called a little saint because her little way consists of trifles, but when we ponder, as we have in this chapter, her marvelously regular and miraculously unfailing performance of these trifles, we must conclude that she is not a little but a great saint, or better, that she is a great, though little saint.*

Rule 4: To offer our joys to give God pleasure.

Life is not, of course, unmingled suffering. Our Divine Lord had His joys; so did our Blessed Mother; so did the Little Flower. As we go through life we encounter lawful joys, some merely permitted, others willed by the good God. Must we then renounce them? Or, if we accept them, if we concede them, shall they remain outside of love as if they escaped its

---

* It is true that her little way is "sweet"; true too that it is "easy" in the sense that anyone can follow it, but in its higher ramifications, in its perfection, it is not easy; it calls for heroic sanctity. Those who have been impressed by the sweetness of the Little Way, and concluded that it was therefore easy, have been misled by this—that her love, in transforming sacrifice, has so permeated it with sweetness and invested it with so many attractions, that in it the cross disappears beneath the flowers. but the cross is ever there, and those flowers have cost much in the gathering, for often have they had to be sought in the very midst of thorns, and at the price of wounds very painful to sensitive nature.

action? And shall there then be hours in life when, with the absence of sorrow, love, too, shall be wanting?

Certainly not! A heart truly loving could not bear that. Love is consuming. It makes fuel of everything, and all serves to intensify its flame. Besides, it purposes to leave nothing in the soul or in life outside its influence. This is why, in the little way where love plays so important a part, where it is the principal resource of the soul, everything, absolutely everything, joys as well as sorrows, can and ought to serve as nourishment for love.

Thus thought and acted St. Thérèse. Besides, she knew too well the heart of the good God, more tender than a mother's heart, to think that our love is not pleasing to Him except when exercised in the midst of suffering. What a strange Father He would be, indeed, if He were pleased only to see us suffering! But no, it is not so. Little Thérèse said, on the contrary, that the good God finds it very hard, owing to His great love for us, to have to leave us on earth to complete our time of trial, and that He must rejoice at seeing us smile. And so, with equal happiness, she offered to Him her joys and her sorrows.

She wrote: "It seems to me that if we take Jesus captive by our sacrifices, our joys enchain Him too. For that it suffices not to concentrate on selfish happiness, but to offer to our spouse the little joys He scatters on our path to delight our hearts and raise them up to Him."

We may well believe that she attached great importance to this point of her "little doctrine," for she returns to it frequently in her writings, and particularly in her poems, where she pours forth the choicest sentiments of her soul.

> "My griefs, my joys, my sacrifices small—
> Behold my flowers."

Let us cite also these words, which seem to us to sum up best her thought: "I wish to suffer for love's sake, and for love's sake even to rejoice." In that short phrase, little Thérèse depicts herself fully, and with a flash of light shows to little souls the road to follow in order to live on love.

An excellent example of this offering of her joys, as well as her sorrows to God, is found in the following passage in which she describes her conduct at the table. Notice that she first determines that Our Lord before her, sat at table, partook of food and of course enjoyed it. So she too will enjoy her meals, she concludes. Then she finds heavenly personages to whom to offer all that which pleases her. That which most pleases her goes to the Infant Jesus. Whenever, however, the fare is displeasing, it is offered, not to any heavenly personage, but "gaily," notice, to herself, whom she calls quaintly and delightfully "my dear little child." Here is the passage: "In the refectory we have but one thing to do: to accomplish this so lowly act with thoughts uplifted. I declare to you that often it is in the refectory the sweetest aspirations of love come to me. Sometimes I am impelled to dwell on the thought that if Our Divine Lord were in my place, with the fare set before Him as served to me, He would certainly partake of it. . . . It is very probable that during His life on earth, He tasted of the like food: He ate bread, fruits, etc. . . .

"Here are my simple little rubrics:

"I picture myself at Nazareth in the house of the Holy Family. If I am served with, for instance, salad, cold fish, wine, or anything of strong flavor, I offer it to St. Joseph. To the Blessed Virgin I give the hot portions, well-ripened fruits, etc.; and the feastday fare, particularly cornflour, rice, preserves, these I offer to the Child Jesus. Lastly, when a bad dinner is brought me I say gaily to myself: 'Today, my dear little child, all that is for you.'"

Rule 5: Always to smile; to ask temporal favors only under the conditions stipulated herein.

St. Thérèse wished that Our Lord should not, as she put it so touchingly "have the least trouble on her account." And because when we love someone very much, we are always grieved to see him suffer, feeling herself loved by the good

God, she strove in some manner to hide her sufferings from Him. To speak the truth, that could only be playfulness or an invention of love on her part, since nothing escapes the divine gaze. But, as she somewhere remarks, when one loves one does and says foolish things. And her love, not knowing how to express itself, was manifested in this touching manner.

Therefore, in face of every sacrifice as of every suffering, she had accustomed herself always to smile.

In the same way she smiled upon the good God when He tried her, and all the more sweetly the more He seemed to try her. And in that smile she found her purest joy. She made it her heaven on earth. She sang:

> "My heaven is to smile on the God I adore,
> When He hideth Himself my faith to prove;
> To smile—awaiting His return once more. . . .
>   My heaven is Love!"

She smiled on a penance which was particularly painful to her so that, she said, the good God, as though deceived by the expression of her countenance, might not know that she was suffering.

She smiled on every manifestation of God's holy will: "I love Him so much," she said, "that I am always content with what He sends me. . . . I love all that He does. . . . My God, Thou fillest me with joy in all Thou dost."

Neither would she have wished to give her heavenly Father occasion to refuse her the least thing, feeling that that might cause Him even the slightest pain. That was why she never asked any temporal grace for herself, fearing lest her desire might not be conformable to the divine good pleasure; and when obedience commanded her to do so, she knew how to arrange in such a way as to leave the good God perfectly free to hear her or not, assuring Him in case of need that if He heard her not, she would love Him all the more. Or else she would turn to the Blessed Virgin, who, she said, then set aright her little desires and submitted them to the good God or not, according as she deemed well.

But we must take good care not to condemn in others or in ourselves a different manner of acting in what concerns the desire of temporal favors, on condition of their not being an obstacle to the acquisition of eternal good. The request for them made to the good God may be very pleasing to Him, and St. Thérèse from the heights of heaven seems to encourage it, as the great number of favors of this kind attributed to her intercession testifies. But before her death, she took care to make known that in heaven she would act as on earth, and that before presenting her requests, she would begin by looking into the eyes of the good God, to see if it be His good pleasure.

Chapter Four

The Unselfishness of the Love of the Little Flower

The unselfishness of the love of the Little Flower has already been brought out in passages in which we showed that her rule was always to give pleasure to Jesus. In her little way of self-surrender, the reader has always been made aware there is no room for thoughts of self. In this section, however, we are to treat expressly and separately of the unselfishness of her love and to illustrate that quality by new examples.

The unselfishness of the Little Flower's love of God is a revelation even to those most intimately acquainted with the lives and writings of the saints. She succeeded in expressing her burning love of God in ways more striking, more beautiful, and more tender than any other saint ever expressed love of God. She says, "God has given me so clear an insight into the mysteries of His love that if I could only express what I know, you would hear heavenly music; but alas, I can only stammer like a child." She does not stammer; she makes heavenly music; let us quote some of the passages that illustrate the unselfishness of her love.

In one passage of her Autobiography she says that if it were possible she would wish that God could not even see her good deeds! She wished that God could not even see what she did for Him! How strange such a disposition appears to us who not only want God but also the world to know our good deeds. But the Little Flower wishes to conceal her virtuous actions even from God. Why? This is her explanation. "If it were possible," she says, "I would wish that God could not

The Little Flower dressed as St. Joan of Arc for
a theatrical production in the Carmel of Lisieux.

even see my good deeds, because I love Him so much I would like to give Him joy without His knowing who gave it." Did ever saint utter such tender sentiments before? But there is more; she continues: "When God sees the gift of good actions being given Him, He is obliged, as it were, to make a return. I would wish to spare Him the trouble." The trouble of rewarding her good deeds! Certainly this is love which, in its unselfishness, resembles the love of the angels.

In another passage the Little Flower tells us that Our Lord for long years gave her no consolation in prayer. "It was," she says, "as if, as of old, Our Lord were asleep in the boat." "But," she adds, "this rather rejoices than grieves me." It rejoices her! Think of it! The apparent inattention of Our Lord; this neglect of His Little Flower rejoices her. Why? The passage in which she explains this strange rejoicing is, I think, one of the most beautiful she ever penned. "It rejoices me," she says, "because I am always content with whatever He sends me. I love all He does." I love all He does! If Our Lord sent her a cross she was not only resigned to the cross but she actually loved the cross. It mattered not whether He sent sunshine or rain, a cross or a rose, she loves all He does.

The one wish of her heart is to give Our Lord pleasure. In her solicitude for Our Lord she goes back through the centuries and tells us that had she been on the ship which carried the apostles, when the sea threatened to overwhelm it and Christ slept on quietly amid the tossing billows and the lashing waves, she would have taken good care not to have awakened Him. Under no circumstances would she have anticipated by even one single instant that moment of time which Jesus might choose to awake and quiet the storm. For to have done so would have been to depart, though ever so little, from her own little way which she has told us is the way of spiritual childhood, the way of trust and absolute self-surrender. Is there love more perfect than this?

The same marvelous unselfishness of love is revealed in a surpassingly beautiful poem which the Little Flower addressed to our Blessed Mother, a poem every lover of St. Thérèse should memorize:

> "All, all that He has granted me, Oh! Tell Him He
>   may take it!
> Tell Him, dear Mother, He may do whate'er He
>   pleases with me;
> That He may bruise my heart today, and make it
>   sore, and break it,
> So only through Eternity my eyes His Face may see!"

Is there in all spiritual literature a passage which surpasses in sheer beauty and depth of spirituality those lines? "Tell Him, dear Mother, He may do whate'er He pleases with me. That He may bruise my heart today, or make it sore or break it.* I love all He does." And just as she lived in and by and on love, so she died. Two nights before she died, the infirmarian, looking in upon the Little Flower during the night, found her with hands joined and eyes raised to heaven and asked, "What are you doing? You ought to try and get some sleep." "I cannot, Sister, I am suffering too much; so I pray." "And what do you say to Jesus ?" "I say nothing—I love Him!"

She wasn't saying anything to Him! She was just loving Him. And she died loving Him, with these words of love upon her lips: "O! . . . I love Him . . . My God, . . . I . . . love Thee!"

What shall we say, my dear readers, in the presence of such love? I can imagine some one of our readers saying, "Oh, if it were only possible for me to love Our Lord so, to love Him as the Little Flower loved Him." But it is possible. Her little way is open to all. We need only ask her to help us. She has promised to spend her heaven in making Love loved, in making others love God as she loved Him. Accordingly, let us confidently set out on her little way, confidently and constantly asking her, "Little Flower, Seraph of Love, make me like thee, a Seraph of Love."

---

* Such sentiments as these need to be vocalized to bring out their full import. The italic type of the printer does not suffice.

Scapular Facts

Chapter One
Why Wear the Scapular?

Mary's Promise to Save
All Who Die Wearing Her Scapular

The feast of Our Lady of Mount Carmel on July 16, is for Carmelites, Carmelite parishioners and members of the Scapular Confraternity, one of the greatest and most joyful feasts of the year. There are two reasons why this feast is so joyful an occasion for Carmelites: First, because today we are reminded of the complete title of Carmelites, the proudest title ever bestowed upon a religious order; namely, "The Brothers of the Blessed Virgin of Mount Carmel." THE BROTHERS OF THE BLESSED VIRGIN! What more beautiful title could be imagined! The brothers of the Blessed Virgin of Mount Carmel—why Mount Carmel? Because on Mount Carmel the order was founded and from Mount Carmel devotion to the Blessed Virgin was propagated by Carmelite priests. The second reason why this feast is such a joyful occasion is that on this day we are reminded of the privileges bestowed upon our order—privileges bestowed because our order is the oldest order in the church and the first order dedicated to the Blessed Virgin. The privileges of which I speak have been conferred on the order by the various popes down through the ages. The popes stamped the order with the seal of their approval; they approved of our glorious title (The Brothers of the Blessed Virgin); they showered the order with indulgences such as the plenary indulgence which one may gain as often as a Carmelite Church is visited on July 16th.

But there is one privilege greater than all others; a privilege bestowed upon Carmelites by the Blessed Virgin herself, bestowed by her through a Carmelite saint, St. Simon Stock.

St. Simon was the Superior General of the order in the thirteenth century. At that time the Carmelites were being persecuted. Some asserted that the very title of the order of which we are so proud was more blasphemous than beautiful. St. Simon had long asked the Blessed Virgin to give to the Order, to her "Brothers," some sign of her approval; some sign of her love; some sign that she approved of their title and of their work; some special privilege which would distinguish the Carmelite Order from all other orders. The Blessed Virgin at last answered his prayer and expressed her approbation of the Order and her love for her earthly brothers by appearing to Saint Simon and giving to him the Brown Scapular, saying to him as she gave the Scapular, "This is the privilege I give to you and to all Carmelites, that whosoever shall die wearing this Scapular shall never suffer the pains of hell." A strange and marvelous promise indeed that is—"Whosoever shall die wearing this Scapular shall never suffer the pains of hell."

Are we reasonable or unreasonable in hoping and trusting in that promise? Non-Catholics, you know, scoff at such a belief. They would say, "What superstition, what absolute nonsense to believe that a piece of cloth worn about the neck can save a man from hell." And in a sense they are right. The Scapular is a piece of cloth—blessed indeed—but still a piece of brown cloth and as such it has no virtue, no power whatsoever, no power to save a man from hell nor to admit a man to heaven. Why then do we nevertheless believe that that piece of brown cloth (or its equivalent, the Scapular medal) worn at the moment of death will, as the Blessed Virgin promised, protect its wearer from eternal punishment? We do not believe that the piece of brown cloth will effect that; we believe that the Blessed Virgin's intercession will do it. The Brown Scapular is the badge of the Blessed Virgin. She has promised to save from hell by her intercession anyone who dies wearing her badge, the Scapular. And she is able to keep her promise.

Once we grant that the Blessed Virgin actually appeared to Saint Simon and made the Scapular promise (and this is as historical a fact as could be wished), we need only prove that the Blessed Virgin is able to keep her promise. If one can prove that, then our confidence in the Scapular immediately appears reasonable

Let us then prove that the Blessed Virgin is able to keep her promise that "whosoever shall die wearing the Scapular shall never suffer the pains of hell." Let us prove that the Blessed Virgin can obtain by her prayers anything she wants, including the grace of salvation to those who die wearing the Scapular.

Before proceeding to the proof, we might remark that our Blessed Mother would of course not make the promise unless she could keep it, and therefore the very fact that she made the promise carries with it for us the certainty that she can and will fulfill it. Nevertheless, let us set forth the grounds upon which our confidence in her rests.

First—Mary's intercession is all powerful because she was actually the Mother of God. "Who can doubt," says Saint Bernard, "but that the Son will listen to His mother—such a Son listen to such a mother." To realize Mary's power over Our Lord we need only recall that He did not bring His body with Him from heaven; He assumed it of Mary. By the fact that she gave to Our Lord His human nature, His flesh and blood, she contracted with Him a natural relationship, the relationship of mother. She was actually His mother—the Mother of God. What incalculable power therefore there must be in her intercession! When she prays, it is to her own Divine Son that she addresses Herself. To His Mother, what can this best of Sons refuse? It is simply inconceivable that her prayers should not be heard.*

---

* I am merely indicating briefly the reasons for Catholic belief in Mary's intercessory power. A full explanation of these points will be found in any advanced Catholic Catechism.

Secondly—Mary's intercession is powerful because of her holiness. It is evident that our prayers increase in power as we increase in sanctity. The soul most holy in God's sight, therefore, will have the greatest influence with God. And we know that the most holy of all souls is Mary, that there is no soul, no saint, no angel who can compare in holiness with Mary. God exalted Mary to the very highest possible point of sanctity —to the very pinnacle of holiness, because she was to be His Mother. He simply showered His gifts and graces upon her. We have no idea of how beautiful and resplendent her soul was. We can gain some glimpse of it, however, if we remember that her soul was God's masterpiece, the masterpiece of the All-Mighty and All-Powerful God. Think of all that means: that upon the beautifying of Mary's soul, God concentrated and, in a sense, exhausted all His infinite, limitless powers. And this because the honor of God demanded that He should proceed from none but a most holy and entirely spotless Mother, from a Mother most splendidly and gloriously adorned with every imaginable grace and glory and perfection. Therefore, since God listens with the most favor to the prayer of the soul that is most holy, and since no one can even remotely compare with Mary in holiness, it follows that Mary's prayers for us excel in power and potency and efficacy those of any and every angel and saint in heaven.

Thirdly—A third reason why Mary's prayers for us are so powerful is this: The soul that loves God will of course be heard by God with the greatest favor. Now, no soul that ever lived loved God as much as Mary loved Him and, therefore, she has more influence with God than any soul that ever lived. Let me explain why it is true that no soul that ever existed loved God as much as Mary loved Him.

There are two kinds of love, natural and supernatural love. Natural love is the love a mother has for her children, love between husband and wife or love between friend and friend. Supernatural love is the love we have for God; we do not love God with a natural love; the saints did not love God with a natural love but with a supernatural love, a love that was above nature. But Mary loved God with a supernatural love and with a natural love also. She had for God as much supernatural love as any of the saints, but she had also what the saints did not have for God; namely, the natural love of a mother for her child. In Mary's heart there burned for God the natural love of a Mother and the supernatural love of the saint. In Mary the natural love of a Mother and the supernatural love of a saint were centered on one and the same object. The Divine Infant was at once her child and her God. When Mary loved her Son, she loved her God. That is true of no other creature that ever lived. No other creature could love God as Mary loved Him, with a natural love, because no other creature was the Mother of God. Therefore, Mary's love was unique. Since these loves, natural and supernatural, were concentrated on one and the same object, it is clear that Mary loved God more than any soul that ever existed.

This then is why Mary's prayers for us are so powerful: (1) because she is the Mother of God (2) because she is of all souls the most holy and (3) because of all souls she loves God most.

That is why we believe in the scapular promise; we do not place our trust in the piece of cloth nor in the medal; we place our trust in Mary who, because she is the Mother of God and of all souls the most holy and of all souls the closest to God, she is able to keep her promise of saving from hell whosoever dies wearing her Scapular.

Her promise is to save those who die wearing the Scapular. The only way to be certain of dying wearing the Scapular is to wear it constantly. To neglect to use this simple and sure means of reaching heaven is certainly carelessness and folly of the highest order.

It might occur to some to ask, "Is it possible that a man who had lived in constant sin should escape God's justice by constantly wearing the Scapular?" The answer is that it is almost impossible to imagine a habitual sinner being careful always to wear the Scapular; the case is so rare that we may regard it as theoretical, not practical. It is true almost without exception that one who is careful always to wear the Scapular will also be careful to live a sinless life. One who never for one moment, day or night, fails to wear the Scapular has firm faith and strong devotion to the Blessed Virgin, and that faith and devotion cannot co-exist with habitual sin. Either sin or the Scapular will be given up.

So if there are times when we have been without the Scapular let us not hereafter make an exception for even one moment. If you haven't a Scapular, or Scapular medal, get one without delay and wear it at all times and in all places.

In conclusion, let me remark that Mary's Scapular Promise (of saving from hell all who die wearing the Scapular), which appears at first thought so marvelous, does not seem wonderful at all, when we consider the constant thoughtfulness of Mary, and the habitual and powerful confidence in her, displayed by a person who is careful always to wear her Scapular. Suppose that you knew of someone who thought enough of you to wear your picture day and night, week after week, year after year, for a lifetime. What kindly feelings towards that person would you not entertain? Would you not do all in your power for a person who manifested such enduring affection for you? Is it so wonderful then that Mary obtains from her Divine Son the grace of a happy death for one who all his life was so thoughtful of her as never to put aside her picture, her badge, her Scapular?

I think, therefore, that we may conclude that the Scapular Promise far from being incredible is not even marvelous, for what Mary promised is just what we would expect our loving, kind and generous Mother to do for those who so love her that they never for a moment in life fail to carry lovingly her image. It is but natural that Mary should provide that as death dims the mortal gaze of the faithful wearer of her Scapular image, his eyes should open in eternity to see Mary herself, beside the judge, smilingly assuring her faithful child of a favorable sentence, a sentence that will insure for her child the eternal companionship of her, whose image on the Scapular he bore so lovingly all his life.

Chapter Two

Brief History of the Scapular and of the Carmelite Order*

Mount Carmel, the Cradle of the Order

The Carmelite Order takes its name from Mount Carmel in the Holy Land, on which mountain the order had its origin. The word "Carmel" means "The garden on the beautiful hill."

In Old Testament times, Elias and Eliseus, great Hebrew prophets, and their successors who were called "Sons of the Prophets", dwelt in caves on the side of Mount Carmel. After the coming of Christ these caves of Mount Carmel were occupied by men who loved a life of solitude and prayer and who wished to live and die in those regions sanctified by the footsteps of Our Lord. In time these hermits came to live under one rule and one superior. After the Crusades, when the Holy Land and Mount Carmel passed into the hands of infidels, the monks from Mount Carmel fled from persecution and massacre into Europe and many found their way into England where monasteries were founded. One of the English Carmelites of the Middle Ages was Saint Simon Stock.

The Order in England—Saint Simon Stock

Little is known of the early life of Saint Simon Stock except that the second part of his name (Stock) is due to the

---

* This chapter is a condensation of the admirable pamphlet, "The Scapular of Our Lady of Mt. Carmel", (Gill and Son, Dublin) by the Most Rev. P. E. Magennis, O. Carm., Prior General of the Carmelites. The author has endeavored to preserve, as far a possible, the exact words of Father Magennis.

fact that he lived in the trunk of a tree, spending his days in spiritual labors and his nights in prayer. Later he became a Carmelite and when the first General Chapter of the Order was held in England in 1247, Saint Simon made such a favorable impression upon his brethren that they selected him General of the Order.

In the many difficulties of his new position the newly elected General turned naturally to Mary, to whom he had always been devout. When Simon was a youth he had been pre-advised by Mary that he would one day join an Order which had been for years on Mount Carmel and which she had taken under her special protection.*

To his characteristic devotion to the Mother of God is due the miraculous power of Saint Simon, whose life abounds in miracles. But of the many supernatural events of his life the most interesting is the "Vision of Saint Simon" in which the Scapular was bestowed.

Our Lady Bestows the Scapular

Saint Simon, burdened with the weight of eighty years and oppressed with difficulties which threatened the very existence of the Carmelite order in Europe, betook himself to prayer and supplicated the Mother of Carmel, asking her, as Mother and Patroness of the order, to have pity on her Carmelite Brothers and relieve them in their hour of trial.

The bountiful heart of God's Mother could not resist the prayers and tears of the General of the Order called by her name, and towards morning, just as the dawn was breaking, she appeared to the holy man. The sight was entrancing, for the Queen of Heaven was surrounded by a great company of angels of dazzling brightness. It was only with great difficulty,

---

* At that time, as now, the members of the Carmelite Order were known as the "Brothers of the Blessed Virgin." The Latin title of the Carmelites today is indicated by the initials "O. F. B. V. M. C.", Ordo Fratrum beataeVirginis de Monte Carmelo which means "The Order of the Brothers of the Blessed Virgin of Mt. Carmel."

then, that Simon could gaze on the glorious vision. There, in answer to his prayer, she presented him with a garment, formed after the manner of a scapular, saying "THIS SHALL BE A PRIVILEGE FOR THEE AND ALL CARMELITES; WHOSOEVER SHALL DIE WEARING IT SHALL NOT SUFFER EVERLASTING FIRE."*

These strange and wonderful words of the Blessed Virgin were rapidly communicated to Carmelites throughout the world, and her promise was in turn made known to the people by the Carmelite monks. The effect was therefore two-fold; first upon the Carmelite habit and secondly upon the laity in the formation of scapular confraternities.

The ritual for profession in the order was changed so as to give the Scapular its rightful place. It is now called "the habit." For a Brother to be found without the Scapular is considered an offense calling for severe punishment. No Carmelite can celebrate Mass without it. When he goes to rest he must have a smaller Scapular to take the place of the one daily worn. It is not, amongst the Carmelites, a question of having a covering for the body; it is a duty to wear (at least in a miniature form) the habit so favored by the Mother of God. Even in death, the ritual (which read differently in the time of Simon Stock) now prescribes that the Brother be robed in "his Scapular."

Scapular Confraternities Organized

More extraordinary still was the effect of the Scapular promise upon the religious life of the faithful. In the thirteenth century, lay people often begged the privilege of being buried in the habit of their favorite order, and this, if granted, was considered a strong guarantee of salvation. After the promise of Mary to Saint Simon, the faithful who were associated with Carmelite priests began gradually to wear the Carmelite habit, not only at death but in life, and these lay friends of the Carmelites formed amongst themselves

---

* Since this marvelous promise of the Blessed Virgin is discussed at length in Chater One, its extraordinary character needs no further comment here.

organizations or unions similar to guilds. Immediately after the death of Simon, we find unquestionable traces of these organizations or combinations of the faithful around Carmelite churches, and, therefore, we conclude that these unions were formed in his time and by reason of the scapular devotion. In the later years of the thirteenth century, a confraternity whose members were united by devotion to God's Mother and whose chief garb or dress was the Scapular, was attached to every Carmelite church. In England, Ireland and Scotland those societies were, and are still named "confraternities"; in Italy generally "companies" (compagnie); in Germany "skapuliersbrüderschaft"; in Spain "hermandades."

The great scapular feast of the sixteenth of July, the solemn commemoration of Our Blessed Lady of Mount Carmel, had its beginnings in the Mass celebrated for the members of the confraternities in their own chapels and by their own chaplains. Finally, it was their mighty influence with the highest ecclesiastical authorities that ensured a place for their feast in the local calendars and later on in the Universal Church. In the sixteenth century it was no uncommon thing to find as many as several thousand in the confraternity of the one town or city.

That the devotion of the people to the Scapular, through the centuries since the days of Simon Stock, was acceptable to Our Lady and her Divine Son is not even called in question by the most ardent of its opponents. On every side one hears of extraordinary favors granted to those who have piously and worthily worn this badge of fidelity to God's Mother.

After the Reformation, with the suppression of Carmelite monasteries, the scapular confraternities dwindled for a time. Consequently, Holy Church, in order to facilitate the wearing of the Scapular, gave leave to any priest, even though not a Carmelite, to enroll the faithful in the Scapular and to receive them into the scapular confraternity.

Thus even down to the present day, lay people who are at a distance from any Carmelite Church, or legally formed confraternity, may become members enjoying all the privileges attached to the scapular devotion. It is merely necessary to be enrolled by a priest having the proper faculties.

The Scapular Medal

At first the Scapular worn by lay people, or by confraternity members, was the same as the Scapular of the habit of the Carmelite priest; later the Scapular for lay people assumed the smaller size that it has today.

Thus far we have spoken of the brown Scapular made of cloth and connected by strings and so placed that one part lies on the breast and the other on the shoulders.

Pope Pius X, being petitioned by people who could not conveniently wear the cloth Scapular in their everyday dress, allowed the substitution of material more durable and less liable to inconvenience the wearer in torrid climes. For the cloth out of which the Scapular was usually made, the Holy Father permitted the use of the medal as a substitute. This permission was later extended to those not in torrid climates and Rome has decided that "all spiritual favors belonging to the Scapular, not excepting the Sabbatine Privilege, could be gained by the wearers of the medal on complying with the requisite conditions."*

The Prestige of the Brown Scapular

Amongst the faithful in English-speaking countries, the name by which the Scapular of Our Lady of Mount Carmel is best known is "the brown scapular," because of the color of the material out of which it is fashioned. In every other country, it is called simply "the scapular," since it is, in reality, the model on which all the other scapulars were fashioned. Furthermore, the Carmelite scapular is unique in its history and also in the sanction* given by the church to the wearing of it.

---

* Nevertheless some who wear the Scapular medal make certain of their position by having a Cloth Scapular in reserve for use in case of serious illness.

* The sanction or privileges given to the wearing of the Scapular are listed in Chapter Three of this book.

Membership in the Scapular Confraternity a High Privilege

The wearer of the Scapular is a participator in the good works of all those who are clothed in the Scapular, the livery of Our Lady of Mt. Carmel, a partner in the mighty volume of praise that daily ascends from monastery and convent and from the homes of the faithful—praise to Mary and through Mary to her Divine Son. In this mighty army of Carmelite wearers of the Scapular there are many supremely holy souls, both lay and religious. What a wave of enthusiasm seized on the faithful when our present Holy Father proclaimed the canonization of the "Little Flower." Yet we cannot doubt that inside the walls of convents and monasteries there are many, not unlike this Little Flower, living lives of sanctity and penance. There are, too, myriads of lay men and lay women in the Catholic Church today who, unknown even to their dearest friends, live lives of great holiness. To be united with the chosen souls in and outside convents and monasteries, as every wearer of the scapular is united, is very consoling, but to be partners with them in the great confraternity of the scapular so that they may be called in the best sense our brothers and sisters, to become heirs to their lives of mortification and holiness, evinces indeed a wonderful condescension of Divine providence.

What wonder then that miracles have accompanied the scapular devotion throughout the ages! What wonder that men and women have clung with such steadfast fidelity to the Scapular of Our Lady of Mt. Carmel! What wonder if the soldier in face of danger wishes to wear the uniform of the Queen of Heaven! What wonder that faithful souls travelling to their Father's home desire to wear what they believe is a guarantee of a Mother's kindly love! We are all children in the spiritual life, no matter how the years have crowded on us. It's a child's prerogative to be clothed by a Mother's kindly hand. Hence the time can never be when the faithful child of Holy Church does not feel a thrill of pleasure as he is being robed in the livery of Mary—the Scapular.

Chapter Three

The Privileges of Membership in the Scapular Confraternity

The privileges* of membership in the confraternity of the Scapular may be reduced to the following heads: The Scapular promise, the Sabbatine privilege, three special favors, and plenary and partial indulgences.

Privilege No. 1—The Scapular Promise

This promise is contained in Mary's words when on July 16th, in the year 1251, she appeared to St. Simon Stock, Superior General of the Carmelites, at Cambridge, England, and gave him the Scapular. Her words are: "Receive, my beloved son, this Scapular of thy order. It is the special sign of my brotherhood. He who dies clothed in this habit shall be preserved from eternal fire. It is the badge of salvation, a protection in danger, a pledge of peace and eternal alliance."

The wearer of the Brown Scapular is in a special manner Mary's child ("My Brothers," she calls them), and enjoys the protection of this powerful Mother in dangers of body and soul, in life, and especially at the hour of death.

Privilege No. 2—The Sabbatine Privilege

In an official papal document, Pope John XXII relates that in a vision in which our Blessed Lady appeared to him, she

---

* Chapter Three of this book is taken almost in its entirety from the "Scapular Booklet," an admirable treatise by the Very Rev. Lawrence C. Diether, O. Carm., Provincial of the Carmelite Order in America. Father Lawrence's book contains valuable information, especially for clerical directors of the scapular confraternity.

graciously granted to the members of the scapular confraternity the great Sabbatine privilege, which she ordered the pope to promulgate and confirm. "I, the Mother of grace," Mary said to the pope, "shall descend on the Saturday after their death, and who so I shall find in Purgatory, I shall free, so that I may lead them unto the holy mountain of life everlasting." She also lays down the conditions for gaining this extraordinary indulgence.

The Holy Roman and Universal Inquisition, under Paul V decreed, on January 20, 1613, that "It is lawful for the Carmelite Fathers to preach that Christians may piously believe in the help promised to the souls of the brethren and the members of the Confraternity of the Blessed Virgin Mary of Mount Carmel, namely, that the Blessed Virgin will assist by her continual intercession, suffrages and merits, and also by her special protection, particularly on the Saturday after death (which day has been consecrated to her by the Church), the souls of the brothers and the members of the confraternity departing this life in charity, who shall have worn the habit and shall have observed chastity according to their particular state of life, and also have recited the Little Office, or if unable to read, have kept the fasts of the Church and have abstained from the use of meat on Wednesdays and Saturdays, unless the feast of the Nativity of Our Divine Lord should fall on one of those days."

Privilege No. 3—Special Favor

A share in the spiritual fruits of the entire order which is applicable to the Poor Souls.

Privilege No. 4—Special Favor

Every altar, when Mass is offered up for a deceased member, is a privileged altar.

Privilege No. 5—Special Favor

At death, the General Absolution with a plenary indulgence can be imparted to every member by a priest having faculties, or in his absence, by any approved confessor.

Privilege No. 6—Indulgences

A. Plenary Indulgences (under the usual conditions).

1. On the day of enrollment.
2. On July 16th, the feast of Our Lady of Mount Carmel, or on one Sunday of July, according to the custom of the place.
3. On the same feast, each time they visit a church or chapel where the scapular confraternity is erected.
4. On Whit Sunday.
5. On November 15th, the commemoration day of the dead of the Order, or on November 16th, if the 15th be a Sunday.
6. At the hour of death, if well disposed and contrite, one pronounces the Holy Name of Jesus, at least in his heart.
7. A plenary indulgence under the usual conditions may be gained on the following days by visiting a Carmelite church, or any church, if a Carmelite or confraternity church is more than a mile distant:

January 1st—Circumcision of Our Lord.
February 2nd—Purification of Our Lady.
February 4th—St. Andrew Corsini.
February 15th—St. Peter Thomas.
February 25th—St. Avertan.
March 6th—St. Cyril.
March 18th—St. Gabriel.
March 19th—St. Joseph (or during octave).
March 23rd—St. Baptist Mantuan.
March 25th—The Annunciation.
March 29th—St. Berthold.
April 8th—St. Albert.
May 5th—St. Angelus.
May 16th—St. Simon Stock.

May 25th—St. Mary Magdalen of Pazzi.
July 2nd—Visitation of Our Lady.
July 16th—Our Lady of Mount Carmel, for each visit from noon on 15th till midnight on 16th. Also one day during the octave.
July 20th—St. Elias.
July 24th—Bl. Martyrs of Compiegne.
July 26th—St. Anne.
August 7th—St. Albert.
August 15th—Assumption of Our Lady.
August 27th—Transverberation of the Heart of St. Teresa.
September 2nd—St. Brocard.
September 8th—Nativity of Our Lady.
October 15th—St. Teresa, or during Octave.
November 14th—All the saints of Carmel.
November 21st—Presentation of Our Lady.
November 24th—St. John of the Cross.
November 29th—BB. Denis and Redemptus.
December 8th—Immaculate Conception.
December 11th or 17th—Bl. Frank.

Also the Feast of the Most Holy Trinity; Ascension of Our Lord; Corpus Christi; Sacred Heart of Jesus; St. Joseph, 3rd Sunday after Easter, or within the octave; St. Joachim; saint under whose name a church is dedicated. Also a choice, once every year; and once during the Forty Hours' Adoration.

B. Partial Indulgences
1. An indulgence of five years and five quarantines*: once a month on any day, when a member receives Holy Communion.
2. Three years and as many quarantines, when receiving Holy Communion in a church or oratory of the confraternity on any feast of Our Lady observed by the Universal Church.

---

* This is according to the old indulgence. Please see 1983, Code of Canon Law for the current indulgence.

3. Three hundred days each Wednesday and Saturday of the year for abstaining on those days.

4. One hundred days for any act of piety or charity.

5. Seven years and as many quarantines for visiting a church or oratory of the confraternity on Wednesdays or Saturdays; three hundred days on any other day.

6. Five hundred days, each time, for reverently kissing the Scapular (Benedict XV).

7. Ten years and 10 quarantines for visiting a Carmelite church, or any church if a Carmelite church is more than a mile distant, on Christmas Day, Easter Sunday, Whit Sunday, Trinity Sunday, feast of Corpus Christi, Immaculate Conception, Nativity, Presentation, Annunciation, Visitation, Purification, Assumption of Our Lady, feast of St. Michael, SS. Peter and Paul, All Saints, Nativity of St. John the Baptist, Finding and Exaltation of the Cross, patrons of Carmelite churches, all Sundays and Saturdays of the year, all Mondays, Wednesdays and Fridays of Lent.

Note 1—All the indulgences mentioned are applicable to the souls in Purgatory, thus constituting a rich field of spiritual favors from which members of the confraternity may reap an abundant harvest for the souls of departed friends or relatives.

Note 2—Last, but not least: "When you are gone and your relatives, growing used to your absence, forget you, the Carmelite Order and its great confraternity will still be alive and mindful of you. You will be remembered once a month in a Mass which is offered up for the deceased members of the scapular confraternity; you will be remembered once a month in the Dead Office, which is offered in all Carmelite communities throughout the world for the departed members of the Order; once each quarter in the Ternary Offices which they recite; once a year in the special commemoration of all Souls of the Carmelite Order; and EACH DAY in the good works performed by the Order throughout the whole world.

Chapter Four

Some Practical Questions Briefly Answered

Question: May the Scapular medal be worn instead of the cloth Scapular?

Answer: Yes.

Question: Are all the privileges attached to the wearing of the cloth Scapular obtained by wearing the Scapular medal?

Answer: All the indulgences and privileges listed in Chapter Three of this booklet are obtained by wearing the Scapular medal.

Question: Does the promise of the Blessed Virgin to save from hell all who die wearing the Scapular apply to the Scapular medal?

Answer: Some authorities answer affirmatively and others negatively. The latter maintain that inasmuch as the decree of the Church does not expressly mention that the promise of the Blessed Virgin applies to the Scapular medal, the matter is uncertain and, therefore, the safest procedure is to wear the cloth scapular. Personally, the author believes that Our Blessed Lady would no more permit the eternal damnation of one who constantly wears the Scapular medal than she would permit the eternal punishment of one who constantly wears the cloth Scapular. All the reasons for the fulfillment of the Scapular promise outlined in Chapter 1 of this booklet apply to the Scapular medal.

Question: If one habitually wears the Scapular medal during the day, is it necessary to wear it at night?*

Answer: Yes. The scapular promise reads "All who die wearing the Scapular." Therefore since death may come at night the medal or the Scapular should be worn at night.*

Question: Should the Scapular or Scapular medal be worn while one is taking exercise such as swimming?

Answer: Inasmuch as death may come at any time the Scapular or Scapular medal should be worn at all times. Many are so intent upon gaining the Scapular promise that they wear the Scapular even in the bath. Certainly the safest rule is never for a moment under any circumstances to be without the Scapular or Scapular medal. It is just this constant thoughtfulness of Mary enduring throughout the years and persisting hourly throughout one's life that makes the Scapular promise credible and reasonable.

Question: If a person does not remember being invested with the Scapular and now wishes to obtain all the Scapular privileges, what procedure is necessary?

Answer: The probability is that almost everyone is invested with the Scapular on his First Communion day because that is almost a universal custom in all countries. If you have well founded doubts that you were ever invested, any Carmelite priest or, if you do not live near a Carmelite Church, any priest will invest you in the Scapular at any time because the ceremony takes but a few minutes. Just bring the Scapular or Scapular medal with you and ask the priest to invest you.

Question: If a person was invested in the Scapular at First Communion but has not worn the Scapular for years and now wishes to gain the Scapular privileges, what procedure is necessary?

---

* There is a Roman decree to wit, if the clothing in which the medal is carried is put aside at night for any necessary purpose, the requisite continuity is not thereby broken and the indulgences may be gained just as if the medal were attached to the night clothing; but, as explained elsewhere, it is uncertain that the scapular promise would in this case be realized, and therefore we have answered the question affirmatively, that is, wear the medal even at night.

Answer: It is merely necessary to procure the Scapular which the individual may put on himself; or to procure a Scapular medal and carry it. No re-investing and no ceremony presided over by a priest is necessary.

Question: Where may Scapulars or Scapular medals be obtained?

Answer: They may be obtained in any Catholic book store, Catholic supply house, or Catholic gift shop. Scapulars may also be obtained from:

The Slaves of the Immaculate Heart of Mary
P.O. Box 524
Vienna, Ohio 44473
330-856-9837

They also publish a beautiful little booklet about the brown Scapular called "Garment of Grace", in either English, Korean, Chinese, Portugese, or Spanish.

Question: How should one answer the objection of a non-Catholic that it is superstitious to believe that the wearing of a piece of cloth could save a man from hell?

Answer: Catholic belief is not correctly stated in the objection.

Question: Would it be just that the habitual sinner who had never worn the Scapular during life would be saved by putting on the Scapular at the moment of death?

Answer: The author has never known of any instance such as the one described and believes that the question is a merely theoretical one. He is of the opinion that the habitual sinner would not even think of the Scapular as death approached. However, if it should happen that the sinner were clothed in the Scapular at the last moment by a pious mother or nun, the salvation of the sinner's soul would be due to the generosity of Our Blessed Mother rewarding the prayers and devotion of the mother or nun.

Question: How may members of the Scapular Confraternity become members of the Little Flower Society?

Answer: By filling out the membership blank which will be sent upon request made to The Carmelite Monastery, 6413 Dante Avenue, Chicago, Ill. 60637

Question: Should the cloth Scapular be of brown color?

Answer: The Scapular may be brown or any shade between brown and black, whereas the strings of the Scapular may be of any color.

Supplement

Supplement

Description of the National Shrine of the Little Flower

The Paintings in the Church Vestibule

The paintings in the vestibule depict various events in the life of St. Thérèse. The three paintings to the left represent events in her girlhood, and the three to the right picture her life in the convent.

The first painting represents St. Thérèse with her father on one of their evening walks. The story reproduced on the canvas is best told in the Little Flower's own words on page 12.

The second painting represents the "Smile of the Blessed Virgin" upon the Little Flower.

The third painting represents the Little Flower strewing flowers before the Blessed Sacrament during a procession of the Blessed Sacrament in the Normandy village in which she lived.

The fourth* painting (to the right of the main entrance) represents St. Thérèse in the midst of her novices. The Little Flower was given the office of Mistress of Novices at the unusually tender age of twenty, and to her novices she addressed the most beautiful spiritual counsels, which are included in the large Autobiography.

The fifth painting depicts the charity of St. Thérèse, tenderly helping an aged and invalid sister whom she cared for with never-failing patience and love.

---

* Three of the paintings are the work of l'Abbé Bouffet, a Carmelite priest of Paris, and three were painted by M. Joseph Gérard, also of Paris. Both artists have been decorated by the French Academy and are ranked high among the artists of France.

The sixth painting depicts the last Holy Communion of St. Thérèse surrounded by the other Carmelite Sisters of the convent.

The Paintings in the Church Interior

To your right as you enter the church the visitor will find in the panel between the confessionals a painting of unusual interest.

In the center, St. Thérèse is pictured kneeling before our Blessed Lady and obtaining from the Infant Jesus in His Mother's arms, the roses, which, according to her promises, she is letting fall on earth.

To the right and left are pictured the miracles approved by the commission of cardinals before the Beatification of St. Thérèse; to the right the cure of Abbe Anne, to the left the cure of Sister Louise.

To your left as you enter the church, also in the panel between the confessionals, there is a rather complicated but comprehensive painting of the beneficent activity of St. Thérèse.

In the center St. Thérèse is represented in the act of letting fall her roses upon the United States in general (the United States are represented by Columbia and the eagle) and upon the pilgrims to the National Shrine in particular (the facade of the National Shrine Church is pictured in the foreground).

In the panel to the right, two conversions wrought by St. Thérèse are commemorated. In the lower part of the panel there is pictured the conversion of a Scotch Presbyterian minister, Mr. Grant.

In the upper part of the panel there is pictured a French soldier who, after having neglected his religious duties for many years during which his life was most viciously sinful, was suddenly converted while reading the Autobiography of the Little Flower.

Thus in this panel, specimens of the constant activity of St. Thérèse in converting both non-Catholics and bad Catholics is happily represented.

In the panel to the left another totally different species of the beneficence of St. Thérèse is pictured. In the lower portion of the panel the miracle wrought by the Little Flower in favor of the Carmelite Nuns of Gallipoli is represented.

In the upper portion of the panel, an instance of the miracles worked by the intercession of St. Thérèse upon the foreign missions is shown.

The Original Painting of St. Thérèse

In the left transept of the church, that is, on the side of the church opposite the relics, in a frame bordered by electric shell roses, is the original picture of St. Thérèse painted by her own sister, Céline, who was still living in France when this book was first published.

The Shrine Proper

The National Shrine of the Little Flower is called "The Rose Bower," and the fitness of that name will be evident from the following description taken from the "Little Flower Bulletin": The National Shrine of the Little Flower is universally declared to be the most beautiful Shrine to the Little Flower in America. It was built by donations large and small given in thanksgiving for favors received from the Little Flower by members of her society. That is the first remarkable feature of the Little Flower's Shrine. It is a monument to the power of the Little Flower's intercession because every dollar of its cost represents someone's thanksgiving offering to the Little Flower.

The shrine was made in Paris by the famous firm of Poussiellgue and is built according to the traditional principle of shrines of saints in Europe around a painting of the saint in glory as its central or focal point. The chandeliers are not merely chandeliers, but each is really a rose bush to symbolize her promise to "let fall from heaven a shower of roses" and to emphasize the chief lesson she teaches, namely, love of God, the rose being for her queen of the flowers, because it symbolizes the queen of the virtues, love of God. The hanging rose bushes or baskets themselves are shaped like roses. They are made of gold-plated bronze and a close view will reveal that the bronze work is all foliage rose leaves done so delicately that one of America's most noted architects declared upon viewing the Shrine: "I have never seen such magnificent bronze work. It is superb." The outer golden bronze rose bushes, which are filled with white roses of crystal, form, you will notice, an arch, which serves as an outer border to the Shrine. The inner arch leads up from within the two side arches of the altar itself to culminate in the large centerpiece or glory made of gold and bronze rays to symbolize light and heat, the light of inspiration and the heat of love sent forth to the world by the Little Flower. The Little Flower herself is painted in the centerpiece in glory, in the ecstasy of her vision of God in heaven. Thus at the national shrine above the altar the painting of the Little Flower represents her as she is, in heaven, and below in the central arch of the altar the statue of the Little Flower represents her as she was on earth. If there is any more beautiful statue of the Little Flower in Europe than the new one in the arch of the National Shrine today, it could not be located by the artists who made the search.

The entire Shrine, counting the roses in the bronze vases in the arches, contains 578 electric roses and the beauty of this ensemble, when illuminated, is indescribable.

The Relics of St. Thérèse—The Most Precious and Largest Collection of Relics in America

To the right of the shrine proper, on the smaller altar of the Little Flower and the Infant Jesus at the end of the transept rest the relics of St. Thérèse.

On the altar table is the golden reliquary with the five major relics of the Little Flower. This reliquary is supported by two kneeling bronze angels and is fashioned in the form of a golden rose branch, each rose of which contains one of the five relics of the Little Flower, all forming the most noteworthy collection of her relics in the world except at her convent home in France. Two of the five major relics—locks of the Little Flower's hair and a portion of her flesh* were given to the shrine by her own sister, Pauline, who was still the Mother Superior of the Carmelite Convent when Father Dolan visited Lisieux, in which the Little Flower lived. The other three relics are portions of her ashes, a piece of the habit in which she died and was buried, and finally several relics of bones of the Little Flower. Where all these rare, and precious relics are, is it strange that the Little Flower dispenses her favors so lavishly?

In the gold and marble reliquary in the left panel of this altar, the visitor will find a little toy, a tambourine which the Little Flower used as a girl.

In the right panel of this shrine of the Little Flower and the Infant Jesus, also in a gold and marble reliquary, there is the map of North America drawn by the Little Flower at twelve years of age and annotated in her own handwriting.

To the left of the altar in a rose-bordered relic case is the Little Flower's chair which was in her cell and which she used during her convent life in the Carmel of Lisieux.

To the right of the relic altar, also in a rose-bordered relic case is one of the most attractive of all the relics to visitors to the shrine. This is the Little Flower's rose bush, now converted into a crucifix.

In the center of the large walnut case still further to the right of the Little Altar on which repose so many Precious Relics of the Little Flower, is the blessing of Pope Pius XI bestowed on the members of the Society of the Little Flower. To the right of the blessing is the original document granting the special indulgences authorized by Our Holy Father to members of the society. To the left of the pope's blessing is the English translation of these indulgences. In the lower right hand of the case is framed a piece of the habit worn by the

---

* The Little Flower's flesh corrupted as she prophesied it would, that is, it was reduced to dust, to ashes, with this exception—that a small portion of her flesh was found clinging to her habit. It is this relic which is referred to above and which is naturally the rarest of relics of the Little Flower.

Little Flower when she took her religious vows. Also framed in the lower left hand side is an Agnus Dei of the Little Flower made by the hands of Pope Pius XI. Also in the case, the visitor will note the framed messages of the four living sisters of the Little Flower to the members of her society in America and the composite make-up of five original photographs of the Little Flower, artistically arranged by her sister Céline.

Other relics which are often not visible to visitors, because they are frequently taken from the national shrine to other churches in other cities for exposition at novenas conducted by Father Dolan, O. Carm., and Father Sullivan, O. Carm., include: a lily or flower made entirely from locks of the hair of St. Thérèse; a piece of the silken silver band which was used to bind the Little Flower's remains when they were transferred from the church to the cemetery, and two reliquaries which served as ornaments on the wall of her cell. Of course it serves to bring St. Thérèse very close to visitors when they can at the National Shrine look upon objects that were actually touched and handled and used by St. Thérèse herself.

The Main Altar

The magnificent main altar is the object of the enthusiastic admiration of both the lay and clerical visitors who come in a steady stream daily to the National Shrine.

The most prominent figure is, of course, Our Lady of Mt. Carmel holding the Infant Jesus so tenderly loved by St. Thérèse of the Child Jesus.

To the left, kneels St. Thérèse in an attitude of supplication before the Queen of Carmel. To the right, is an angel holding in one hand the shield of the Carmelite Order, and in the other, the sword of Elias, typifying the spirit of the Order: zeal for God, zeal for souls.

From the description given, the visitor will realize how fitting it is that the design of the main altar of the National Shrine of the Little Flower should be exactly what it is: Our Lady of Mt. Carmel with the Infant Jesus and with them, Our

Lady's latest sainted Carmelite daughter, St. Thérèse of the Child Jesus.

The Windows of the Shrine Church*

The windows of the Church tell the history of the Carmelite Order, the first and oldest religious order to be dedicated to Mary. The color-scheme of the Carmelites, brown and white, is carried out in the windows of the church. On them is depicted the history of the order, its peculiar spirit and mission, its privileges and its glories.

---

* Unfortunately, the shrine described in the text was destroyed by fire in 1975. A new shrine has been constructed in honor of the Little Flower in Darien, Illinois which is currently owned and operated by the Carmelite sisters: National Shrine of St. Thérèse 8501 Bailey Road Darien, Illinois, 60561 (630) 969-3311 www.saint-therese.org . The editor of this book chose to leave the description of the former shrine because it was one of the most magnificent pieces of Catholic architecture in the United States. The original shrine was widely known and its memory merits a place in Catholic history. (Editors Note)

THE GREAT COMMENTARY on THE FOUR GOSPELS by Cornelius aLapide, S.J.

QUOTES FROM THE REVIEW by SCOTT HAHN

Cornelius aLapide, S.J. (1568-1637) is a giant figure in the history of Catholic biblical interpretation. Born in a tiny Catholic enclave in the Calvinist Netherlands in the bloody generation after the Reformation, Lapide grew to be one of the Church's most gifted scholars and spiritual interpreters of the sacred page.

Between 1614 and 1645, Lapide wrote commentaries on every book of Scripture except Job and Psalms.

To read Lapide four hundred years later is to enter a nearly forgotten world of biblical interpretation ...more striking – the sheer breadth and density of Lapide's interpretative matrix or his audacity in summoning all these resources to the interpretation of the sacred text.

Lapide himself takes a breathtaking high view of Scripture's purpose: Lapide prefaces his commentary with thirty-eight "canons of interpretation," which reflect a wise and prayerful method. "

It is clear that the Fathers hold pride of place for Lapide in his interpretative work.

- *6"x 9" Book format*
- *2900+ Pages in four volumes*
- *First complete English translation*
- *Sewn Binding & Headbands*
- *Bonded Leather Covers & Satin Ribbons*
- *Greatest Catholic Bible Commentary ever*
- *Extensive discussion of Greek and Hebrew words*
- *$199. Per four volume set*

A List of Small Books
Available from Loreto Publications

Boy Heroes - Ernst Wagner/Dom Alban Fruth O.S.B.	$4.95
Breaking With The Past - Abbot Gasquét	$5.95
Calvary and the Mass - Bishop Fulton Sheen	$5.95
Counsels to Confessors - St. Leonard of Port Maurice	$6.95
The Conversion of Alphonse Ratisbonne - Baron deBussieres	$7.95
The Wisdom of St. Francis De Sales	$4.95
The Dogma of Faith - St. Benedict Center	$4.95
Explanation of the Veni Sancte Spiritus - Fr. Nicholas Gihr	$6.95
The Gift of Self to God - Fr. Nicholas Grou S.J.	$6.95
50 Meditations on the Passion - Fr. Alban Goodier	$5.95
Meet Brother Martin - Fr. Norbert Georges O.P.	$5.95
Money Manipulation and Social Order - Fr. Denis Fahey	$7.95
The Mystical Body and Its Head - Msgr. Hugh Benson	$6.95
Our Lady of Perpetual Help - Fr. Francis Connell, C.SS.P.	$5.95
Poems of Her Heart - Poetry of Virginia Teehan	$6.95
Poems of Joseph Mary Plunkett	$6.95
Storm Novena - St. Benedict the Moor Mission	$4.95
Treatise on the Spiritual Life - St. Vincent Ferrer	$5.95
The Battle for Oscar Six - Eugene DeLalla	$7.95
The Ballad and the Message - Br. Charles Madden OFM Conv.	$7.95
The Difficult Commandment - Fr. C.C. Martindale, S.J.	$5.95
The Wife Desired - Fr. Leo Kinsella	$7.95
The Mystery of the Wizard Clip - Raphael Brown	$5.95
The Woman of Genesis - Bro. T.M. Sennott, M.I.C.M.	$7.95
The Tragedy of James Connolly - Fr. Denis Fahey	$6.95
The Rulers of Russia - Fr. Denis Fahey	$7.95
The Rulers of Russia & the Russian Farmers - Fr. Denis Fahey	$7.95
Workingman's Guilds of the Middle Ages - Fr. Denis Fahey	$7.95

Loreto Publications

P. O. Box 603
Fitzwilliam, NH 03447
Phone: 603-239-6671
www.LoretoPubs.org

The most popular autobiography ever written may well have been that of Saint Thérèse of Lisieux. Unlike the stigmatist Padre Pio, who is the only saint of modern times to compare in popularity with the Little Flower's universal appeal, Sister Thérèse of the Child Jesus, during her mortal life (1873-1897), was hardly known outside the walls of her Carmelite cloister. And, she may have never been well known this side of heaven had she not been ordered by her superiors to write a personal journal of her own exquisite growth and fruition in the spiritual life – a growth that never idled from the time she was three. "From the age of three years," she testified, "I never refused anything to the Great God." Before the youngest child of Louis and Zelie Martin left this world, she prophesied that her greatest active work would "begin" in heaven and that she would employ herself in beatitude "doing good upon earth." From there, just as she promised, she has never ceased to "let fall a shower of roses" upon all who invoke her. Such devotion of the universal church, as that bestowed upon Sister Thérèse of the Child Jesus, was quickly rewarded by the Vicar of Christ. She was canonized only twenty-eight years after her death by Pope Benedict XV.

Loreto Publications is thrilled to publish Carmelite Father Albert Dolan's unique collection of eight monographs, each of which deals with the temporal spiritual journey of our chosen vessel of grace, either as the saint saw herself in the eyes of God, or as she was intimately known by her parents, four sibling sisters, fellow religious, childhood friends and others whose lives she touched after her death. One might call this redolent nosegay of inspirational testimonies, an anthology, in the Greek sense of that word, for *anthos* literally means a "gathering of flowers."

In order to compose his octave of devotion, Father Dolan traveled, in 1924, to France: to Normandy's Alencon, where Saint Thérèse was born, to her family home in Buissonnets, to the Carmel at Lisieux, and to other French towns. Then, he went to Rome, where he and Pope Pius XI had a mutually productive discussion of his apostolate to make the "Little Way" of the Little Flower better known in homes and monasteries in America. At the Carmelite convent he was blessed with priceless interviews with Saint Thérèse's three sisters (who were nuns there), and one of her teachers. At Caen, he visited a fourth sister, who had joined the Visitation order. One third of this book is dedicated to these precious recollections gathered from her living siblings. In fact, one of the eight monographs, "Book Five," is completely devoted to the Little Flower's saintly mother Zelie, who died when Thérèse was only four years old.